America's Voucher

What explains the explosive growth of school vouchers in the past two decades? In *America's Voucher Politics*, Ursula Hackett shows that the voucher movement is rooted in America's foundational struggles over religion, race, and the role of government versus the private sector. Drawing upon original data sets, archival materials, and more than 100 interviews, Hackett shows that policymakers and political advocates use strategic policy design and rhetoric to hide the role of the state when their policy goals become legally controversial. For over sixty years of voucher litigation, white supremacists, accommodationists, and individualists have deployed this strategy of attenuated governance in court. By learning from previous mistakes and anticipating downstream effects, policymakers can avoid painful defeats, gain a secure legal footing, and entrench their policy commitments despite the surging power of rivals. An ideal case study, education policy reflects multiple axes of conflict in American politics and demonstrates how policy learning unfolds over time.

Ursula Hackett is Senior Lecturer in Politics at Royal Holloway, University of London. Her Oxford doctorate won the Political Studies Association's Sir Walter Bagehot Prize in Government and Public Administration. She researches religion, race, public policy, and American political development and speaks on American politics regularly at Chatham House and the UK Foreign Office.

America's Voucher Politics

How Elites Learned to Hide the State

URSULA HACKETT

Royal Holloway, University of London

CAMBRIDGE
UNIVERSITY PRESS

University Printing House, Cambridge CB2 8BS, United Kingdom

One Liberty Plaza, 20th Floor, New York, NY 10006, USA

477 Williamstown Road, Port Melbourne, VIC 3207, Australia

314-321, 3rd Floor, Plot 3, Splendor Forum, Jasola District Centre, New Delhi - 110025, India

103 Penang Road, #05-06/07, Visioncrest Commercial, Singapore 238467

Cambridge University Press is part of the University of Cambridge.

It furthers the University's mission by disseminating knowledge in the pursuit of education, learning and research at the highest international levels of excellence.

www.cambridge.org
Information on this title: www.cambridge.org/9781108812054
DOI: 10.1017/9781108868594

First published 2020
First paperback edition 2021

A catalogue record for this publication is available from the British Library

Library of Congress Cataloging in Publication data
Names: Hackett, Ursula, 1988- author.
Title: America's voucher politics : how elites learned to hide the state / Ursula Hackett, Royal Holloway, University of London.
Description: Cambridge, United Kingdom ; New York, NY, USA : Cambridge University Press, 2020. | Includes bibliographical references and index.
Identifiers: LCCN 2019058647 | ISBN 9781108491419 (hardback) | ISBN 9781108812054 (ebook)
Subjects: LCSH: Educational vouchers--Law and legislation--United States. | Education and state--United States.
Classification: LCC KF4137 .H33 2020 | DDC 344.73/076--dc23
LC record available at https://lccn.loc.gov/2019058647

ISBN 978-1-108-49141-9 Hardback
ISBN 978-1-108-81205-4 Paperback

Contents

Figures

Tables

Acknowledgments

I am grateful to have a generous circle of colleagues who graciously read and commented upon all or parts of early drafts of this book. Nigel Bowles, David Campbell, Chris Hanretty, Nadia Hilliard, Desmond King, Lisa Miller, Chris Prosser, and the anonymous Cambridge University Press reviewers: thank you all. This book improved immeasurably as a result of my colleagues' friendly and forensic engagement. It has also been a pleasure to work with my editor at Cambridge University Press, Sara Doskow, who facilitated a wonderfully smooth and helpful review process.

Over the years many scholars have helped to bring *America's Voucher Politics* to completion. At Oxford, Christopher Hood, Desmond King, Nigel Bowles, and David Campbell posed a series of searching questions that would shape my postdoctoral research plans and ultimately inspire this book. An alfresco conversation with Sid Milkis helped clarify the conceptual apparatus of attenuated governance when the book was in its early stages. Over a series of coffees in Chicago, Suzanne Mettler kindly gave her feedback and encouragement to various iterations of this project. Over brunch in Boston, Andrea Campbell pushed me to think more about the extent to which attenuation strategies are symmetrically available to conservatives *and* liberals. My work improved greatly as a result.

It would not have been possible to write this book without deep conversations with coauthors and friends. Conversations with Desmond King are never dull. It was a delight to coauthor a paper with Des on vouchers and racial policy alliances, which ultimately fed into Chapter 3. I am grateful for Des's pathbreaking scholarship, continued friendship, and encyclopedic knowledge of the literature. I am also grateful to my excellent colleague Andrew Lewis. When he won a grant to retrieve materials from Ohio governor George Voinovich's archive, Andy and I had many fruitful discussions about the Ohio voucher effort. We received great feedback on the resulting paper at the Midwest Political Science Association conference, and Andy generously allowed me to utilize some of those materials in Chapter 4.

I presented parts of this book at the annual meetings of the American Political Science Association, the Midwest Political Science Association, and the European Consortium for Political Research. I particularly appreciated helpful conversations on school choice with Linda White, Jim Farney, and Clark Banack over a very expensive dinner in Oslo. And I am grateful to Charlotte Haberstroh and Julian Garritzmann for inviting me to present at the Political Economy of Education workshop in Oxford, where I sharpened up Chapter 5 on the recommendations of Leslie Finger and Tim Hicks.

At the Toronto Political Development Workshop, I found my tribe. This annual event is an extraordinary forum for junior scholars: sharply focused, hour-long discussions of every paper by a team of intellectual heavyweights, coupled with a warm welcome and dinner at Rob Vipond's own home. I am enormously appreciative of the analytical firepower provided over the years by David Bateman, Gerry Boychuk, Andrea Campbell, Gerald Gamm, Nicholas Jacobs, Jeffrey Jenkins, Peter John, Richard Johnson, Richard Johnston, Desmond King, Robert Lieberman, Jack Lucas, Jim Morone, Adam Sheingate, Carolyn Tuohy, Rob Vipond, Tim Weaver, Margaret Weir, Linda White, and Christina Wolbrecht.

I am glad to have many wonderful colleagues at Royal Holloway who regularly lend me their support and intellectual engagement, including Nicholas Allen, Michael Bacon, Sofia Collignon, Yoav Galai, Andreas Goldthau, Chris Hanretty, Oliver Heath, Cassilde Schwartz, and Kaat Smets. I am proud to be part of such an open and collegial department.

To my husband, Chris, my emotional support, relentless cheerleader, fellow political scientist, and dearest friend – thank you for everything.

Abbreviations

ACA	Affordable Care Act
AFT	American Federation of Teachers
BAEO	Black Alliance for Educational Options
CBT	child benefit theory
ESA	education savings account
FHA	Federal Housing Administration
HHS	Department of Health and Human Services
MPCP	Milwaukee Parental Choice Program
NAACP	National Association for the Advancement of Colored People
NAP	No-Aid Provision, a.k.a. Blaine Amendment
NEA	National Education Association
RFRA	Religious Freedom Restoration Act
STO/SFO/SGO	Scholarship Tuition/Funding/Granting Organization
UFT	United Federation of Teachers

Introduction

Subtle Forms of Circumvention

On January 23, 1964, seven-year-old Bryan Poindexter and his mother Lorraine went to the office of Principal Ethel Walker of the private Ninth Ward Elementary School at 1231 Japonica Street, New Orleans, Louisiana. Lorraine attempted to enroll Bryan in the school, but the principal refused to meet them. A legal battle was about to begin. Following the public school desegregation landmark *Brown* v. *Board of Education* (1954),[1] Louisiana had created "tuition grants," a program awarding parents public money for private – segregated – education, and schools such as Ninth Ward Elementary sprung up to cater to new demand. The state paid students $2 per day to attend segregated private schools, while most black children – Bryan among them – were confined to public schools rapidly hemorrhaging whites and funds. The National Association for the Advancement of Colored People pursued the Poindexters' case, and on August 26, 1967, the district court for the Eastern District of Louisiana struck a blow to the white supremacist regime by striking down the tuition grants in its decision *Poindexter* v. *Louisiana Financial Assistance Commission.*[2]

[1] *Brown* v. *Board of Education of Topeka*, 347 US 483 (1954).

[2] *Poindexter* v. *Louisiana Financial Assistance Commission*, 275 F Supp 833 (E.D. La. 1967). This decision was the second of four *Poindexter* rulings: 258 F Supp 158 (E.D. La. 1966) disposed of the defendants' motion to dismiss the suit. The US Supreme Court affirmed the district court's judgment in *Louisiana Financial Assistance Commission* v. *Poindexter*, 389 US 571 (1968). After these rulings the state attempted to resurrect the tuition grants, which were again struck down in *Poindexter* v. *Louisiana Financial Assistance Commission*, 296 F Supp 686 (E.D. La. 1968).

Forty-four years later, two armies of litigants bristling with amicus curiae briefs met in Washington, DC, to fight for the future of Arizona's tax credit voucher scholarships, a program funding parents' choice of private, mostly religious, education through tax credits. Pastor Glenn Dennard, his wife, Rhonda, and their five children joined Luis Moscoso and his family as parent-intervenors[3] in the suit defending the vouchers. Battle-weary after a decade of lower-court litigation, their opponents were a group of Arizonan taxpayers led by community organizer Kathleen M. Winn, history professor Diane Wolfthal, librarian Maurice Wolfthal, and educationalist Lynn Hoffman. On April 4, 2011, the US Supreme Court found in favor of the scholarship parents, by upholding the program as constitutional in *Arizona Christian School Tuition Organization* v. *Winn*.[4]

Two legal decisions, four decades apart. At issue in both cases were voucher programs granting parents public money for private education.[5] One program was deemed constitutional; the other was not. Seemingly disparate, these programs were united by a crucial political maneuver: an effort to distance the government from legally contentious policy goals – the subsidy of segregated, or religious, education. In both cases, policymakers pursued their aims through private service mechanisms, using third-party organizations, individuals, or the tax system to provide benefits. This book unpacks this distancing phenomenon by asking how elites use policy design and rhetoric to advance their policy goals when those goals become legally controversial.

Since *Brown* v. *Board of Education*, Louisiana's segregationists had been desperate to deploy state power to prevent the mixing of black and white students without seeming to do so. They applied a veneer of constitutionality by policy delivery, channeling money through parents and delegating administration to private commissions. But the veneer was thin. Segregationists failed to obscure their true purpose

[3] Parent-intervenors are parents who join ongoing litigation because they claim an interest related to the subject of the lawsuit, in this case school vouchers.

[4] *Arizona Christian School Tuition Organization* v. *Winn*, 563 US 125 (2011).

[5] For simplicity, in this book, I use the term "voucher" to mean all programs that pay tuition at private K–12 schools. I show in Chapter 2 that vouchers come in many different designs and demonstrate in Chapter 6 that the use of the term "voucher" is highly politicized. My use of the term is a space-saving shorthand. Where needed, I use the term "tax credit voucher" or "tax credit scholarship" to indicate voucher programs that are funded through tax expenditures instead of direct appropriation.

in communications. They trumpeted their efforts to combat the federal government, using nakedly racist language and boasting about the artifice that supported segregation. In *Poindexter*, the court found them out.

> For a hundred years, the Louisiana legislature has not deviated from its objective of maintaining segregated schools for white children. Ten years after *Brown,* declared policy became undeclared policy. Open legislative defiance of desegregation orders shifted to subtle forms of circumvention.... *But the changes in means reflect no change in legislative ends.* (Wisdom 1967) [italics added]

The court concluded with a flourish: "The United States Constitution does not permit the State to perform acts indirectly through private persons which it is forbidden to do directly" (Wisdom 1967).

In the Supreme Court's 2011 *Winn* decision, the controversy was religious, not racial, because most vouchers are used at religious schools. Like Louisiana's segregationists, Arizona's legislators had been stung by previous court verdicts. After a 2009 defeat by the state supreme court on religious entanglement grounds, policymakers got creative. By funding the program through tax credits rather than direct legislative appropriation, and having private organizations administer the scholarships, policymakers sought to avoid the First Amendment challenge. An enormously complicated piece of administrative machinery obscured the role of public money. Supporters were careful to avoid mentioning benefits to religious schools, focusing instead upon benefits to children. The Supreme Court majority was satisfied that the tax credit design distanced church from state: "Any injury the objectors may suffer are not fairly traceable to the government" (Kennedy 2011). The court's four liberal dissenters were unpersuaded: "A subsidy is a subsidy (or a bailout is a bailout), whether accomplished by the one means or by the other" (E. Kagan 2011).

Both *Poindexter* and *Winn* dealt with efforts to distance the government from legally controversial policy purposes, with varying success. A white supremacist regime, hitherto free to pursue its policy objectives openly, sought to minimize the appearance of state action in an attempt to circumvent legal challenges. Facing church–state jurisprudence prohibiting public aid for religious institutions, policymakers utilized tax credits to avoid religious entanglement. In both cases, policymaking elites and advocates acted strategically to pursue their objectives amid hot-button political contestation. In this book, I show that when policymakers anticipate legal losses, they turn toward purposefully obscure communications strategies and hidden, private delivery mechanisms.

The Growth of the Hidden State

Hidden, delegated, or "submerged" forms of governance have expanded rapidly across America in health care, education, housing, and many other policy arenas over the past several decades (Hackett 2017; K. J. Morgan and Campbell 2011; Faricy 2011; Mettler 2010; Hacker 2002). These governance arrangements utilize private organizations and the tax system to deliver government social policy, accentuating the role of individual choice in social policy marketplaces and attenuating the connections between consumer-citizens and the state. Since 2008, tax credit programs funding private K–12 tuition have tripled in number, the amount devoted to the home mortgage interest deduction rose 24 percent, and the net federal subsidy of health-care plans for under-65s reached $704 billion, with projected future rises (Joint Committee on Taxation 2008, 2013; Congressional Budget Office 2017).

The rapid growth of privatized forms of governance presents a puzzle, because such policies apparently offer policymakers few opportunities to claim credit for policy successes, and exacerbate government's principal-agent problems by delegating functions to others. Such policies are also typically regressive, often expensive and involve government growth "under the radar" – that is, failing to register with most ordinary voters – issues of concern to both liberals (worried about their distributive consequences) and conservatives (publicly committed to shrinking the state). So why do privatized forms of governance pass, grow, and spread?

The explanation lies in the strategic use of *attenuation* to avoid political and legal challenges when losses are likely. Attenuation is the process by which policymakers in local, state, or federal government hide the state's role in promoting a particular policy output. One way to distance the state from certain policy goals is to utilize third-party organizations or the tax system to deliver a benefit (attenuated delivery). Another is to obscure the state's role in delivering certain policy outputs through communications strategies (attenuating rhetoric). In this book, I argue that doubling up two forms of *attenuated governance* – pursuing *both* attenuated delivery and attenuating rhetoric together – helps policies pass and survive by thwarting legal opposition.

Scholars root the growth of the submerged state in a conservative public philosophy's dominance of public discourse over the past thirty years (Mettler 2009). Conservatives deploy third-party delivery or tax system funding arrangements to create the appearance of public spending restraint. Once passed, the programs acquire a fiercely protective interest group support network consisting of the private beneficiaries of government subsidy. Any efforts to reform or eliminate such policies are hobbled by an enthusiasm gap born of informational asymmetries between beneficiaries and the public.

This explanation is sound but incomplete. The thirty-year time frame overlooks the fact that hidden forms of governance predate this conservative era by at least four decades. In addition, emphasizing the *political* stability of hidden governance obscures the ways in which such policies are also insulated from successful *legal* challenges. Their political and legal advantages extend beyond the appearance of public spending restraint to the achievement of multiple state purposes under the radar, from regulation of private providers to more contentious goals. And attenuation strategies are pursued by both conservatives and liberals – white supremacists and racial egalitarians, accommodationists and secularists, and communitarians and individualists – when those elites expect their policy commitments to arouse strong oppositional advocacy and lose in court.

Suzanne Mettler's submerged state is a form of policy design, whereas attenuated governance has both rhetorical and design dimensions. This book disaggregates attenuated governance into its constituent parts: rhetorical framing and policy delivery. Drawing upon the case of school vouchers – an umbrella term used in this book to denote programs that pay tuition at private K–12 institutions, including tuition grants, education savings accounts, and vouchers funded either by direct appropriation or through tax credit scholarships – I argue that policies are more likely to be successful if they *combine* deeply attenuated policy delivery with deeply attenuating rhetoric. By "successful" I mean more likely to be passed into law and upheld in court and less likely to be overturned by voter referendum or subjected to legal challenge. As Clint Bolick, former voucher litigator for the Goldwater Institute, argues, "Any successful reform strategy is necessarily at least a two-step process, legislative and judicial" (Bolick 2003, 17). True success is broader than mere program passage; it must be sustained (Patashnik 2008).

Legal Battles in the States

Judicial action at both state and federal levels is key to the survival and growth of school vouchers because these policies activate constitutional questions about race, religion, and civic institutions. "Lose the courts, lose the war" (MacLean 2017, 229). Existing accounts of the submerged state omit the role of the courts, yet elites' concerns about legal challenges help drive political behavior as they focus upon legal vindication (Glendon 1991; Tulis and Mellow 2018). As De Tocqueville famously wrote, "Scarcely any political question arises in the United States that is not resolved, sooner or later, into a judicial question" (De Tocqueville 1998, 110). Legal challenges to vouchers come at *state*, as well as federal, level, because state constitutions are thronged with educational mandates, prohibitions, obligations, and positive rights (Zackin 2013). Many of the greatest legal obstacles and opportunities lie at the state level. I demonstrate in this book that state lawmakers forestall legal opposition by strategically utilizing attenuated governance: downplaying the role of the state and deploying private delivery mechanisms to avoid constitutional challenges.

This is an account of policymaker learning and *elite*, rather than mass, feedback effects. Much recent work deals with the effect of privatized delivery upon public attitudes (Ellis and Faricy 2011; Gingrich 2014), whereas I examine elites' strategic use of attenuation to survive judicial scrutiny. Attenuated governance is primarily aimed at fending off legal challenges (although it can also serve to reduce the likelihood of political challenges) by providing courts with a powerful rationale in favor of program constitutionality: the idea that *the state is not involved* in a constitutionally suspect policy output.

Unlike the public, judges and justices are not hoodwinked by the hidden nature of tax expenditures,[6] nor is their decision-making swayed by a program's popularity or distributional consequences but rather by ideas and ideology, institutional preservation, policy design, and determinations of policymaker intent. Case law is a source of policy feedback because courts are constrained by precedent (Stone Sweet 2002) and because court decisions provide information to policymakers and advocates about which policy designs and communications strategies are most likely to survive in future.

[6] A tax expenditure is a policy tool that allows policymakers to spend money through the tax code.

Conservatives, in particular, have been astonishingly successful at utilizing attenuated governance to achieve their ends. Patiently, tactically, and iteratively, over more than sixty years of voucher litigation, conservatives have honed their legal strategy by testing different communications strategies and policy designs in court. Although, as I show in Chapter 1, both liberals and conservatives have incentives to attenuate when they fear legal losses, the privatization strategy meshes well with many conservatives' preference for market-based policy solutions. Today's explosion of school vouchers is the result of decades of policymaker learning about which sorts of programs and communications are most resilient in the face of legal attack.

Organization of the Book

The first two chapters lay out the analytical frameworks that animate this book. Chapter 1 explains why policymakers have an incentive to engage in attenuation by situating the politics of the hidden state within America's *three foundational identity struggles*: age-old, divisive, and recurrent contestation over race, religion, and civic institutions. Elites use attenuated governance to pursue their policy goals amid intensive contestation when more visible programs would be struck down as unconstitutional. Sometimes these programs are also electorally unpopular, but policymakers' chief fear is a legal one – that opposition groups will mobilize and hostile judges will strike their programs down.

Chapter 2 demonstrates that disaggregating the hidden state into underlying dimensions is theoretically valuable. The rhetorical and policy design dimensions are analytically separable. They occur in different spheres of political activity: policymaker communications and policy design. Combining these two dimensions produces different sorts of politics, with implications for the survival and growth of submerged policies. I term these phenomena "two dimensions of attenuated governance."

In the next six chapters, I show how particular policy designs and communications strategies help programs pass, survive, and grow, avoiding legal entanglements and opposition mobilization. This book demonstrates that while passage, growth, and spread of attenuated policies can occur under many circumstances, such policies are most likely to succeed when policymakers combine a deeply attenuated policy design with a deeply attenuating communications strategy.

These *doubly distanced* policies provide one major advantage to policymakers: distancing the government from legally contentious purposes. "Legally contentious purposes" are policy goals that attract substantial constitutional controversy, whether support for racially segregated institutions, defunding public education, subsidy of religious activity, policing voter access to the polls, abortion counseling, contraceptive provision, or other polarizing issues. Attenuated governance deemphasizes the role of government in attaining these controversial goals. By placing responsibility for program management with third-party organizations or individual service users, policymakers can avoid or limit pushback.

1

America's Foundational Identity Struggles

THREE FOUNDATIONAL IDENTITY STRUGGLES (AND SIX INSTITUTIONAL ORDERS)

Attenuated governance is an indirect governance arrangement in which local, state, or federal government distances itself from policy outputs, either rhetorically or through third-party policy delivery. *Attenuation* is the process by which elites – that is, policymakers, organized interests, donors, and power-holders of all stripes – hide the role the state plays in promoting a particular policy goal. Policy-design attenuation involves the use of private organizations and tax expenditures – money spent through the tax code – to deliver social policy. Rhetorical attenuation involves policymakers distancing themselves from particular policy initiatives in their communications, by claiming that the state is *not* involved in producing a policy output. Figure 1.1 displays an example of an attenuated policy design, by which state funds ultimately support private schools. The complexity of the policy (administration by private organizations – to individual parents rather than directly to schools – and funding through the tax code rather than direct appropriation) serves to distance the policymakers from the private school at the other end of the chain.

It makes strategic sense for policymakers to attenuate when their policy goals provoke substantial controversy, mobilize opposition forces, and draw legal challenges, which those policymakers expect to lose. The most enduring of these controversies are the *three foundational identity struggles*: race, religion, and civic institutions. I term these contests "foundational identity struggles" because they are age-old, divisive, recurrent, and highly emotional battles over American national identity.

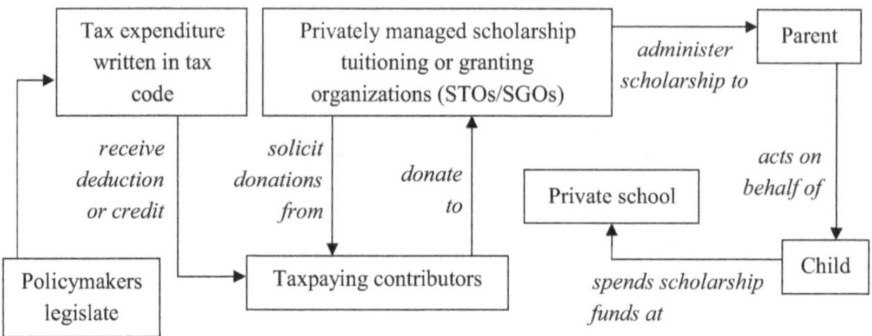

FIGURE 1.1. Example of an attenuated policy design.

The opposing sides in these great racial, religious, and civic foundational struggles form three sets of competing orders: constellations of institutions, practices, and ideas that hang together over time, each claiming to embody America's essence. These orders are coalitions of state institutions, advocates, groups, and other elites, which seek to gain and exercise governing power (D. King and Smith 2005). Attenuated governance is advantageous to elites facing a resurgent rival order, when rival ideas and interests start to gain control of governing institutions, because it enables members of the weakened order to achieve their aims indirectly while avoiding direct confrontation with powerful opponents.

The next section outlines the clash of ideas in America's three foundational identity struggles, which I term the "religious struggle," the "racial struggle," and the "public–private struggle." This book shows how all three struggles inspire political leaders and advocates to advance their aims and undermine rival views about the relationship between church and state, the role of the state in upholding or demolishing racial hierarchies, and the appropriate boundaries between state and markets.

The Religious Struggle

American history can be understood as a series of contestations between two rival forces and rationales, both of which claim to represent America's founding moment: a secularist order derived from Enlightenment thinking and an accommodationist order derived from religious thought and the legacy of Puritanism (Lacorne 2011). The former considers America to be a secular nation in essence, committed to a high and impregnable separation of church and state. The latter sees America as essentially religious and Christian, ultimately deriving its laws and government from God. What is America: a religious or a secular nation? Both sides claim the mantle of religious freedom, but they differ in their vision for achieving it.

For members of the secularist order, drawing from the legacy of Thomas Jefferson, the fullest expression of religious freedom comes when church and state are separated most completely (G. Thomas 2015). This expression entails strict adherence to the Establishment Clause, avoiding entangling the state with religious activity through subsidy of religious institutions or promotion of overtly religious purposes. For secularists, religion should be entirely a private matter. For members of the accommodationist order, by contrast, religious freedom means that the state should encourage the fullest flourishing of religious activity. Accommodationists place weight upon the Free Exercise prong, rather than the Establishment prong, of the First Amendment. The chief goal of the accommodationist order is for the state to avoid burdening religious freedom with onerous regulations but instead to support religious actors and institutions in their moral mission. Accommodationists think that it is the business of government to encourage and protect religion (Justice and Macleod 2016).

The religious struggle between rival accommodationist and secularist orders predates the founding of the United States. It was present in the tensions between colonial governments in their various establishments and differing laws on religious liberty and accommodation. Puritan colonies flourished, and few colonies – bar Rhode Island – established any great degree of religious tolerance. Just as the neo-Puritan, accommodationist order was partially dethroned by the disestablishment of the state churches (1786–1833), so the Second Great Awakening (1790–1840) elevated Evangelical Protestantism by inspiring religious revivals and infusing public life and state institutions with the Protestant religion (Noll 2002). Protestantism was institutionalized in the nation's public schooling system, and Catholicism firmly excluded.

Vying for power in the battles over public aid for denominational institutions (1835–1959), the secularist and accommodationist orders entered the twentieth century with accommodationism ascendant. But even as accommodationism won public commitments from the Eisenhower administration amid the postwar rise in religious affiliation and devotion, the Warren Court's school prayer decisions (1962–3) began to dismantle it. The federal courts turned toward a secularist understanding of church–state jurisprudence for much of the remainder of the twentieth century, although by the twenty-first century, accommodationists had once more begun to make inroads among jurists in cases such as *Pleasant Grove City* v. *Summum* (2009), *Salazar* v. *Buono* (2010), *Burwell* v. *Hobby Lobby* (2014), *Masterpiece Cakeshop* v. *Colorado Civil Rights Commission* (2018), and *the American Legion* v. *American Humanist Association* (2019).[1]

The Racial Struggle

American history can also be understood as a series of contestations between *white supremacist* and *transformative egalitarian* orders (D. King and Smith 2005, 2011). The racial controversy returns several different answers to the following question: Is America a white, racially "pure" nation or a racially diverse one – a nation committed to upholding racial hierarchies or demolishing them? The white supremacist order elevates those defined as "white" and associated with "whiteness" – a shifting category – than those defined as "black" or associated with "blackness." Instantiated in chattel slavery systems and later in the Jim Crow laws, the white supremacist order committed and, indeed, constrained elites to uphold a rigid racial hierarchy.

After a brief flourishing during Reconstruction (1865–76), the transformative egalitarian order's gains were eroded by the reinforcement of white supremacy by southern Congressional committee chairs within a divided Democratic Party and in the policy commitments of the New Deal (1933–6). With the hard-won gains of the civil rights movement and the extraordinary achievements of the Great Society (1964–8), the transformative egalitarian order secured governing commitments, turned some state institutions to its cause, and continued to fight "private" discrimination.

In its modern incarnation, the two sides in the racial struggle consist in those who do and those who do not consider the appropriate role of government to include directly addressing persistent material racial inequalities (D. King and Smith 2005). King and Smith term the institutions and organizations devoted to remedying material racial

[1] *Pleasant Grove City* v. *Summum*, 555 US 460 (2009); *Salazar* v. *Buono*, 559 US 700 (2010); *Burwell* v. *Hobby Lobby Stores, Inc.*, 573 US _ (2014); *Masterpiece Cakeshop, Ltd.* v. *Colorado Civil Rights Commission*, 584 US _ (2018); *The American Legion* v. *American Humanist Association*, 588 US _ (2019).

inequality through government action a *race-conscious* policy alliance. It sets itself in opposition to a *color-blind* policy alliance, which disclaims race-targeted measures such as affirmative action (D. King and Smith 2011; Hackett and King 2019). In the twenty-first century, the color-blind alliance has gained the upper hand, as the federal courts turn against affirmative action, endorse voter ID laws, and loosen some of the electoral commitments established under the Voting Rights Act.

The Public–Private Struggle

In combination with the *religious struggle* and the *racial struggle,* America is also an arena of battle between communitarian and individualistic orders, which I term the "public–private struggle." The former derives an explanation for America's successes from its communities and civic institutions, and the latter, from the character and actions of individual citizens and leaders. Both communitarians and individualists consider the promotion of liberty to be central to American politics, but they differ in their interpretation of this core American value.

The nation's founding documents draw intellectual succor from individualist intellectuals such as Thomas Paine and John Locke, for whom true liberty could be secured only through the efforts of property-owning individuals free from an overweening state. But for leaders such as George Washington and Benjamin Rush, liberty was understood to be "a blessing bestowed on the entire community rather than a privately held benefit distributed to rights-bearing individuals" (Balogh 2009, 24).

In the constitutional commitment to individual rights, America owes a debt to Lockean classical liberalism. The Civil War amendments, particularly the Fourteenth Amendment, further elevated the autonomous, rights-bearing individual (Balogh 2009, 16). Nevertheless, the early spread of public education in the United States and other civic institutions embodied the communitarian vision of the common good and classical republicanism. Nineteenth-century courts consistently favored the welfare of the community when it conflicted with the private property rights of individuals (Novak 1996).

The Progressive Era (1890–1920) furthered the communitarian order by expanding civic institutions and public education, yet by the twentieth century, the "laissez-faire" state began to grow, embodying a more individualist principle that elevated personal rights and property claims. This contestation between communitarian and individualistic orders

TABLE 1.1. *Three foundational identity struggles*

Foundational identity struggle	What is America?	Rival orders in America's foundational identity struggles (notable proponents and inspirations)	
Religious struggle	Religious or secular?	*Accommodationist America* John Winthrop John Edwards Frederick Frelinghuysen Billy Graham	*Secularist America* Roger Williams Thomas Jefferson James Madison Clarence Darrow
Racial struggle	Racially pure or diverse?	*White supremacist America* John C. Calhoun Strom Thurmond George Wallace	*Transformative egalitarian America* Abraham Lincoln Frederick Douglass Martin Luther King
Public–private struggle	Individualistic or communitarian?	*Individualistic America* John Locke Thomas Paine Milton Friedman	*Communitarian America* George Washington Benjamin Rush Horace Mann

continued into the second half of the twentieth century with the growth of unionization and the expansion of state administrative capacity during the New Deal and Great Society years, followed by conservative retrenchment and the rise of individual rights jurisprudence (Lewis 2017). Americans, like their northern neighbors, are fundamentally ambivalent about the appropriate role of the state (Tuohy 1992).

Table 1.1 outlines the three foundational identity struggles and the six institutional orders that compete within them. These fundamental struggles prompt the questions: What is America? Who are we as a people? Over the course of American history, political elites have asked these questions repeatedly (Huntington 2004). This book focuses upon elites, not the public, because it is elites who develop and articulate the systems of meaning that frame public discussion on these core questions (Hunter and Wolfe 2006). Elites adjudicate competing claims. And each side in these great struggles returns different answers, with one side or the other in the ascendance in different periods.

These political–institutional orders are united by their policy commitments, concepts, and ideas. Ideas are central to the struggles between rival orders because, as this book argues, the key to the growth of the hidden state lies in the elaboration of *rationales* for policy by political elites: policymakers, advocates, lawyers, judges, and organized interests. Ideas are enacted as policy by courts and legislatures through "practices of reason-giving and reason-taking" (Justice and Macleod 2016, 26). Ideas define rival orders' goals and desires, meanings and interpretations, and judgments and expectations (R. C. Lieberman 2002). They take on significance here because of the importance of rationales in the legal defense of controversial policies and because the particular ideas at issue in these struggles concern the very foundations of American identity and nationhood: religious freedom, racial hierarchies, and civic commitments. Ideas have power.

Of course, I am not the first to uncover foundational identity struggles, although I am the first to label them as such. Each of these rivalries attracts scholarly attention by virtue of their pivotal importance in American political thought and action. But few scholars deploy the same terminology and theoretical assumptions or consider these battles as clashing institutional orders animated by ideas and in search of political power. Political scientists King and Smith, who created the racial institutional orders framework, and historian Denis Lacorne, who considered America's religious history as a clash between Enlightenment and neo-Puritan forces, are exceptions. This book is the first to translate debates in political theory between communitarians and individualists into an institutional orders framework, showing how these ideas animate political coalitions in the real world.

America's foundational struggles do not neatly align, and the same patterns of interest recur across broad swaths of time. Patterns of the past leave traces in today's politics (Orren and Skowronek 2004). The study of religious, racial, and public–private struggles is typically siloized by subfields, being the preserve of scholars of religion, race, and political economy, respectively. In this book, I consider how these foundational struggles operate *together* to structure American political development.

The rival orders within America's religious, racial, and public–private struggles align and crosscut in multitudinous ways. They are analytically distinct, since the adoption of one order's commitments in a particular foundational struggle does not necessitate the adoption of another's, although in recent years, these struggles have aligned on either side of the growing partisan divide. Communitarianism aligned with accommodationism within nineteenth-century Protestantism. Early Baptist groups combined religious fervor with both individualism and strict regard for church–state separation. Today, white evangelicals tend to adopt accommodationist and individualist positions in the modern culture wars. White supremacists during slavery and its aftermath leaned upon religious justifications, but their opponents also drew intellectual succor from these sources. The segregated schools rejecting Bryan Poindexter and his classmates were strictly nonsectarian in orientation; yet modern conservatism marries accommodationism with color blindness, even as it grapples with the tenacious white supremacist vision emboldened by the Trump administration.

These rival orders are not to be interpreted as monolithic in any period of American history. America's foundational identity struggles exhibit intercurrence (Orren and Skowronek 2004). Multiple, incongruous authorities, policies, ideas, and institutions created at different times operate simultaneously. Nevertheless, it is possible to discern eras in which one side or the other predominates over the other. By "predominate" I mean that an order has gained temporary ascendance within the governing institutions of the state: executives, legislatures, and – importantly for the purposes of this book – the judiciary. Each side seeks to repudiate its opponents' ideas in courtrooms and legislatures.

Although I identify the courts as key sites of order creation and displacement, they are not the only such sites. Rival orders fight in legislatures, in bureaucracies, and on the field of electoral battle. States, representatives, executives, and judges vie with one another to determine the Constitution's meaning (Orren and Skowronek 2004). Judges are situated in politics. "Adversarial legalism" characterizes American politics, policy, and governance because American judges are more political, and their decisions less uniform, than judiciaries in comparable countries (R. A. Kagan 1991). The American state is a legally constrained decision-making system in which party influence on the process is strong (R. A. Kagan 1991; McCann 1986). As this book demonstrates, courts are often partisan institutions, susceptible to lobbying, and called upon to adopt political roles alongside policymakers, bureaucrats, and advocates.

At certain critical junctures, the balance tips in favor of one or the other side under the pressure of change fashioned by political entrepreneurs, that is, individual actors and organizations seeking to achieve their ends by harnessing political rules, ideas, and institutions and by exploiting their opponents' weaknesses (Skowronek and Orren 2016). This displacement of extant arrangements of power and authority is evidenced by the expressed ideas, membership, and public commitments of the governing organs of the state. For example, the rise of the racial egalitarian order occurred by means of the dismantlement of Jim Crow laws, the institutionalization of anti-discrimination practices in government, and the turn of the judiciary toward such ideas as "disparate impact" and "affirmative action."

Recently, the changing behavior of conservative organizations, such as the Koch network, the Goldwater Institute, and the Cato Institute, presages the growing power of the individualist order. In particular, Koch grantees, once hostile to an activist Supreme Court, have started to press for an activist judiciary to secure their objectives (MacLean 2017). What should white supremacists, racial egalitarians, accommodationists, secularists, individualists, and communitarians do when rival ideas and interests start to gain a degree of legitimacy? Is it possible for elites to achieve their policy goals when their enemies start to amass power and mobilize opposition? How can losers stop winners from sweeping aside their policy commitments?

Legacies of Losing

In the broadest terms, this book is an account of what happens when an order is (temporarily) dethroned and its rival elevated. I argue that combatants in America's three foundational identity struggles often utilize indirect means to achieve their aims despite rival orders' institutional and ideational power. Repeated interactions between winners and losers in American politics sustain multiple, intercurrent traditions.

American political development can be understood not only as a series of constitutional "moments" but also in terms of powerful "antimoments" – that is, robust challenges to the key transformative eras in American politics: the Founding, Reconstruction, and the New Deal (Tulis and Mellow 2018). The "losers" at these critical junctures – Barry Goldwater, Andrew Johnson, and the anti-Federalists – ultimately became "winners" because the manner of their losing sowed the seeds for the eventual triumph of their cause. The ideas the losers advanced did not dissipate but instead persisted, inspiring incursions against the dominant regime and ultimately achieving success for the losers' preferred ideas and policies.

This book does not concern itself with "losers" in the sense of those beaten at the ballot box in pivotal elections. I am concerned with the policy forms *policymakers in power* choose to utilize when they expect their policies to attract substantial controversy and be struck down as unconstitutional. These policymakers are "winners" in the sense that they have the power to make policy. They are "losers" in the sense that they perceive their guiding commitments – to secularism or accommodationism, white supremacy or transformative egalitarianism, communitarianism or individualism – to have become controversial and, hence, vulnerable.

As rival orders gain adherents among advocates, policymakers, and judges, policymakers strategically attempt to protect and insulate their policy goals. Legislators anticipate policy feedback as policies reshape political opportunities and adjust their designs and communications strategies accordingly (Schneider and Ingram 2019). Policymakers are "forward-looking" by disposition, in that they consider the effect of their decisions upon future political opportunities and costs (Skowronek and Orren 2016, 40). They pay attention to the nature of the rival orders they seek to dislodge when they make strategic political choices (Teles 2008, 3). When they anticipate legal losses, they act to preserve their interests.

In Robert Dahl's classic treatment of Supreme Court decision-making, preference mismatches between justices and elected policymakers should only occur for very short periods because "the Supreme Court is inevitably a part of the dominant national alliance" (Dahl 1957, 293). If this were true, court challenges would not make much difference to political elites' governing commitments. Electoral winners would not need to fear legal overthrow of their policies because the values of justices and politicians should always align.

But Steven Teles demonstrates that there is a lag between winning at the ballot box and reshaping the composition of the judiciary at federal and state levels. It takes longer for the legal market to clear, that is, for justices to become aligned, politically, with policymakers who have become politically dominant, than is anticipated by some versions of the "political court" theory (Teles 2008, 10–11). Hence, those in the position to make policy sometimes face courts whose allegiance lies with rival ideas and interests: courts exhibit "ideational entrenchment" (Teles 2008, 268). Attenuated governance can help here. By obscuring the role the state plays in promoting legally vulnerable policy ends, policymakers can successfully avoid or weather constitutional challenge – even when their goals do not align politically with those of the courts.

In modern times, the two sides in the *racial, religious*, and *public–private foundational identity struggles* align along partisan lines to a much greater extent than at any time in America's past. The Democratic Party is secularist, diverse, and communitarian. The Republican Party is accommodationist, white, and individualistic. This partisan alignment is symptomatic of the intensive polarization that characterizes modern American politics – more contentious, with more confrontational rhetoric and a fractured, compartmentalized society (Bernhard and O'Neill 2018). Polarization heightens the strategic value of attenuation, as the next section explains.

How Foundational Identity Struggles Give Rise to Attenuation

Why would governments wish to hide their role in promoting a policy output? We know that voters' negativity bias – their tendency to ascribe greater weight to public failures than successes – makes anticipative blame avoidance a powerful impetus (Hood 2002; R. K. Weaver 1986). For controversial issues, the dangers of associating with a polarizing program are even greater. Aside from the political mobilization of opposition forces, there may be constitutional matters in play. After the Supreme Court struck down segregated education, state governments' attempts to perpetuate it were vulnerable to legal challenge. Similarly, forty state constitutional provisions prohibiting public aid for denominational schools make it risky to fund religious education openly (Hackett 2014a).

The three foundational identity struggles are continuously contested, but the temporary triumph of one side or the other gives rise to situations in which it is strategically advantageous for policymakers to engage in attenuated governance. For example, the rise of the racially egalitarian policy alliance in the dying years of Jim Crow made it politically difficult for segregationist regimes in the South to identify the state *publicly* with the white supremacist cause. One of their solutions was education tuition grants, an attempt to utilize attenuated policy designs to uphold segregationist institutions *without appearing to do so*. White supremacists infamously sought to avoid the Fourteenth Amendment challenge by deemphasizing the role of the state in supporting restrictive covenants,[2]

[2] Restrictive covenants are legally binding conditions written into a property's deeds that dictate what all future homeowners can and cannot do with their property. Enforced by the state until the landmark Supreme Court decision *Shelley* v. *Kraemer*, 334 US 1 (1948), racially restrictive covenants deepened segregation by preventing homeowners from selling to people of color.

"privatizing" white primaries,[3] and transferring public property (parks, swimming pools, and other recreational facilities) to private hands – all while maintaining it with public funds.

Several decades later, as the transformative egalitarian achievements of the Great Society years faded, Congress launched Section 8 and Housing Choice Voucher schemes, which provided a level of public subsidy of tenants almost identical to that of public housing projects but delivered in disguised form. By using taxpayers' money to subsidize private rentals rather than build new projects, public subsidy of low-income housing could continue to grow even as welfare became stigmatized. Housing vouchers enabled policymakers to use public money to relieve welfare needs without the necessity of actually naming the program "public housing" (Vale and Freemark 2012). It was difficult for federal policymakers to commit to public housing publicly because of the backlash against race-conscious measures to ameliorate inequalities. Attenuated policies, such as housing vouchers, could help low-income African Americans (a core goal of the race-conscious alliance) without arousing so much controversy.

Similarly, the ascendance of secularist understandings of church–state relations during the Warren Court (1953–69) and its immediate successors made it difficult for accommodationists in government to support religious institutions publicly – hence the turn toward attenuated forms of governance in an effort to avoid entangling the state with religious purposes, with mixed success. Third-party "circuit-breakers," to use Justice Souter's felicitous phrase, help sidestep Establishment challenge by breaking the link between religious institutions and the state (or at least, *appearing* to do so). In one church–state case in Virginia, Souter dissented with the argument that "[h]ere there is no third-party standing between the government and the ultimate religious beneficiary to break the circuit by its independent discretion to put state money to religious use" (Souter 1995). His reasoning implies that indirect subsidy

[3] White primaries were primary elections in which only whites were allowed to participate. In response to the Supreme Court decision in *Smith* v. *Allright*, 321 US 649 (1944) outlawing the white primary, several states sought to make their systems legally acceptable by repealing primary laws on the books and renouncing all state control. This effort to distance the state from controversy by delegating the elective process to private groups was only partially successful, however, because courts generally found the state to be unconstitutionally entangled with these racist institutions, e.g. *United States* v. *Classic*, 313 US 299 (1941); *Elmore* v. *Rice*, 72 F Supp 516 (E.D. S.C. 1947); *Terry* v. *Adams*, 345 US 461 (1953).

of religious institutions via third parties is less constitutionally suspect than direct payments.

As the secularist order was eroded in turn by the accommodationist order – instantiated in the passage of federal and state Religious Freedom Restoration Acts (RFRAs) and a more conservative judiciary – it was the turn of the *secularists* to pursue their goals obliquely. It became important to avoid the impression that the state was violating religious free exercise. Hence, secularists defended policies on LGBT rights, anti-discrimination, and contraceptive coverage using an "attenuation" escape hatch, allowing legal recharacterization of their purposes in court (Walsh 2014). For example, members of the secularist order defended the contraceptive mandate under the Affordable Care Act (ACA) by introducing policy mechanisms that relieved religious organizations from having to provide contraceptive coverage *directly*. Organizations were merely required to signal their moral opposition to contraception, triggering a process by which a third-party administrator would instead provide the controversial coverage (Cartwright-Smith and Rosenbaum 2012).

Attenuated governance is necessary to avoid the charge that the ACA unconstitutionally burdens the exercise of religion under RFRA. Writing for the court majority in *Burwell* v. *Hobby Lobby* (2014),[4] Justice Samuel Alito summarized the Department of Health and Human Services' (HHS) argument:

> In taking the position that the HHS mandate does not impose a substantial burden on the exercise of religion, HHS's main argument... is basically that the connection between what the objecting parties must do (provide health-insurance coverage for four methods of contraception that may operate after the fertilization of an egg) and the end that they find to be morally wrong (destruction of an embryo) *is simply too attenuated*. (Alito 2014) [italics added]

Similarly, the core of the *Zubik* v. *Burwell* case was whether the ACA preserved religious freedom by distancing the Little Sisters of the Poor order and other religious organizations from what they saw as a morally objectionable purpose: the provision of contraception (Per Curiam 2016b; Matheson 2015).[5]

For the accommodationist *Hobby Lobby* and *Zubik* court, these efforts to attenuate the connections between corporations and a legally contentious purpose were insufficient, but the attenuation escape hatch

[4] *Burwell* v. *Hobby Lobby Stores, Inc.*, 573 US _ (2014).

[5] *Zubik* v. *Burwell*, 578 US _ (2016).

was successful in other cases. The DC Circuit found in favor of the secularists using a version of the attenuation defense in the 2006 case *Village of Bensenville* v. *Federal Aviation Authority* (FAA).[6] At issue was an accommodationist challenge to the secular order under the auspices of the RFRA. A church and its allies sued to protect a religious cemetery from the expansion of O'Hare Airport. Their opponents successfully employed an attenuation defense, arguing that although the FAA subsidized the expansion, it was sufficiently removed from the plan's administration (by the City of Chicago) that the connection between government and the controversial purpose – the destruction of hallowed ground – was attenuated. Hence, RFRA did not apply. The court argued, "[E]ven in instances in which the federal government plays some role, constitutional standards do not attach to conduct by third parties in which the federal government merely acquiesces" (J. W. Rogers 2006). Critics argue that these attenuation arguments "illegitimately shield such instances of state action from constitutional review" (Metzger 2003, 1446).

Attenuation through tax subsidy and private delivery mechanisms has also been used to defend institutions that practice racial, religious, or gender discrimination[7]: private transportation networks subject to free speech lawsuits;[8] religious practices by private childcare providers on army bases;[9] Health Maintenance Organizations litigated for denying Medicare services;[10] and company towns subject to Establishment and Free Exercise claims.[11] The constitutionality of these programs and practices depends crucially upon the extent to which "state action" can be said to have taken place. Attenuated governance defends by denying state action.

Table 1.2 shows how the six competing orders in America's foundational identity struggles have utilized attenuated governance to overcome challenges and achieve their goals amid intensive contestation.

[6] *Village of Bensenville* v. *Federal Aviation Authority*, 457 F 3d 52 (2006). This case was heard in the DC Circuit because the Federal Aviation Administration was the respondent. The City of Chicago was an intervenor for the respondent, arguing that "its plan does not burden petitioners under First Amendment precedent" and that "the relocation of the cemetery does not implicate RFRA because the City, not the FAA, is responsible for the imposition of the claimed burden on religious exercise" (J. W. Rogers 2006).

[7] For example, *Kerr* v. *Enoch Pratt Free Library of Baltimore City*, 149 F 2d 212 (4th Cir. 1945); *Schumacher* v. *Argosy Education Group*, 2006 US Dist. LEXIS 88608; *Grove City* v. *Bell*, 465 US 555 (1984).

[8] *Lebron* v. *National Railroad Passenger Corporation*, 513 US 374 (1995).

[9] *Hartmann* v. *Stone*, 68 F 3d 973 (6th Cir. 1995).

[10] *Grijalva* v. *Shalala*, 152 F 3d 1115 (9th Cir. 1998).

[11] *Marsh* v. *Alabama*, 326 US 501 (1946).

TABLE 1.2. *The value of attenuated governance in three foundational identity struggles*

Order	Aim	Need for attenuation	Means of attenuation	Success of attenuation
Racial struggle				
White supremacist order	Segregate schools; resist desegregation	End of "separate but equal" with *Brown* v. *Board of Education* decision, 1954[12]	Arm's-length administration through private commissions	Struck down: e.g. *Poindexter*, 1967, 1968 *Hall* v. *St Helena*, 1961[13]
White supremacist order	Enable housing discrimination, "redlining," and restrictive covenants	Outlawing of racial restrictive covenants in *Shelley* v. *Kraemer* decision, 1948[14]	Channel housing benefits through private housing providers	Limited success: civil rights advocates place responsibility with state
Racial egalitarian order	Boost racial diversity of student bodies and worker hiring pools; combat historical discrimination	Rise of affirmative action challenges, e.g. *Fisher* v. *University of Texas*[15]	Race used in as limited a way as possible; flexible individualized consideration; Rhetoric: affirmative "opportunity." Design: "diversity"	Mixed: Roberts Court favors "color-blind" approaches

(continued)

12 *Brown* v. *Board of Education of Topeka*, 347 US 483 (1954).

13 *Harrison* v. *Day*, 106 S.E. 2d 636 (Va. 1959); *Hall* v. *St Helena Parish School Board*, 197 F Supp 649 (E.D. La. 1961); *Pettaway* v. *County School Board of Surry County, Va.*, 230 F Supp 480 (E.D. Va. 1964); *Griffin* v. *County School Board of Prince Edward County*, 377 US 218 (1964); *Lee* v. *Macon County Board of Education*, 231 F Supp 743 (M.D. Ala. 1964); *Poindexter* v. *Louisiana Financial Assistance Commission*, 275 F Supp 833 (E.D. La. 1968); *South Carolina Board of Education* v. *Brown*, 393 US 222 (1968); *Coffey* v. *State Educational Finance Commission*, 296 F Supp 1389 (S.D. Miss. 1969).

14 *Shelley* v. *Kraemer*, 334 US 1 (1948).

15 *Fisher* v. *University of Texas at Austin*, 570 US _ (2013) (Fisher I); *Fisher* v. *University of Texas at Austin*, 579 US _ (2016) (Fisher II).

TABLE 1.2 *(continued)*

Order	Aim	Need for attenuation	Means of attenuation	Success of attenuation
		Religious struggle		
Accommodationist order	Support religious schools	First Amendment applied to states, 1947; Warren Court	Child benefit theory defense[16]	Growing success: e.g. *Zelman*, 2001 *Winn*, 2009[17]
Secularist order	Achieve secular goals over religious objections	Passage of federal and state Religious Freedom Restoration Acts	State action defense[18]	Succeeded in some cases: e.g. *Village of Bensenville*, 2006[19]
Secularist order	Prevent religious organizations from blocking contraceptive coverage	Passage of federal and state Religious Freedom Restoration Acts	Exemptions from government mandates	Failure to uphold mandate for closely held corporations: e.g. *Hobby Lobby*, 2014[20]

16 Child benefit theory (CBT) is the legal rationale that states money granted to an individual child and not *directly* to the private school at which they spend the money is constitutional in a way that direct grants would not be. For a full explanation of CBT, see Chapter 4.

17 *Zelman* v. *Simmons-Harris*, 536 US 639 (2002); *Arizona Christian School Tuition Organization* v. *Winn*, 563 US 125 (2011).

18 State action is a legal rationale invoked by private parties in their defense against lawsuits. The defense is that the private conduct in question is actively supervised by the state, and therefore, the private party reasonably relies upon state action. By repudiating the state action defense, opponents *attenuate* the connection between state policy and private action, arguing that the private conduct was *not* the result of deliberate and intended state policy.

19 *Village of Bensenville* v. *Federal Aviation Administration*, 457 F 3d 52 (2006).

20 *Burwell* v. *Hobby Lobby Stores, Inc.*, 573 US _ (2014).

Order	Aim	Need for attenuation	Means of attenuation	Success of attenuation
Public–private struggle				
Individualistic order	Reduce the amount spent on public education	Growth in federal funding for education after the Elementary and Secondary Education Act 1965	Redeploy public money to private providers; solicit private funds for education initiatives	Substantial growth of tax expenditures but traditional spending also continues to grow
Communitarian order	Increase control over private schools	Increase in private schooling; Every Student Succeeds Act reduces federal leverage	Require third parties to regulate schools and voucher holders	Regulations vary greatly by state; limited success in some states
Individualistic order	Decrease union strength	Rise of public sector unions, 1950s–70s	Promote freedom of choice for parents to choose weakly or un-unionized private and charter schools	Decrease in public and private sector union membership
Communitarian order	Grow the social welfare apparatus of the state; increase redistribution	Conservative state retrenchment during and after the Reagan presidency	Use tax expenditures; "private" funds to increase the state contribution invisibly; "choice-based rationing" of welfare benefits[21]	Substantial growth of tax expenditures but problem of control and equity

21 "Choice-based rationing" is an informal system of rationing that discourages eligible beneficiaries from claiming instead of denying their claim formally. The claimant's failure to receive benefits can be attributed to the claimant's own choices instead of choices made by the state (Super 2003).

In each case, the order members' desire to achieve their aims (column 2) generates an incentive to *attenuate* (column 3) because the order has temporarily lost predominance within state institutions. As adverse litigation and political confrontations mount, individuals and organizations deploy attenuated governance (column 4) to insulate their preferred policies from challenge, with varying success (column 5).

Why Choose Attenuated Governance rather than Other Tactics?

Attenuated governance is not the only means by which elites can seek to avoid entangling the state with racial, religious, or civic controversy that they expect to lose. Table 1.3 displays multiple strategies deployed by policymakers to achieve their purposes even when an order opposed to their interests holds power. These strategies are not always mutually exclusive but may sometimes be pursued simultaneously, for example, tax credit scholarship programs (attenuation) aimed at disabled students (targeting) (Table 1.3).

Attenuated governance, however, is the most powerful of the strategies in Table 1.3, for four reasons. First, attenuated governance emphasizes the role of private interests, a strategy that appeals to the political value of market-based solutions to public policy in the United States. Americans prefer the national government to "enable rather than command" (Balogh 2009, 3). This preference for market solutions is manifested in long-standing support for private enterprise and mistrust of government authority. Attenuation provides an opportunity for advocates to draw upon market-based, private sector rhetoric that can serve to reduce hostility to government programs, especially among Republicans (Lerman, Sadin, and Trachtman 2017; Huntington 2004; R. A. Kagan 1991).

Second, attenuated governance has the greatest degree of plausible deniability. Unlike onerous regulations, policy targeting, or focusing on marginal spaces, attenuated governance explicitly distances the government from a legally contentious purpose. Third, attenuated governance is valuable because it enables policymakers to pursue controversial policy goals vigorously (yet invisibly). Although policy drift also distances the state from policy outputs by enabling policymakers to merely avoid updating policies rather than purposely enacting new ones, drift is a slow, passive, and unwieldy option that binds policymakers to outdated legislation.

Fourth, attenuated governance is more suitable than ordinary policy targeting or direct taxing and spending for policy areas that invoke value claims. Unlike regulative or distributive policy areas, the three

TABLE 1.3. *Strategies for avoiding political controversy*

Strategy	How it helps avoid policy challenges	Examples
Attenuation	Distance government from contentious issues. Use private delivery circuit breakers in policy design or focus on private action in communications strategies, deemphasizing the role of the state in producing policy outputs.	Tax credit voucher scholarships Indirect contraceptive delivery under ACA "Dollar Diplomacy" partnerships with bankers (Moore 2011)
Regulation	Create, expand, and administer complex, visible regulations in the interests of "fraud prevention" or "women's health," which can indirectly achieve the policy goal.	Voter ID laws Regulation of abortion providers Right to Work legislation
Targeting	Target sympathetic constituencies to make overt opposition difficult. Direct action at a small, defined group to minimize concerns about broader ramifications.	Funds for disabled children to attend private schools Home loans for veterans through the Department for Veterans Affairs
Marginal action	Federal action at the margins of the nation, and taxes assessed indirectly at the nation's borders (Balogh 2009, 52).	Remove Native Americans in marginal lands Deportations and immigration enforcement
Drift	Deliberately fail to update policies such that their coverage becomes increasingly incomplete or their regulations are superseded.	Welfare state retrenchment through "risk privatization" (Hacker 2004)

foundational identity struggles invoke morality policy debates, animated by values embedded in ethical conceptualizations of the world. These are grand, deep-seated, powerful and mobilizing, recurrent, and highly contested hot-button political issues. They are, therefore, closed to the sorts of compromises common in other areas of policy (Hollander and Patapan 2017). These racial, religious, and public–private struggles are firmly rooted in America's history and self-understanding, provoking constitutional questions that cannot be resolved through ordinary political channels. The urgent moral claims pressed by combatants in America's foundational struggles are at odds with the slow, frequently frustrating pace of political change in a separated, federal system with many veto points.

Attenuated governance helps policymakers sustain their programs (by insulating them from legal challenges) and gain reelection (by reducing the danger of angering powerful opponents). Reelection-focused policymakers are keen to avoid arousing legal attacks by powerful opposition forces, so they are expected to avoid entangling the state with controversial issues as far as possible. A Cato Institute interviewee described these incentives:

> Politicians hate to lead, they'd much rather follow public sentiment, and until public sentiment and public education is improved with respect to school choice, voters know what the possibilities are, politicians will be afraid to get out in front and lead voters along towards school choice programs. (Coulson 2010b)

The result of these strategic imperatives – concern for program passage, defense, and reelection – is attenuated governance.

What about Playing to the Base Instead?

One source of possible counterarguments to this explanation for the origins of attenuated governance arrangements is the observation that tribal partisanship is strengthening, priming ordinary citizens to consider policy in light of their partisan commitments (Jacobs and Mettler 2018). Accordingly, we might expect policymakers to jettison low-reward, blame-avoidance measures in favor of a full-throated endorsement of their own side's commitments, mobilizing their base. In this scenario, the growing prominence of the three foundational identity struggles could be expected to reduce, rather than increase, the strategic value of attenuation.

My response is that this scenario does indeed arise. For example, when the white supremacist order was ascendant within southern institutions (1876–1954), it could pursue its aims openly, without attenuation. Conversely, the egalitarian order's achievements during the heyday of the liberal legal network described by Teles (around 1960–90) allowed it to achieve policies such as busing and affirmative action, which conservatives see as "durable policy outcomes far from the center of public opinion" (Teles 2008, 55). Moreover, there have been instances in American history when policymakers have yielded to the desire to emphasize, rather than attenuate, the government's role in producing a controversial policy output *even when they expect to lose*, including efforts to reinstitute school prayer, crush labor unions, or instigate government-sponsored affirmative action programs. But I also demonstrate that emphasizing the government's role comes with a cost of which policymakers are aware: it raises the likelihood that a policy will be overturned by legal challenges.

Partisan polarization among rival orders in America's racial, religious, and public–private struggles increases the strategic value of attenuation for elites – policymakers, advocates, donors, and organized interests. As the Republican Party has aligned itself more closely with white, colorblind, accommodationist, and individualist forces and the Democratic Party with rival secularists, egalitarians, and communitarians, the prospects of compromise have diminished. Drawing upon an increasingly professionalized party infrastructure, electronic communications, and an organized, well-funded constellation of public interest law firms, members of rival orders have powerful backing but must contend with a robust response from their opponents. The need to distance the government from legally controversial purposes becomes more pressing in proportion to the growth in political controversy and the institutional power of rivals.

Policymakers certainly engage in posturing – voting for policies that cannot become law or are certain to be struck down by the courts – in order to mobilize copartisans. But they are also concerned with policy and posterity: sustaining their legislative achievements into the future. American governance is better understood as "politics as organized combat" rather than "politics as electoral spectacle" (Hacker and Pierson 2010). In other words, most voters are weakly informed or unaware, with little or no knowledge of policy or the political process, so the true competitors in American politics are organized groups rather than atomized voters (Hacker and Pierson 2010). The prize for which these organized groups fight is a *policy* rather than electoral victory. America is a "policy state," in which, since the Founding, policymaking has consumed more and more of the business of government as the state has expanded (Skowronek and Orren 2016). Increasingly, policymakers care about policy and preserving it for the future.

Insofar as policymakers are interested in sustaining their policies for posterity, there is a strategic incentive to insulate such programs from legal challenges when these programs face intensive contestation. The strength of partisanship can be complementary – rather than opposed – to the logic of attenuated governance, in two ways: First, sustaining a program offers policymakers concrete achievements to help mobilize their base and consolidate support. Second, the strength of partisan heuristics and the segmentation of media markets allow leaders to dog-whistle, rather than holler, to their copartisans about legislative achievements (Albertson 2015). Hidden forms of attenuated governance insulate programs from legal challenges without precluding partisan mobilization.

This book demonstrates that the supposed trade-off between program defense and credit-claiming or control opportunities is illusory. Policymakers can claim credit and exert control through attenuated governance; they just do so in an oblique, coded way. Although it is typically less visible to the general public than are directly administered programs, attenuated governance presents no *credit-claiming* problem when policymakers use language such as "empowerment," "choice," and "quality education" to microtarget relevant issue publics (as I discuss in the concluding chapter) or when they create programs targeted at sympathetic constituencies such as foster children, military families, or disabled students (as I show in a survey experiment in Chapter 7).

Although funding is delivered indirectly via intermediaries or the tax system, attenuated governance presents no *control* problem when the money is tied to certain criteria and hedged about by regulations (as I show in Chapter 4). And attenuated governance has significant legal and political advantages over direct forms of governance because it insulates controversial programs from attack (Chapter 6). Distancing mechanisms may diminish *some* types of control and credit claiming, but they also enhance the chances that a program will pass, survive, and spread.

CONCLUSION

The puzzle that animates this book is this: Why does the hidden state grow when it is so expensive, expansive, elaborate, and regressive? The answer I offer is that it can be strategically valuable to attenuate the connection between state and policy outputs in certain circumstances.

By utilizing indirect policy delivery mechanisms and obscuring the role of the state in providing a policy benefit (forms of policy delivery and articulation that I call *attenuated governance*), policymakers can avoid or limit pushback from rival interests.

These rival interests arise from deep-seated controversies in politics, which I term "America's foundational identity struggles." These foundational struggles are the most enduring controversies in American political life: race, religion, and civic commitments. American political development is structured by competition within these foundational struggles by six institutional orders, that is, coalitions of institutions, ideas, and practices that hang together over time, motivating action.

The *racial struggle* consists in the opposition between white supremacists committed to upholding a rigid racial hierarchy and racial egalitarians seeking to demolish racial hierarchies and ameliorate racial inequalities directly. The *religious struggle* is the opposition between secularists committed to the most complete separation between church and state and accommodationists who think that the state should encourage the fullest religious flourishing. The *public–private* struggle is the contest between individualists who believe that the state should give the widest latitude to individuals and market activity and communitarians who believe government should build civic institutions and promote the collective good. Each of these institutional orders – white supremacists and racial egalitarians, secularists and accommodationists, and communitarians and individualists – claims to embody America's essence, so competition between them is intense and recurrent.

Although the six institutional orders are analytically distinct, in practice they have become more closely connected with growing partisan polarization in America's culture wars. In America's "politics as organized combat," politics is a fight over policy demands of organized groups. With growing partisanship, fights between America's institutional orders become fiercer. Elites use attenuated governance to pursue their aims amid hot-button political contestation when they need to sustain their programs against legal and political attack.

But exactly *how* do elites mount an attenuation defense? That is the subject of the next chapter. Attenuation can be pursued not only through policy design – utilizing private organizations or the tax system to deliver benefits – but also through communication strategies – obscuring the role of the state in providing a particular benefit and emphasizing that of the marketplace. Historically, some efforts to attenuate the connection between state and policy outputs have been more successful than others.

In the next chapter, I argue that the rival orders in America's foundational identity struggles have prevailed over their opponents to the extent they are mindful of the fact that attenuation is multidimensional. Programs are most likely to pass and avoid legal challenge when policymakers *combine* a deeply attenuated policy design with a deeply attenuated communications strategy. I show how attenuated governance differs from other forms of hidden, submerged, or delegated governance and why it is theoretically valuable to disaggregate the hidden state into *two dimensions of attenuated governance*.

2

Two Dimensions of Attenuated Governance

VOUCHERS IN AMERICA'S FOUNDATIONAL IDENTITY STRUGGLES

Foundational struggles over race, religion, and civic institutions give rise to attenuated governance when one order is displaced by its rival. As political elites contemplate legal challenge – and possible overthrow – of their cherished commitments, they act strategically to forestall it. Outright defiance is dangerous, but there is another way. By privatizing, delegating, denying certain intentions, and using coded, oblique speech – acting indirectly, in other words – policymakers can hope to avoid entangling the state with legally vulnerable policy outputs, thus preserving the policy supports of white supremacy or racial egalitarianism, secularism or accommodationism, and communitarianism or individualism, even after their opponents gain a degree of legitimacy and power within governing institutions.

Vouchers – policies that deliver a sum of public money to individuals for the purchase of services in private markets that would otherwise be provided by the government direct – are one tool by which combatants in America's foundational identity struggles have sought to preserve legally vulnerable policy commitments. Vouchers individualize policy choices, by gifting (or burdening) the individual consumer with funds to make his or her own purchasing decisions in social policy. This element of individual choice helps to distance the state from controversial policy outputs, because any benefit to private, segregated, or religious organizations is mediated by the consumer.

In place of government-built social housing, voucher programs give families money to spend on private rental accommodation. School voucher programs offer tuition payments for parents to spend at private institutions rather than send their child to a neighborhood public school. Voucher arrangements in health care provide government money for consumers to use in private health insurance markets to supplement or supplant publicly funded options such as Medicaid and Medicare.

The injection of market-based choice mechanisms makes it easier for political elites to distance the state from controversies. For example, by giving public funds through the independent decisions of families, the state can plausibly claim not to be involved in the operational choices of schools where school vouchers are spent (Eckes, Mead, and Ulm 2016). The state has created the benefit and registers or approves private providers. But because the connection between state and school is attenuated through the intercession of the consumer-citizen,[1] voucher schools could (and sometimes do) discriminate on the basis of race, sexual orientation, ability, and other factors (Eckes, Mead, and Ulm 2016). These rapidly expanding programs are transforming the state by delegating responsibility for core policy functions to private actors: shifting risk and attenuating chains of accountability.

The Rise of Vouchers

Much of the growth in American voucher programs has occurred since 2010. School voucher programs, for example, numbered eight in 2000, twenty-five in 2010, and sixty-two by 2019, covering more than half a million children across twenty-eight states. Despite concerns that the passage of the Affordable Care Act (ACA) would reduce enrolments in the voucher-based Medicare Advantage by cutting reimbursements to insurers offering such plans, the number of enrollees has doubled – to more than 20 million, from a quarter to a third of Medicare beneficiaries – since the ACA passed (Galewitz 2018). The 2008 passage of Veterans Affairs legislation increased the number of housing vouchers distributed by 10,000 per year. More than 2 million American households – veteran and nonveteran – currently utilize housing vouchers.

In particular, the growth of school voucher programs has been recent and explosive (Figure 2.1). The earliest vouchers were segregation tuition grants established, as I show in Chapter 3, by white supremacists in America's racial struggle (Hackett and King 2019).

[1] "Consumer-citizens" is a term used by Kimberly Morgan and Andrea Campbell to emphasize individuals' marketplace transactions rather than their participation in democracy.

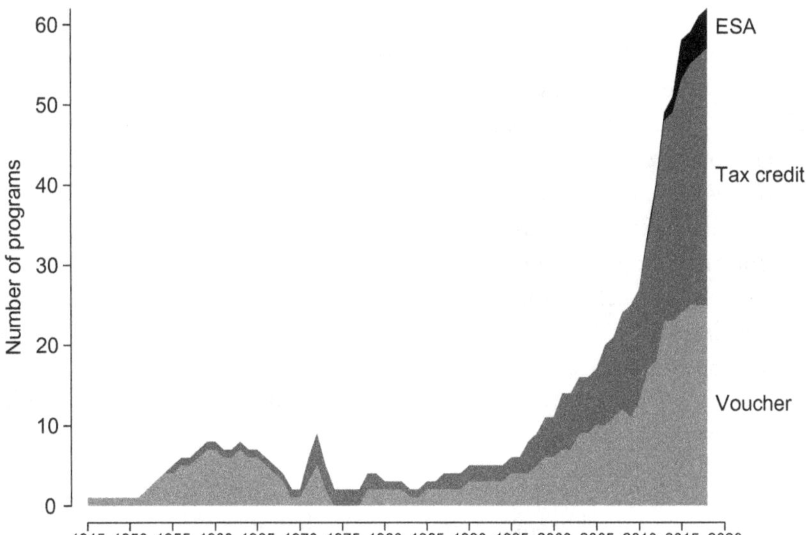

FIGURE 2.1. The growth of vouchers: cumulative total of voucher programs in the United States, 1945–2018.

Attempting to accomplish indirectly what they could not do directly – support segregated education – such programs were struck down because their racist purposes were easily exposed. Their successors, regular voucher programs of the 1990s and 2000s, received court approval in 2001 but suffered voter-led setbacks. Voters in four states holding referendums on voucher plans during this period – Michigan (1978 and 2000), Oregon (1990), Colorado (1992), and California (1993 and 2000) – rejected vouchers by a two-to-one margin (Molnar 2001).

After many years of such failures, two Midwestern states enacted voucher programs in the early 1990s: Wisconsin in 1990 and Ohio in 1995. Despite a favorable Supreme Court ruling on voucher constitutionality, voucher programs failed to multiply as quickly as proponents hoped. The slow growth in vouchers helped spur a strategic shift among voucher advocates. Instead of subjecting the proposed legislation to the public scrutiny of the referendum, advocates switched to a quieter legislative route detailed in Chapter 4. They were "legislating what can't be done by referendum" (Elam 1999). Increasingly they also turned to a more attenuated form of design: the tax credit scholarship. Tax credit scholarships are vouchers funded not by direct appropriations but through *tax expenditures*: departures from the normal tax treatment of income for particular people, institutions, or activities.

Receiving Supreme Court endorsement in 2010, in conjunction with Republican gains across the nation, vouchers achieved rapid growth, as Chapter 6 demonstrates. The year 2011 was declared "the year of school choice." It was merely a starting gun. Seven programs were created in 2011, six in 2012, nine in 2013, and twelve more by the end of 2016. Design varied. Some utilized tax credits and intermediary organizations for the distribution of grants, but all subsidized parents' choice of private school, including religious ones. Policymakers also experimented with a new breed of voucher policies – education savings accounts, which do not require legislators to establish such a convoluted program design as that of tax credit scholarships – and (as Chapter 7 explains) sought to avoid the antivoucher scrutiny by softening their rhetoric and emphasizing individual choice.

Disaggregating the Hidden State

As they learned about which sorts of programs might survive and flourish, policymakers adopted a wide variety of program designs, funding mechanisms, and communications strategies. But all programs subsidized parental choice of private school tuition. Vouchers require individuals to intercede between the government and the private organizations on which public funds are spent. This form of policy delivery is quintessentially attenuated because the money is transferred indirectly, rather than directly, to the private institutions that ultimately bank the money. In other words, such programs operate indirectly.

"Indirect action" is not a monolithic concept but rather a quiver of arrows in a policymaker's armory. Strategic policymakers can shore up their programmatic commitments by obscuring the role of the state rhetorically or through any number of policy design variants. With voucher policies, government gives individual consumer-citizens public funds to spend in private markets (K. J. Morgan and Campbell 2011). Hence, the relationship between the funder (government) and funded (the private organization that ultimately banks the money spent by the consumer) is indirect. "Indirect" is a slippery term. It can mean *unintended*, but it also means *opaque* (in its description), *circuitous* (in design), or *untraceable* (public understanding is weak). The multidimensionality of this concept is loosely evident in the literature but, until recently, has rarely been disaggregated explicitly in theoretical or empirical work (Hackett 2019). The result is a set of concepts that are theoretically rich but fuzzy around the edges.

Various forms of indirectness can be usefully distinguished, because hidden governance has differential effects in different spheres of political and legal activity. Some policies are both complex in design *and* hidden from the public. For instance, "submerged policies," including the tax expenditures that constitute the "hidden welfare state," are identified not only by their complex *design* – utilizing private organizations or tax expenditures to deliver government benefits – but also by the fact that they are *invisible* to ordinary people: the public knows little about them and is typically misinformed about their scope and purpose (Mettler 2009; Howard 2007). The term "submergence," then, could refer to either of two analytically separable phenomena: complexity or low visibility.

Submerged policies seem to be *both*, but these dimensions do not necessarily stand and fall together. For instance, a policy may be indirect in design without generating misunderstandings in a court of law: well-informed judges give legal weight to the indirectness of a policy design despite full knowledge of its intended purpose. When judges consider the constitutionality of religious school aid programs, indirect modes of program delivery are more likely to be found constitutional (Hackett 2017). Only policy design – not public visibility – is relevant here.

Tax expenditures are indirect in policy design, since they are delivered via the tax system, but the defining feature of this "hidden welfare state" seems to be its hiddenness to the general public, since explaining it will make it "start to disappear" (Howard 2007, 3). The best-known tax expenditures, such as the Home Mortgage Interest Deduction (HMID) and the Earned Income Tax Credit (EITC), are both hidden (by design) and not so hidden (in terms of public understanding). There are complex policies with relatively high visibility to the public (tax-efficient Section 529 college savings accounts, for instance) and directly provided policies with relatively low visibility (most environmental regulations). Submergence has powerful effects, but we need to know which aspects do the explanatory work.

Defining the hidden state leads to a further conceptual quagmire: From whom are the programs hidden? Is partial or incomplete information among the many equivalent to full information among the few? Do hidden policy designs and weak public understanding always rise and fall together? The HMID and EITC cases suggest not. The Treasury Department and Congress's Joint Committee on Taxation promote transparency by producing regular estimates of the revenue cost of tax expenditures (Hacker 2016). Ironically the burgeoning scholarship on the "hidden" welfare state might contribute to its demise (but only in the public understanding sense; the policy design remains).

Some of this "government out of sight" is deliberately hidden by elites, through explicit delegation of functions to individuals, private organizations, or other governments (Balogh 2009; K. J. Morgan and Campbell 2011). Other policies are misunderstood by the public despite the state's best efforts to inform them of their existence, scope, and purpose. For example, Mettler's data reveal that even a quarter of food stamp recipients – designed to be a more visible service – are unaware that they use a government social program (Mettler 2009). Most programs are ignored or misunderstood by ordinary citizens. Fewer are explicitly designed to downplay the government's role.

Policies with a high level of delegation, privatization, and complexity – such as America's health-care system – are often "kludges": clumsy but temporarily effective policy fixes that add up to a complicated system with no clear organizing principle (Teles 2013). But is a kludge a "kludge" because it is corrupt, or complex, or incoherent, or because the intentions of its creators have been lost in a rising tide of impenetrable policy fixes? Consumer-choice delegation such as Medicare Part D is rhetorically indirect – policymakers engage in distancing rhetoric in an attempt to alleviate public skepticism toward government – but also "indirect" in that, it creates unintended consequences: fraud, abuse, "market stickiness," and consumer frustration (Rai 2001; K. J. Morgan and Campbell 2011). "Pork barrel markets" can unintentionally empower producers at the expense of the state's own goals (Gingrich 2011). Yet most complex policies are neither corrupt nor incoherent. Divergence from policymaker intention is an additional conceptual layer to "kludgeiness" that is analytically separable from its other features.

Indeed, complexity or incoherence may themselves become the goals of policymaker action – rather than an unfortunate side effect to be avoided – in situations where it is advantageous to obscure policy purposes. Some tuition grant programs during the era of segregation, for example, were specifically designed to obscure the goal of racial discrimination by utilizing intermediary organizations for policy delivery (Hackett and King 2019; Forman 2007). These cases had kludgey features – complexity that obscures policy purpose – but were otherwise not kludgey at all, because these programs stood alone rather than existing as mere temporary bolt-ons. Distinguishing the effects of kludgeiness from similar forms of indirectness, incoherence, and complexity requires a differentiated approach and a conceptual map.

Two Dimensions of Attenuated Governance

Scholars do not typically distinguish different forms of indirectness. These characteristics are considered complementary to one another. Indeed, a policy that is indirect in that policymakers use rhetorical devices to distance themselves from its administration is often *also* a policy that utilizes a submerged policy design and is poorly understood by the public, with unintended consequences for democratic governance and market efficiency. But these manifestations of indirectness are in fact analytically separable. They do not stand and fall as one. They occur in different spheres: politicians' speechmaking and policy design as articulated by policymakers. Here I examine *two dimensions of attenuated governance*: attenuated delivery and attenuating rhetoric. A policy can be attenuated on one of these dimensions but not the other, both, or neither.

Attenuated governance obscures the state's role, a purpose that may be accomplished through rhetorical means as well as through the formal transfer of powers from one institution to another. Delegated governance, the submerged state, tax expenditures, and some kludges are versions of attenuated governance that lean upon the attenuated design dimension. "Government out of sight" and the hidden welfare state are versions of attenuated governance that tend toward the rhetorical, communications dimension.

The disjunction between attenuated delivery and attenuating rhetoric helps solve certain persistent puzzles in American political development. For example, although the postwar state channeled housing benefits in racially discriminatory ways through private organizations, those excluded from such benefits became *politicized* rather than depoliticized, as the classic submerged state literature would expect (Thurston 2015). One way to explain this surprising observation is to consider the disjuncture between attenuated delivery and attenuating rhetoric.

The Federal Housing Administration (FHA) utilized an attenuated delivery: utilizing private housing providers to distance the government from politically contentious issues of racial discrimination. But it could not prevent civil rights organizations from *de*-attenuating communications about such programs by revealing the role of the state. Advocates traced back patterns of racial exclusion to the government, contesting the FHA's efforts to disguise its own role in excluding blacks from housing (Thurston 2015). The result of this disjuncture was growing agitation by members of the racial egalitarian order, pressing for government to demolish, rather than reinforce, racial hierarchies.

TABLE 2.1. *Two dimensions of attenuated governance*

Dimension	Arena	Form of attenuated governance	Voucher politics example
Attenuating rhetoric	**Policy articulation:** how policymakers publicly describe their policies.	Policymakers engage in distancing rhetoric to increase the perceived distance between government and policy administration, or they obscure the government's role entirely.	Supporters describe school vouchers as "loans" or "scholarships" rather than "grants," emphasizing private individual choice. This linguistic sleight-of-hand *rhetorically attenuates* the connection between government and private academies.
Attenuated delivery	**Policy design and delivery:** how the policy functions and is administered.	Policy utilizes private organizations or the tax system to deliver benefits.	Tax credit scholarships are administered by a complex system of scholarship tuition organizations and tax deductions or credits. This *attenuated policy delivery* helps protect such programs from legal challenge by distancing the state from private school beneficiaries.

The distinction between attenuating rhetoric and attenuated delivery matters because these dimensions diverge in real cases, with legally and politically significant effects. Table 2.1 displays the policy articulation and policy design dimensions with illustrative examples from the field of voucher politics.

Attenuating rhetoric involves policymakers distancing themselves from a policy in speechmaking by obscuring the state's role in delivering policy outputs. Rhetorical attenuation involves the claim that the state does *not* deliver a particular policy, whereas rhetorical *de*-attenuation is the claim that the state *does* deliver a particular policy. In communications, school choice supporters often seek to weaken the connection between state and private schools, while their opponents seek to link the state to the private institutions it funds.

Policymakers can attenuate by emphasizing the way individual consumer-citizens intervene between government and policy delivery, rhetorically distancing the state from policy outputs.[2] For example, in recently reported debates over school choice legislation in Virginia and Arizona, Virginia attorney general Ken Cuccinelli said the program involved no direct appropriation of public funds, and Arizona state schools superintendent John Huppenthal argued that it "only indirectly benefits private schools" (Fischer 2013b; J. Walker 2012). In their press comments, opponents highlighted the role of the state. For Arizona School Boards Association general counsel Chris Thomas, "[i]t's a voucher program that results in government money being used potentially for an unconstitutional program" (Ringle 2011). For Virginian delegate Scott Surovell (D-Fairfax), "[i]t allows people to do through the back door what you're not allowed to do through the front" (J. Walker 2012).

Similarly, during the 2013 passage of voucher bills in Mississippi and North Carolina, the executive director of the NC Values Coalition, Tami Fitzgerald, attenuated the connection between state and school by emphasizing parental intervention: "It puts control back in the hands of the parents and it removes the state-created barrier to success for children with disabilities" (Bonner 2013). Her opponents sought to *de*-attenuate the connection between state and private schools by highlighting the role of the state. The *Fayetteville Observer* editorialized, "It may be going there indirectly, but public money would nevertheless send our kids to schools that are unaccountable to public oversight" (White 2012). The *Northeast Mississippi Daily Journal* also highlighted the state's role in subsidizing private schools: "It diverts tax dollars – indirectly, but still at public expense – into private schools" (Northeast Mississippi Daily Journal 2012). Attenuating rhetoric distances the state from policy outputs. De-attenuating rhetoric emphasizes the role of the state.

[2] With *attenuating rhetoric*, a speaker disclaims state responsibility, often attributing policy outputs to somebody else: a private organization, individual service users, or some other actor. The opposite, *direct rhetoric*, involves the government taking direct responsibility for policy goals or outputs. Distinguishing attenuating and direct rhetoric is necessarily a qualitative endeavor because meaning is highly contextual. But judges pay close attention to the distinction. Table A4 in the Appendix provides an extensive list of attenuating and direct policymaker statements cited by judges in voucher cases.

Distancing rhetoric is a common feature of policymaking, particularly in a federal polity. For example, regional officials rhetorically shift blame toward the central government in order to downplay their role in making unpopular spending cuts (Mortensen 2012). Emphasizing the role of individuals and markets can help downplay state action. Voucher supporters often emphasize the way individual consumer-citizens intervene between government and schools, rhetorically distancing the state from policy outputs.

The multivocality of attenuating rhetoric – its essential ambiguity – can be useful. Tax expenditures are politically appealing in part because they can be defended on many different grounds: "as aid to individuals in need; subsidies to third-party providers in the private sector; tax relief; and a means of limiting the growth of traditional government programs" (Howard 2007, 179). Elites engage in "dueling communications" about policy benefits and burdens (Jacobs and Mettler 2018, 347). I show in Chapters 3–8 that the decision to rhetorically emphasize or attenuate the role of the state in producing certain policy outputs has *legal*, as well as political, ramifications.

Attenuated policy delivery utilizes private mechanisms for the delivery of policy, *attenuating* the connection between government and ultimate beneficiary compared with directly funded provision: for example, subsidies to private lenders for student loans (as opposed to direct federal loans or grants), vouchers that provide a sum of public money to be spent in the private rental market (as opposed to public housing), tax expenditures for childcare, medical expenses, home-mortgage interest, and earned income tax credits (as opposed to in-kind benefits funded by direct spending or lower headline tax rates) (Hackett 2017). The intervention of the consumer-citizen in voucher politics is one sort of attenuated policy delivery, but some types of voucher further attenuate the relationship between government and ultimate beneficiaries using the tax system.

Weakly and Deeply Attenuated Policy

Scholars identify the hidden or submerged state as having different degrees of visibility to the general public: from the most direct spending programs with visible benefits, such as Social Security, to tax breaks with social policy purposes, to the least visibly governmental provision, such as regulated private benefits supported by tax breaks (Hacker 2016). All voucher programs are attenuated in the sense that they encourage private providers to take on the state's education function and rely upon the choices of individual consumer-citizens to distribute program benefits. But some forms of voucher *further* attenuate the connection

TABLE 2.2. *Deeply and weakly attenuated policy delivery schema*

Level of attenuation	Level I Weakly attenuated	Level II Deeply attenuated
	Definition	
Attenuated policy delivery	*Quasi-direct transfer of public money to private providers* Subsidize private providers to deliver services through contracts and leases.	*Tax exemption or reimbursement delivered through several intermediaries* Delivered entirely through private channels or tax exemption or subsidy.
	Consequences	
Effect on public knowledge of program	Greater degree of public knowledge but lower than direct spending. Political challenges more often.	Hidden. Low levels of public knowledge. Infrequent citizen involvement and political challenge.
Effect on interest group strategy	Organized interests have smaller informational advantage over public.	Groups have large informational advantage over public. Organized interests are energized.
Effect on policymaker strategy	More opportunities for credit claiming but harder to avoid blame for policy failures.	Many blame-avoidance opportunities. Some credit claiming ("reducing government involvement").
Effect on legal challenges	More likely to be challenged in court. More likely to be struck down if challenged.	Less likely to be challenged in court. More likely to be upheld if challenged.

between education providers and the state (Hackett 2017). For example, tax credit vouchers are funded by deducting taxation from donations to third-party organizations, which administer the scholarships. I term those policies "deeply attenuated." By contrast, vouchers funded by an ordinary appropriation without additional layers of administration or third-party delivery are "weakly attenuated" (Table 2.2).[3]

[3] Deeply attenuated programs are tax expenditures, rebates and credits, and policies delivered by third parties with more than one private organization interceding between the state and policy outputs; weakly attenuated ones are quasi-direct contractual arrangements between the state and private providers.

To identify the degree of attenuation of program design, I examine all fifty state constitutions and relevant legislative bill jackets and pieces of legislation, in conjunction with the federal Department of Education's private school regulatory information (Department of Education, Office of Innovation and Improvement, Office of Non-public Education 2009). I develop a twofold typology that defines two subcategories of attenuated governance: weakly attenuated (Level I) and deeply attenuated (Level II), corresponding to the distinction between spending and tax expenditures.

Both categories are part of the submerged state because they utilize private mechanisms for the delivery of social policy, but the latter is more attenuated than the former because it utilizes the tax system and additional private organizations to deliver funds. Two features of voucher and tax credit programs make in-depth qualitative readings of these policies necessary for categorization: (1) The complexity of the statutes and of the concept of submergence requires human readers to evaluate the relevant legislation and precludes automated computer coding. No numerical proxies have yet adequately captured the concept of submergence. (2) The policies' very attenuation – particularly long-standing programs buried in tax codes – requires detailed archival research and qualitative understanding of history and context.

In Table 2.2, I detail the criteria for determining membership of each category on the basis of policy design and summarize the information. In the attenuation schema presented in Table 2.2, regular vouchers are weakly attenuated (Level I), and tax credit scholarship vouchers are deeply attenuated (Level II).[4]

Level I: weakly attenuated – quasi-direct transfer of public money to private providers. Weakly attenuated Level I policies are the least attenuated part of the submerged state but can be meaningfully distinguished from policies that are *not* part of the submerged state at all. Unlike ordinary tax-and-spend policies, weakly attenuated policies subsidize private providers to deliver services. But unlike their more attenuated counterparts, weakly attenuated policies are not provided through tax exemptions, rebates, or credits but typically consist of contractual arrangements with private providers, hedged about by caveats that place limits on the assistance private school students can receive.

[4] Although there is within-category variation in policy design – differing eligibility requirements, for example – each program has more in common with other programs of its type than it does with other types of program along the dimensions elucidated in Table 2.2.

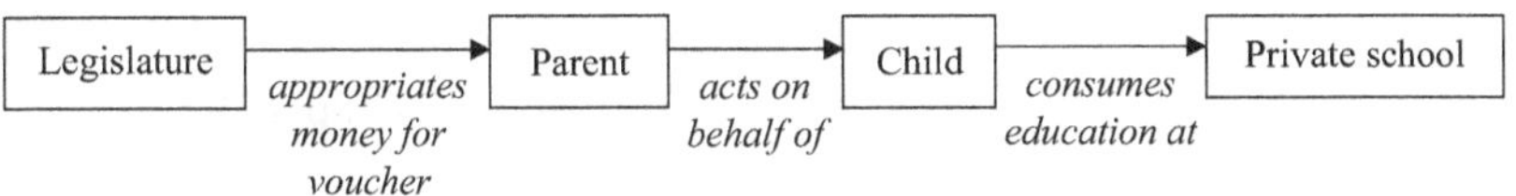

FIGURE 2.2. Weakly attenuated policy delivery.

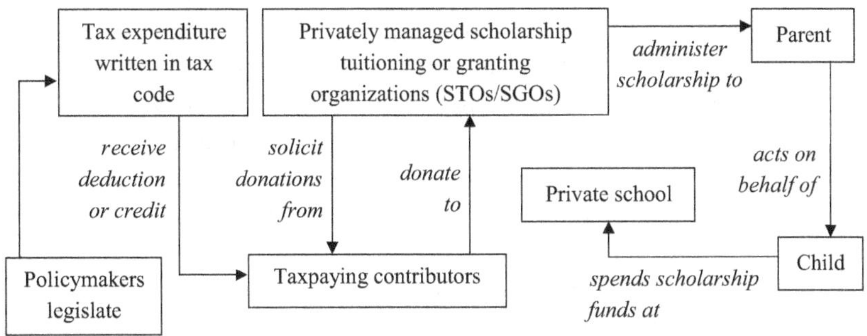

FIGURE 2.3. Deeply attenuated policy delivery.

Regular voucher schemes are a weakly attenuated policy (Figure 2.2). Unlike policies that utilize the tax system or additional third-party organizations for the delivery of policies, vouchers are relatively straightforward in design: they set aside a sum of public money for parents to spend on private education. While vouchers fund private mechanisms for the delivery of education, their relative lack of complexity and their use of appropriated funding make them less attenuated than many other types of aid.[5]

Level II: deeply attenuated – tax exemption, credit, or reimbursement delivered through several intermediaries. The more attenuated category consists of policies that deliver funds through a series of complex channels and the tax system. All tax exemptions, deductions, and credits fit this category, as do policies that provide funds through reimbursement for expenditure via several intermediate organizations. Tax credits are deeply attenuated (Level II) because they are delivered through public subsidy of donations to private organizations that award tax credit scholarships (Figure 2.3).

In states such as Florida, for example, corporations are entitled to redirect up to 100 percent of their corporate income or insurance

[5] Consequently, these lump-sum payments for tuition are subject to many divisive political confrontations, particularly over race: as a means either for southern whites to escape desegregation efforts or for urban minorities to obtain a better education (Forman 2007; O'Brien 1996; D. King and Smith 2011). See Chapter 3.

premium tax[6] liability annually by contributing to a Scholarship Funding Organization (SFO), which awards private school scholarships to low-income children (Florida Statutes 2001). Private providers tend to play a much larger role with tax credits than with voucher scholarships (Suitts and Dunn 2011; American Federation for Children 2012; Berner and Miksic 2014). The links between government and private schools are more attenuated.

The political ramifications of tax *deductions* can be distinguished from that of tax *credits*. Deductions subtract money for a specified activity from a taxpayer's gross income in determining his or her taxable income, either "below" or "above" the line, i.e. computed alongside an individual's gross income or after itemization. Credits reduce an individual's tax liability and come in "nonrefundable" and "refundable" varieties, the latter offering checks even to individuals whose tax liability has been eliminated entirely. The distinction between deductions and credits can be politically consequential because the former are regressive and the latter progressive. Hence, Republican administrations favor deductions, and Democrat ones favor credits (Faricy 2016).

But the distinction between deductions and credits is less consequential when it comes to voucher politics, because the regressivity of the program does not bear upon its constitutionality (although it might bear upon its political acceptability). In my statistical analysis (detailed in Chapters 3–6 and in the Appendix), there is no statistically significant difference between Republican and Democratic legislators in their likelihood of voting in favor of the passage of individual tax deductions in comparison to tax credit scholarships. The key distinction is between directly funded programs (Level I) and tax expenditure – funded programs, which include both deductions and credits (Level II).

Relationships between the Dimensions of Attenuated Governance

As Table 2.1 makes clear, policy design is not the only way to attenuate the connection between the service provider and the state. Policymakers use public utterances to take ownership of, or distance themselves from, policy outputs. Deeply attenuating rhetoric involves a speaker disclaiming governmental responsibility, attributing policy delivery to somebody else: a private organization, individual service users, or others (Table 2.3). Weakly attenuating rhetoric involves politicians' efforts to "own" an issue and take clear, direct responsibility for a policy output (Table 2.3).

[6] The Florida insurance premium tax is a state tax on insurance premiums that is levied on all authorized insurance companies issuing policies covering risks in Florida.

TABLE 2.3. *Divergence and convergence between dimensions of attenuated governance*

	Weakly attenuating rhetoric	**Deeply attenuating rhetoric**
	Quasi-direct	**Distanced-direct**
Weakly attenuated policy delivery	*Policy design and justification are relatively direct, making clear the government's role in delivering a policy output* • Regular school vouchers • Section 8 housing vouchers • GI Bill educational benefits • Food stamps or the Supplemental Nutrition Assistance Program • Public–private partnerships (P3s) through the Build American Bureau (e.g. modernization of air-traffic control)	*Policy design is straightforward, but politicians engage in distancing rhetoric that obscures the role of the government in providing the policy output* • In-kind aid programs for private schools (e.g. textbooks, transportation, science, and sports equipment) • Education savings accounts • Voter ID laws justified in "color-blind" terms
	Contested attenuated	**Doubly distanced**
Deeply attenuated policy delivery	*Policy design attenuates state-policy output connection, but policymakers rhetorically reveal the role of the government in delivering the program* • Segregation vouchers or tuition grants • Postwar subsidy of housing by the Federal Housing Administration • Subsidized health-care markets under the Affordable Care Act • (Recently) The Home Mortgage Interest Deduction, Section 529 college savings accounts, and the Earned Income Tax Credit • Mortgage securitization through the government-sponsored enterprise, the Federal National Mortgage Association a.k.a. "Fannie Mae" (during the financial crisis)	*Complex, attenuated policy delivery. In communications, policymakers obscure the government's role in the provision of policy outputs* • Tax credit scholarships • Tax expenditures such as lifetime learning tax credits • The exclusion of interest on owner-occupied mortgage subsidy bonds and of employer-provided defined benefit pension plans • Mortgage securitization through the government-sponsored enterprise, the Federal National Mortgage Association a.k.a. "Fannie Mae" (during "normal" times)

The rhetorical and delivery dimensions of attenuated governance correlate, but not always. Attenuating rhetoric has value even for policymakers creating a directly administered program because it helps them to avoid blame for policy failure (e.g. criticizing "irresponsible" gun owners or "predatory" mortgage lenders for policy disasters). Conversely, even extremely attenuated policy delivery may be "revealed" if advocates are able to communicate the state's role in delivering a policy effectively (e.g. policymaker communications about subsidized Section 529 savings accounts or ACA health-care exchanges). There is a disjuncture between the rhetoric of tax reform and policymakers' willingness in practice to embrace tax breaks and loopholes (Patashnik 2008). The components of attenuated governance do not necessarily rise and fall as one.

Elites attempt to avoid blame through "presentational strategies," an effort to influence public perceptions, and "agency strategies" or "policy strategies" to remove discretion or delegate policy responsibilities (Hood et al. 2009; Hood 2007). But attenuated governance differs from the blame-avoidance framework on three key dimensions. First, blame avoidance focuses on efforts to avoid "media blame crises" rather than policy litigation. Attenuated governance is primarily aimed at forestalling legal challenges and opponent mobilization rather than necessarily avoiding public opprobrium. This is an account of clashes between organized interests in courts and statehouses – "politics as organized combat" – rather than a description of the voter – politician relationship or "politics as electoral spectacle" (Hacker and Pierson 2010).

Second, attenuated governance is primarily a legislator and advocate, rather than an executive and bureaucrat, strategy because it concerns the design of a policy and associated communications. Blame avoidance is both anticipative and reactive, often responding to policy disasters in real time. Attenuated governance is entirely anticipative, grounded in a desire to avoid legal challenge by members of an opposed order.

Third, blame-avoidance techniques are efforts to avoid blame for error. In the attenuated governance framework, by contrast, policymakers attempt to distance the government from legally contentious purposes, not necessarily policy misjudgments or mistakes. Members of the white supremacist order during the dying years of the Jim Crowera, for example, used attenuated governance mechanisms to promote their purposes – which were popular with many whites – amid the transfer of the judiciary to the racial egalitarian cause.

Table 2.3 displays the divergence and convergence between two dimensions of attenuated governance. The most deeply attenuated policies are *doubly distanced*: policy delivery is indirect, and policymakers rhetorically obscure their role in the provision of policy outputs. These classically attenuated policies form the core of Mettler's submerged state, including tax expenditures such as corporate tax deductions and the exclusion of interest on owner-occupied mortgage subsidy bonds in which the role of the government is almost wholly obscured. School tax credit scholarships are doubly distanced.

Quasi-direct policies at the opposite end of the scale are funded through quasi-direct transfer, and the state's role in the provision of the benefit is clearer. In this category are social welfare programs, which may utilize private providers for the delivery of services, but policymakers and advocates clarify who is responsible for policy delivery. The direct funding of regular vouchers, and the publication of information about their administration and take-up, makes these quasi-direct programs easily traceable.

In other cases, the two dimensions of attenuated governance come apart. Some policies are deeply attenuated in design, insofar as they utilize a variety of third-party providers and tax expenditures to deliver benefits, but policymakers reveal their responsibility for the policy outputs through public communication. Tuition grant payments made by segregationists in the immediate aftermath of *Brown v. Board of Education* follow this *contested-attenuated* pattern. The weakly attenuated political rhetoric belied their deeply attenuated delivery.

Conversely, many programs with a straightforward policy design, funded by public appropriation and featuring a relatively direct connection between state and service providers, are obscure to the public because of a lack of high-quality political communication about the government's role in providing the policy benefit. These are the *distanced-direct* policies in Table 2.3. Many policy programs fit into this category because political communication is often ineffective in explaining the government's role in producing policy outputs.

Strategic Learning about Attenuated Governance

I argue that elites are strategic and that they actively seek the most effective way to instantiate their policy goals and preserve them from challenge. If politics is indeed organized combat rather than an electoral spectacle, as Chapter 1 asserts, then policymakers consider the fate of their policy commitments primarily as a function of elite politics, playing out in statehouses and courtrooms. The core argument of this book is that high-quality policy feedback from judicial decisions, ballot initiatives, and legislative proceedings helps elites construct a policy design and adopt a communications strategy most likely to achieve success. The *doubly distanced* policy form is most successful, so it has come to be adopted more frequently. Learning is a source of endogenous change.

Hypotheses

Combining attenuating rhetoric and attenuated policy delivery is key to the growth of the hidden state.

H1: The hidden state grows relative to the size of the direct state because policymakers have learned to combine attenuated policy delivery with attenuating rhetoric (doubly distanced policies).

I do not suggest that deploying attenuating mechanisms is the sole cause of hidden state growth but that it is crucial. Partisan control of government is strongly related to voucher passage, but partisanship arguments cannot explain why some Democratic legislatures support voucher policies while some Republican regimes eschew them. Market-based reforms to public services, such as New Public Management, have become more common, but any explanation based upon a consumerist reform impulse cannot account for specific patterns of voucher policy growth across states. Contracting out to third parties can save money, but not invariably. Policy feedback accounts for citizens' weak knowledge of attenuated policies and explains the uphill struggle facing reformers. Yet citizen knowledge varies widely over time and cannot explain patterns of legal challenges. This book asserts that attenuation spurs the passage and endurance of private school choice programs.

H2: Doubly distanced policies are more likely to pass and avoid or survive litigation.

The reason attenuated governance explains voucher growth is that it offers a legal cushion to policymakers seeking to create and protect their policy gains in constitutionally sensitive areas. Where there is a danger of intensive contestation, attenuating the connection between government and policy outputs makes strategic sense. In the case of vouchers, I argue that judges are more likely to uphold doubly distanced programs because government is not (or at least does not *appear* to be) excessively entangled in legally contentious areas of race and religion. If a policy is delivered by private organizations, then it is less vulnerable (though by no means invulnerable) to successful separationist challenge in the courts (Boyer 2009).

H2 stands in tension with the claim that tax expenditures are *more* vulnerable to elimination than traditional spending programs (Howard 2007; Haselswerdt 2014). Jake Haselswerdt finds that tax expenditures are more vulnerable to legislative elimination because they include more weakly justified programs, frustrate legislators, and lack a base of support from federal bureaucrats. I propose that the opposite logic applies in the legal realm: more attenuated policies such as tax expenditures are attractive to policymakers seeking to insulate them from legal attack and are protected by complex legal justifications based on the attenuation of the connection between government and religious institutions.

I leave to lawyers arguments about the actual entanglement of government with racially and religiously sensitive subjects. This book makes no judgment about the merits of claims about private religious schooling or parental choice. I simply observe that policymakers, litigants, and judges make, defend, and reject such claims. Attenuated policy design and rhetoric support programs in court by furnishing an argument in favor of program constitutionality – that the government is *not* entangled with illegitimate purposes – which may persuade judges. Arguments and rationales affect legal decision-making and outcomes (Spriggs and Wahlbeck 1997; Collins 2004, 2007).

Unlike Mettler's submerged state, the politics of attenuated governance does *not* hinge upon the general public's ignorance of its existence or scope. Judges are not duped by obscure delivery mechanisms. Doubly distanced policies are more likely to survive litigation because the intervention of private delivery mechanisms furnishes a persuasive argument in favor of their constitutionality. Supporters can more easily argue in court that the state is not entangled with an unconstitutional purpose.

H3: The politics of doubly distanced policies is quieter and less polarizing than that of quasi-direct or contested-attenuated policies.

The character of political debate is expected to vary according to the degree of attenuation of a policy on each dimension. The doubly distanced combination of attenuating rhetoric and attenuated policy delivery tends to produce the quietest form of politics: muted public debate and limited public understanding about the program's nature, scope, and effects. By contrast, a quasi-direct policy is likely to produce loud politics: vigorous, polarized public debate. Distanced-direct and contested-attenuated policies are expected to lie between these extremes, with a much more polarized debate for contested-attenuated policies than for the more rhetorically attenuated distanced-direct policies.

H4: Once a supportive legal precedent exists, policymakers can experiment with policy designs that are less attenuated (distanced-direct) without penalty.

By *H1* and *H2*, policymakers grow the hidden state because of the insulating qualities of attenuated governance. Attenuated governance hides the government's role in supporting politically polarizing policy outputs, insulating it from political and legal challenges. Once a supportive body of legal precedent exists, however, it may be possible to relax some of these safeguards without raising the prospect of legal catastrophe. If a body of case law establishes that a certain policy design attenuates the connection between government and legally contentious purposes, then the need for attenuating rhetoric lessens. This need may also diminish if public opinion shifts in a favorable direction. Remove the danger – entanglement with hot-button issues – and the incentive to engage in attenuation is diminished.

Sometimes the attenuation mechanism itself becomes politically contentious (e.g. contestation over the use of market mechanisms for the delivery of social policy). However, both Right and Left have incentives to create social policy marketplaces (Gingrich 2011). I do not imply that all social policy marketplaces are *intended* by their creators to hide the government's role in the provision of certain benefits; market mechanisms are pursued for many reasons. Instead, I argue that (a) marketplaces do have that effect (attenuated delivery) and (b) at least some social policy marketplaces are used for the purpose of hiding the role of the state in supporting legally contentious policy outputs. Attenuation can occur through multiple channels, of which social policy marketplaces are one.

CONCLUSION

Conceptual fuzziness afflicts the existing scholarship on the hidden, indirect, delegated, or submerged state because these concepts' underlying dimensions are rarely distinguished explicitly. My theory of attenuated governance is distinct from the theoretical constructs that animate these literatures, in part, because it delineates *two dimensions of attenuated governance*: policy articulation and policy design and delivery. These dimensions diverge in real cases, with real-world implications for the programs' passage, survival, and defense against legal challenges.

I have argued in Chapter 1 that America's foundational identity struggles give rise to the strategic imperative to attenuate, that is, to distance the state from controversial policy outputs. When the rise of rival ideas among judges, advocates, and policymakers makes certain policy commitments vulnerable to legal challenge, elites can help insulate their ideas by means of attenuated governance. This chapter considers *how* they do this. All voucher programs are attenuated in the sense that a consumer-citizen intervenes between the state and the ultimate beneficiary of the funds, but not all attenuation strategies are created equal. Some are more successful than others, by which I mean that some strategies provide a greater legal cushion for programs liable to attract fierce opposition from rivals.

If the power of a rival order makes it hazardous to pursue certain policy aims directly, then using indirect, attenuated delivery channels offers an alternative pathway to success. But the manner of that pursuit matters too. I distinguish weakly and deeply attenuated programs on both rhetorical and policy design dimensions. The policies most likely to escape overthrow by adherents of a rival order are *doubly distanced*, because their deeply attenuated design and associated communications offer the greatest degree of plausible deniability in court about the connections between the state and a controversial policy commitment.

Why does the hidden state grow? Because it serves at least three purposes for policymakers facing hostile forces in America's foundational struggles: increasing the likelihood of legislation passage, decreasing the chances of successful challenge, and enabling policymakers to pursue a variety of other goals under the banner of consumer choice. As voucher supporters become more adept at achieving their purposes, modifying their tactics in response to setbacks such as court challenges and referendum rebuff, they switch to attenuated governance.

The following chapters show how elites learn about the most successful policymaking strategies. They acquire knowledge by trial and error, observing other states' successes and failures. The earliest of these "errors" were committed by white supremacists during the dying years of the Jim Crow era. As civil rights advocacy forced the federal government to start addressing racial inequality more forcefully, and as the

Supreme Court under Earl Warren's leadership granted racial egalitarian forces some legal victories, white supremacists in America's racial struggle sought to protect the racial hierarchies they cherished by indirect means. But I show in the next chapter that white supremacists' failure to attenuate their rhetoric, as well as their policy design, doomed their *contested-attenuated* tuition grant legislation in court.

Chapter 3 introduces readers to the first of America's three foundational identity struggles – the racial struggle, the religious struggle, and the public–private struggle – which shape policymakers' strategic incentives to distance the government from legally contentious purposes. When those purposes become vulnerable, as white supremacist policy goals did during the 1950s and 1960s, policymakers turn to attenuated governance in an effort to insulate their programs from legal challenge.

3

The Racial Struggle

Segregation Grants in the Brown *Era*

VOUCHERS AND SEGREGATIONIST AMERICA

The racial component in America's foundational identity struggles consists in the opposition between two major rivals – a white supremacist order elevating whites over other races and a transformative egalitarian order committed to overturning rigid racial hierarchies (D. King and Smith 2005). After Reconstruction's failure in the 1870s, the white supremacist order reasserted itself in the South. White supremacist ideas and institutions dominated for decades through Jim Crow laws and informal systems of racial control. They did not go uncontested. By the second decade of the twentieth century, the transformative egalitarian order had begun to reassert itself, although it would take many more years before the white supremacist edifice would start to collapse.

Opponents of white supremacy cut their teeth litigating lynching during the early decades of the twentieth century, after legislative and executive-centered strategies failed (Francis 2014). They turned to the courts in a strategic attempt to realize their objectives. Long before institutional circumstances were ripe for change or political allies available, the National Association for the Advancement of Colored People (NAACP) utilized legal strategies in an attempt to curtail racist violence. Legal challenges to white supremacy precede the school desegregation case *Brown* v. *Board of Education* (1954), including such landmarks as *Moore* v. *Dempsey* (1923).[1]

Yet with *Brown* v. *Board of Education*, the white supremacist order that had dominated the South, and the North for much of its history, truly began

[1] *Brown* v. *Board of Education of Topeka*, 347 US 483 (1954); *Moore* v. *Dempsey*, 261 US 86 (1923).

to crumble. The civil rights movement undermined a system based on the racialized allocation of opportunity (Pager 2007). In *Brown*, southern elites saw an existential threat to the racial hierarchies that had underpinned their dominance. The federal courts could no longer be relied upon to "defer reflexively to states' rights arguments" (MacLean 2017, xiv). Dogged litigation by the NAACP had begun to turn the federal courts against the "separate but equal" doctrine. To counter this threat, the white supremacist order set out to undermine the newly emboldened racial egalitarian forces.

These white supremacists turned to attenuated forms of governance in an attempt to hide their efforts to avoid desegregation. Table 3.1 displays the ways combatants in America's racial struggle have distanced the government from legally contentious purposes. By distancing the government from controversy using attenuated policy delivery and communications, white supremacists and their opponents hoped to avoid legal challenges.

Drawing upon policy proposals developed by James Buchanan and other members of the emerging "public choice" discipline, members of the white supremacist order sought to win the war through ideas. They founded policy think tanks and commissions to push the cause of vouchers for private schooling, free from government interference.

Thus, the first school voucher programs were adopted in the South in response to *Brown* (Ladson-Billings 2004; Harter and Hoffman 1973).[2] Their purpose was defined by ardent defenders of the segregationist racial order (Hackett and King 2019; Carr 2012; Bonastia 2012; Wolters 1984). These programs were designed to enable white families to escape any desegregation of the public schooling system by utilizing publicly funded vouchers distributed by all-white school districts to send their children to private de facto segregated academies (Ford, Johnson, and Partelow 2017). This tactic was embraced to maintain the South's system of white supremacy (Schickler and Rubin 2016).

The laws authorized public funding for grant payments to parents to spend on private education for their children. Seven southern states

[2] Segregation tuition grants were not the first forms of school choice but the first programs of any scale that offered grants to parents to exercise their "freedom of choice" of a private school. Scattered programs enacted after World Wars I and II had paid for tuition for the children of returning servicemen. Town tuitioning programs in rural areas of Maine and Vermont, established in the late nineteenth century and still in operation, pay for public or nonreligious private school for students from towns without a public school, but fewer than 5 percent of students in each state are eligible for these programs, and tuition is paid directly to the receiving school rather than to parents.

TABLE 3.1. *The value of attenuated governance in the racial struggle*

Order	Aim	Need for attenuation	Means of attenuation	Success of attenuation
White supremacist order	Segregate schools; resist desegregation	End of "separate but equal" with *Brown* v. *Board of Education* decision, 1954[3]	Arm's-length administration through private commissions	Struck down, e.g. *Poindexter*, 1967, 1968; *Hall* v. *St Helena*, 1961[4]
White supremacist order	Enable housing discrimination, "red-lining," and restrictive covenants	Outlawing of racial restrictive covenants in *Shelley* v. *Kraemer* decision, 1948[5]	Channel housing benefits through private housing providers	Limited success. Civil rights advocates place responsibility with state
Racial egalitarian order	Boost racial diversity of student bodies and worker-hiring pools; combat historical discrimination	Rise of affirmative action challenges, e.g. *Fisher* v. *University of Texas*[6]	Race used in as limited a way possible; flexible, individualized consideration; rhetoric: affirmative "opportunity"; design: "diversity"	Mixed. Roberts Court favors "color-blind" approaches

[3] *Brown* v. *Board of Education of Topeka*, 347 US 483 (1954).

[4] *Harrison* v. *Day*, 106 S.E. 2d 636 (Va. 1959); *Hall* v. *St Helena Parish School Board*, 197 F Supp 649 (E.D. La. 1961); *Pettaway* v. *County School Board of Surry County, Va.* (230 F Supp 480 (E.D. Va. 1964); *Griffin* v. *County School Board of Prince Edward County*, 377 US 218 (1964); *Lee* v. *Macon County Board of Education*, 231 F Supp 743 (M.D. Ala. 1964); *Poindexter* v. *Louisiana Financial Assistance Commission*, 275 F Supp 833 (E.D. La. 1968); *South Carolina Board of Education* v. *Brown*, 393 US 222 (1968); *Coffey* v. *State Educational Finance Commission*, 296 F Supp 1389 (S.D. Miss. 1969).

[5] *Shelley* v. *Kraemer*, 334 US 1 (1948).

[6] *Fisher* v. *University of Texas at Austin*, 570 US _ (2013) (Fisher I); *Fisher* v. *University of Texas at Austin*, 579 US _ (2016) (Fisher II).

passed tuition grant laws: Georgia (1953[7]), Alabama (1955), Virginia (1956[8]), North Carolina (1956), Louisiana (1958[9]), South Carolina (1963), and Mississippi (1964). For these states, buttressing separate schools was a pivotal component of segregation. In an eighth state, Arkansas, a publicly funded tuition grant bill was introduced but never reached the governor's desk. Instead, policymakers successfully solicited private funding for tuition grants (Special to the New York Times 1959, 1961) (Figure 3.1).

The tuition grant programs were to be used for segregation academies: single-race private schools, established in direct response to *Brown*. Catholic or "sectarian" schools were excluded from these tuition grant programs, partly due to anti-Catholicism in the South and partly due to the fear that Catholic schools would soon start to desegregate (as, indeed, they did in many parts of the South during the early 1960s) (Carl 2011; Special to the New York Times 1964). The programs diverted millions of dollars of public funds into tuition grants for parents to send their children to private segregated academies.

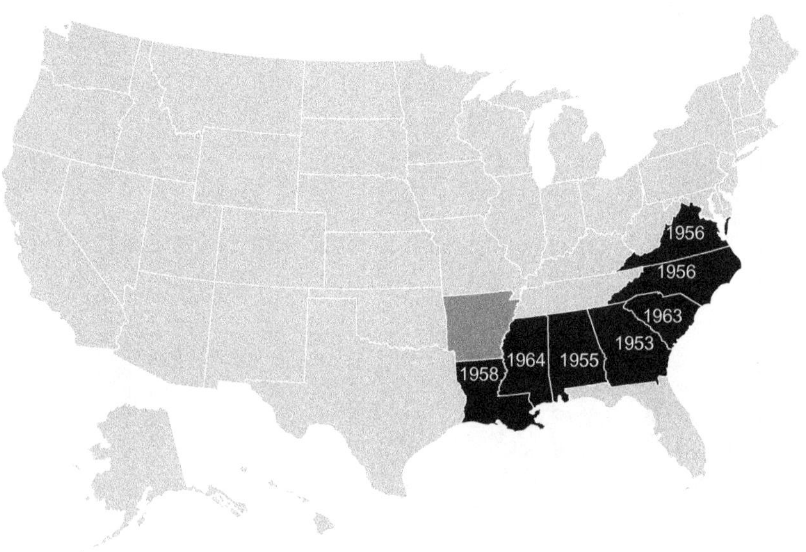

FIGURE 3.1. Segregation tuition grant bills passed, 1953–64.

[7] Grants were not distributed until 1961.

[8] After being struck down as unconstitutional, the program was repackaged by state legislators in 1959.

[9] Grants were not distributed until 1962.

Compiling data on the number of grants issued during this period is challenging because official records are inadequate and incomplete. I triangulate between contemporary newspaper sources, judicial rulings, and reports of the US Commission on Civil Rights in order to piece together the trajectory of grant issuance and usage across states.

Of the tuition grant states, Louisiana and Virginia distributed the largest number of grants. In its first year of operation, Louisiana issued 535 tuition grants, but the number quickly rose to 7,093 in its second year (1962–3) and to 11,000 the following year (Hannah et al. 1964; Wisdom 1967; McBee 1963). In 1966, the number of grants peaked at 15,177, followed by 14,059 in 1967–8, after which the program was struck down by a federal district court (Wisdom 1967).

The value of the grants was initially set at $1.67 per day and later raised to $2 per day, or $360 for an assumed school year of 180 days, which was typically sufficient to cover all or most of private school fees (Wisdom 1967). I utilize data appendices attached to the *Poindexter* v. *Louisiana Financial Assistance Commission* case (1967) to calculate the average tuition charge in private schools set up in Louisiana after the *Brown* decision: $414 per annum.[10] The grants covered, on average, 87 percent of fees. Judges in many states noted that tuition grants were calibrated to the level of school fees and vice versa (Wisdom 1961, 1967; Rives, Grooms, and Johnson 1964). Many segregated schools established after *Brown*, such as Carrollton Private School, Mirabeau Elementary School, United Elementary School, and Jefferson Academy, charged precisely the cost of the tuition grant.

These vouchers were used almost exclusively by whites, although a small number of black students did use tuition grants to attend segregated black academies (Godbold, Cox, and Russell 1969). In *Coffey* v. *State Education Finance Commission* (1969), the vigilant judges provided a detailed data appendix on patterns of voucher usage to justify their conclusion that Mississippian tuition grants were unconstitutional.[11] The court found that all but one of the private schools receiving the $240 tuition grant payments in the school year 1967–8 had an

[10] *Poindexter* v. *Louisiana Financial Assistance Commission*, 275 F Supp 833 (E.D. La. 1967).

[11] *Coffey* v. *State Educational Finance Commission*, 296 F Supp 1389 (S.D. Miss. 1969).

all-white attendance (the other school was entirely African American) (Godbold, Cox, and Russell 1969).

In Virginia, the state dispensed 4,750 grants in the school year beginning in 1959 at a cost of just over $1 million (Carper 1960), each grant amounting to $125 per child for elementary students and $150 for high schoolers, supplemented by local sources (Black 1964; Butzner 1964). By 1964, Virginia had spent more than $7 million on tuition grant payments. Even after the passage of the 1964 Civil Rights Act and a 1965 Supreme Court decision striking down the Prince Edward County's policy of closing the public school system to avoid desegregation, Virginia continued to fund private tuition grants (Black 1964). Numbers rose to almost 14,000 in 1967.

Despite declining enthusiasm for the program on the part of some whiter Virginian counties toward the end of the decade, particularly Roanoke, Arlington, and Alexandria, the number of tuition grants issued in 1968 (after which they were struck down by a three-judge federal court) was in excess of 13,000 (Associated Press 1969). Over the course of a decade, Virginia spent nearly $20 million in tuition grants.

By contrast, the Georgia tuition grant program's early promise – the state spent $1.4 million in 1961–2 alone – was quickly snuffed out after the legislature adopted additional regulations. "The legislature provided [in 1963] that local school systems must participate in the costs and certify the students for private school grants, an action that virtually killed the plan" (Special to the New York Times 1967). State outlay for the grants dropped to a mere $112,000 in 1963 and came to a halt the following year without the need for court action (Wearne 2013). Figure 3.2 displays the rise and fall of tuition grant payments in Virginia, Louisiana, and Georgia. At their peak, around 2 percent of the school-age population in Louisiana and Virginia utilized tuition grants. But the impact of these grants was felt across the South.

The temporality of early tuition grant vouchers reveals four different legal and political strategies on the part of southern states to stop desegregation using both direct and indirect methods (Table 3.2). Vouchers were an element in these strategies.

First, states such as Virginia and Louisiana pursued immediate massive resistance policies in response to *Brown*, a belligerent, all-in, up-front approach that incorporated school closings, outlawing public school desegregation, tuition grant payments, and open defiance, and that ran the greatest risk of legal challenges. Vouchers were one part of the miasma of violent incidents and legal challenges by white

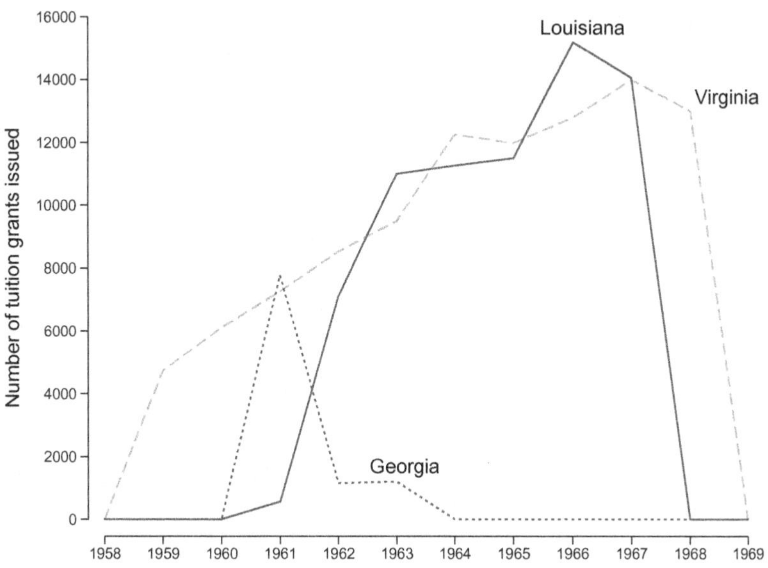

FIGURE 3.2. Selected southern states' issuance of vouchers in the era of segregation.

TABLE 3.2. *Vouchers in the era of segregation*

Four approaches	Characteristics	States
Massive resistance	Early adopters of tuition grants alongside an all-out assault on the *Brown* ruling: school closures, abolition of compulsory attendance, interposition, etc.	Virginia, Louisiana, Georgia, Alabama
Safety valve	Adoption but no actual distribution of public tuition grants. An effort to strike a balance between placating segregationists and avoiding legal challenge	North Carolina, Arkansas
Resignation	No tuition grant legislation. Slow and unenthusiastic but steady progress toward desegregating the public schools	Maryland, West Virginia, Kentucky, Tennessee
Violent suppression	Tuition grant legislation not needed at first because fear of violent reprisals stifles the prospect of legal challenges. Much later adopters of tuition grants, after barriers to desegregation finally start to fall	Mississippi, South Carolina

supremacists. Second, other states including North Carolina deployed a measured approach to slow the pace of desegregation, placate segregationists, and reduce the likelihood of court override by authorizing (but not implementing) tuition grants.

Third, border South states – Maryland, West Virginia, Kentucky, and Tennessee – did not pursue tuition grants because they were resigned to at least token integration, particularly in those with a small African American population. Fourth, states such as Mississippi and South Carolina did not pursue tuition grants at first because, at least initially, they were unnecessary. Policymakers were committed to absolute school segregation, and "most blacks understandably feared violent or fatal repercussions if they chose to press their case legally" (Bonastia 2012, 77). This last group of states did eventually adopt tuition grants but many years later than the "Massive Resistance" group and only when these states' bulwarks against desegregation had begun to crumble at last.

In sum, vouchers were part of the general white supremacy effort to get white children out of the public school system to avoid interracial contact. This imperative was most acute in states such as Virginia that overlapped the southern Black Belt, which had adopted a defiant position to federal desegregation lawsuits but could not rely upon sheer brute suppression to prevent public school desegregation.

Patterns of Support for Vouchers in Defense of Jim Crow

White supremacist Democratic governors, including George Wallace and then his wife Lurleen Wallace of Alabama, Eugene Talmadge and Ernest Vandiver Jr. of Georgia, Earl Long and James Davis of Louisiana, Paul Johnson of Mississippi, and Thomas B. Stanley of Virginia, were vociferous supporters of tuition grant vouchers (Catsam 2009; Kruse 2005). They and their legislative allies established commissions to devise strategies to avoid desegregation. The Sibley Commission in Georgia (the Committee on Schools of the Georgia General Assembly), the Pearsall Committee in North Carolina, and the Gray Commission in Virginia recommended tuition grants as part of packages of measures designed to thwart desegregation (Chin et al. 2006).

Committee memberships were almost exclusively white and male – three African Americans sat on the sixteen-member Pearsall Committee in North Carolina, but the Gray Commission in Virginia was drawn from the state legislature, which had no African Americans and only one woman serving in it (Bonastia 2012, 56). Members of the Gray Commission were drawn disproportionately from south Virginian legislative districts with smaller populations but larger concentrations of black residents, a pattern of support that would be repeated when it came to voting on tuition grant packages across the South.

White segregationists shepherded tuition grant legislation through state legislatures. The bills did not garner uniform support. Some votes were close. However, closeness reflected no principled objection to the racist ends of the measures but doubt about their efficacy in achieving widely shared segregationist goals. Virginia's 1956 tuition grant law passed the upper house by just four votes. There were legislators willing to speak out against tuition grants – but for pro-segregationist reasons, such as expressing their fear that the massive resistance approach would make federal court challenge more likely. For example, Senator Bob Wilson of Walker County, Alabama, argued that federal courts would force private schools to accept black students as long as white pupils received state aid (Associated Press 1965b).

Revealingly, support for tuition grants was concentrated among members with the largest proportion of black residents in their districts. These were the districts that would feel the impact of desegregation most keenly (Bonastia 2012, 73; Muse 1961; Catsam 2009). As in Key's (1949) classic treatment of southern politics, racial conservatism and support for vouchers varied in proportion to the size of each community's African American population.

Attenuated Policy Delivery Helped Avoid Legal Challenge

Many of the very earliest educational expense grants in Georgia, Louisiana, Virginia, and Alabama were directed according to racial criteria to support segregation academies, entangling the state with racist purposes. Several tuition grant programs paid state funds not only to parents but also to the schools directly (Figure 3.3).

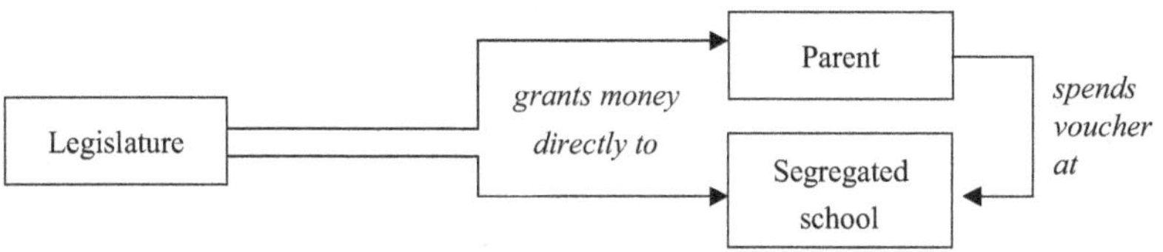

FIGURE 3.3. Direct educational expense grants for children at segregated schools.

New segregation academies were "private in name only" (Crespino 2007, 240). Their boosters' notionally color-blind "freedom of choice" rhetoric notwithstanding, these earliest voucher programs were designed specifically to sustain the racial hierarchies of the Jim Crow era by embedding racial categories in the design and administration of policy.

Unsurprisingly, segregation grants soon ran into difficulties. The NAACP and its allies litigated the programs in state and federal courts (Bonastia 2012; Catsam 2009; Muse 1961). Virginia alone faced four successful lawsuits in the space of a decade. For policymakers keen to safeguard the segregation grants from court challenge, defending the programs against lawsuits necessitated an attenuated policy delivery.

The key to insulating segregation grants from legal challenge was to avoid granting public money directly to segregated schools. States attempted to camouflage the connection between government and segregated academies by funding parents and not schools directly (Figure 3.4).

Some states went further in attenuating the state–segregation academy connection through strategic policy design and delivery. Louisiana, for example, created an arm's-length institution, the "education expense grant fund," to channel public money to parents. In 1962, it established another quasi-private agency to administer tuition grants: the Louisiana Finance Assistance Commission. In Arkansas, Governor Orville Faubus assisted the Little Rock Private School Corporation, a private organization, in purchasing private buildings with public funds to operate a school (Verney and Sartain 2009; Associated Press 1958). Alabama governor George Wallace made similar use of "private school foundations" (Rives, Grooms, and Johnson 1964). Utilizing private buildings and arm's-length intermediaries, segregationists attempted to insulate their programs from legal challenges (Figure 3.5).

This effort to attenuate the relationship between state and segregated schools was deliberate and calculated. Every single time its tuition grant legislation was struck down as unconstitutional – Act 258 (1958), Act 3 (1960), Act 147 (1962), and Act 99 (1967) – the state of Louisiana further attenuated its program design. A district court judge remarked,

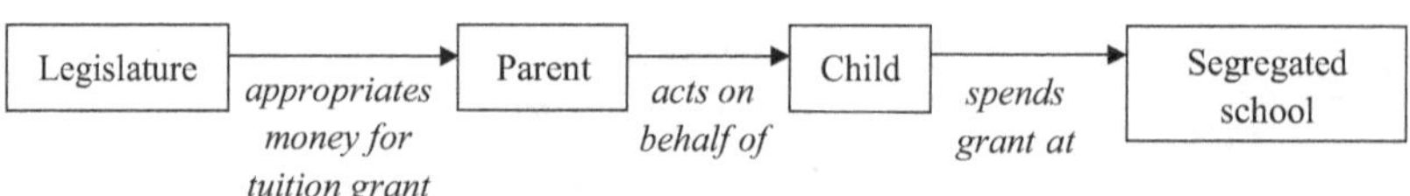

FIGURE 3.4. Tuition grants for children at segregated schools.

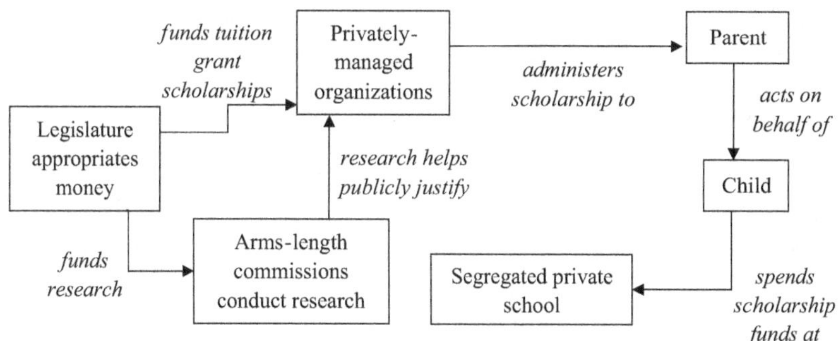

FIGURE 3.5. Attenuating the connection between the state and its segregationist purposes.

"In each succeeding act the scheme became more subtle, the language more sophisticated" (Wisdom 1968). State Senator E. W. Gravolet Jr., who was Senate floor leader for the passage of tuition grant legislation in Louisiana, vice-chairman of the Joint Legislature Committee on Segregation, and chairman of the Financial Assistance Commission from its inception, stated the following in 1962:

> It was primarily because of that federal court decision, [*Hall* v. *St. Helena Parish School Board*][12] combined with the one in Virginia [*Harrison* v. *Day*][13] that the Louisiana Legislature took away the administration of the tuition grants from the State Board of Education and the local school boards and created a new commission to disburse the tuition grants directly to the child, following the constitutional theory that grants directly to the child by the states were legal. The federal court went out of its way in the *St. Helena* case to point out that grant-in-aid could be attacked as being state action under the 14th amendment of the United States Constitution if they were administered by the local school board, because the various private schools would be classified by federal courts as private-public schools. (Wisdom 1967)

Gravolet acknowledged that he and his colleagues deliberately resorted to attenuated policy delivery to forestall legal challenges to segregation grants. By publicly attenuating the connection between state and school through the use of private intermediary organizations, segregationists hoped to avoid a legal confrontation.

> After *Brown* v. *Board of Ed* you had a reaction in the South where literally whites fled the public schools and they started their own school systems and

[12] *Hall* v. *St Helena Parish School Board*, 197 F Supp 649 (E.D. La. 1961).
[13] *Harrison* v. *Day*, 106 S.E. 2d 636 (Va. 1959).

> these were non-religious but they were effectively a means of bypassing *Brown* v. *Board of Ed.* So Prince [Edward's] County, Virginia, you had basically a separate school system that was attended by many of the whites who didn't want their kids going to school with blacks. (Maisel 2012)

Policymakers calculated that using an attenuated governance arrangement would help achieve white supremacist ends by indirect, less legally vulnerable, means than massive resistance. James Buchanan, the public choice scholar and voucher proponent, helped conduct a multiyear study of Virginia's tuition grant system for the Virginia Commission on Constitutional Government, the body created by the Virginia General Assembly in 1958 to defend its school policies. The study concluded that private school subsidies were "a model for evading government control" (MacLean 2017, 83).

Unfortunately, for the segregationists, it was not sufficient to simply attenuate policy *design*. Policymakers also had to conceal their segregationist intent and purposes. Gravolet's statement about his deliberate efforts to avoid legal challenge was published in the *Times-Picayune* in December 1963 and subsequently cited in the Louisiana Supreme Court's 1967 decision striking down the constitutionality of tuition grants for schools that excluded Bryan Poindexter. Being open about segregationist purposes was dangerous.

Veneer of Color Blindness amid Intensive Contestation

The problem for the segregationists was that their attenuated policy delivery was not accompanied by attenuating *rhetoric*. Policymakers proved unwilling or unable to obfuscate their racist goals by communicating obliquely. There were some limited exceptions. Some policymakers changed the designation of the vouchers to help minimize the association between racist purposes and state action. Virginia relabeled its tuition grants "scholarships" in 1959, and Mississippi rechristened its grants "loans" in 1969 (Bonastia 2012, 96; Bolton 2005, 175; Muse 1961, 134). Many referred to vouchers as part of "freedom of association" plans, and some sought to excise mention of race in tuition grant legislation.

Segregation tuition grant efforts attempted to employ notionally color-blind arguments about "freedom of choice." Mindful of the risk of judicial challenges, some politicians publicly justified their tuition grant policies without recourse to race. In Alabama, for instance, the tuition grant law made no mention of race or color, providing that children could qualify for grants if, in the judgment of their parents, it would be detrimental to their "physical or emotional health" or subject them to "hazards to personal safety" if they attended public school (Associated Press 1965a).

These supposedly race-neutral frames formed part of a broader "freedom of choice" response to desegregation, purportedly allowing black children to transfer to white schools but in practice subjecting would-be transfer students to harassment or intimidation and the rejection of their applications on notionally race-neutral grounds.

Even in states such as Arkansas and North Carolina that passed but did not distribute tuition grants, the passage of tuition grant legislation had powerful symbolic functions for segregationist elites. It rallied supporters, roused segregationists, and placated fears of federal takeovers. In Arkansas, Governor Orville Faubus – famous for refusing to protect black children at Little Rock in 1957 – deployed the individualized rhetoric of color blindness to express confidence that his tuition grants proposal would not be overturned by the courts. "It is just carrying a little bit further the rights of an individual. All students have constitutional rights – not just members of one race or group, although the present Supreme Court seems interested in only one race" (Special to the New York Times 1959). Grants were justified on the grounds of "individual liberty" of association for parents and students (Carl 2011, 29).

In Virginia's Prince Edward County, local segregationists closed the public school system for five years rather than submit to desegregation. Officials justified public funding of tuition grants for students at the whites-only Prince Edward Academy in terms of opaque "patriotic constitutionalism" rather than full-blown "diehard segregation." In this view, it was merely black parents' irksome rejection of tuition grants for African American private schools that prevented black children in the county from receiving an education. This logic exposes the segregationist intent of tuition grants beneath the superficial color blindness.

Mostly, however, legislators were open about their segregationist purposes and the state's role in sustaining Jim Crow through vouchers. Despite occasional homage to color blindness, policymakers in the Jim Crow South were not circumspect about their segregationist goals. Establishing the Gray Commission to consider tuition grants, Virginian Governor Stanley declared, "I shall use every legal means at my command to continue segregated schools in Virginia" (Muse 1961, 7). Louisianan segregation leader Representative Wellborn Jack was explicit about the purpose of the grants: "It gives the people an opportunity to help fight to keep the schools segregated. ... This is just to recruit more people to keep our schools segregated, and we're going to do it in spite of the federal government, the brainwashers and the Communists" (Wisdom 1961).

Segregationists were open about the state's role in aiding segregated institutions. The chairman of the State Sovereignty Commission in Louisiana, Frank Voelker Jr., stated, "If the present grants in aid is carried to the federal courts it probably would be knocked out because it is really the state operating the schools" (Wisdom 1967). In his Executive Orders of September 2 and 9, 1963, Governor Wallace referred to the "unwarranted integration" being forced by the federal court (Rives, Grooms, and Johnson 1964). Representative Risley C. Triche of Assumption Parish, Louisiana, argued in the Louisianan House of Representatives in December 1960 that the grant-in-aid system was the most effective weapon against the integration of public schools (Peltason 1971, 228–29). Segregationists boasted that the grants "help your children go to a private segregated school of your choice, instead of having to go to a racially integrated school" (Wisdom 1967). The policy design might have been attenuated, but its associated rhetoric was not.

"The Nonobvious Involvement of the State in Private Conduct"

Judges deciding the fate of tuition grant vouchers remarked upon this disjuncture between attenuated policy delivery and (lack of) attenuating rhetoric. The US district judges in *Hall* v. *St Helena*, a 1961 challenge to Louisiana's tuition grants, noted, "The sponsors of this legislation, in their public statements, if not in the Act itself, have spelled out its real purpose" (Wisdom 1961).[14] Similarly, Governor Wallace's revealing rhetoric about his opposition to "unwarranted integration" was cited by his opponents in subsequent voucher litigation (Rives, Grooms, and Johnson 1964). The *Poindexter* judges quoted the US Supreme Court's *Burton* v. *Wilmington Parking Authority*[15] decision on racial discrimination: "Only by sifting facts and weighing circumstances can the nonobvious involvement of the State in private conduct be attributed its true significance" (T. C. Clark 1961; Wisdom 1967).

Advocates working on behalf of the racial egalitarian order argued that the segregation tuition grants had indelibly marked the state's imprimatur upon white supremacist policy ends. Nancy MacLean writes that

[14] *Hall* v. *St Helena Parish School Board*, 197 F Supp 649 (E.D. La. 1961).
[15] *Burton* v. *Wilmington Parking Authority*, 365 US 715 (1961).

Oliver Hill, one of the NAACP attorneys who fought on behalf of the Prince Edward students, stated their opposition to the grants with the following principle: "No one in a democratic society has a right to have his private prejudices financed at public expense" (MacLean 2017, 69).

The racist motives of the state sponsors of the voucher schemes did not escape judges' attention. A federal district court noted in its 1967 *Poindexter* ruling that Louisianan officials enacted tuition grants to deny black students equal educational opportunities (Wisdom 1967). A contemporaneous news article argued, "Paying the public funds for tuition in private all-white schools is a 'transparent evasion' of the Fourteenth Amendment designed to perpetuate segregated education" (Chapman 1964).

The federal courts in this case, and in other segregation voucher cases, saw through the color-blind justifications proffered by southern politicians, and so struck them down as unconstitutional. As US Appeals Court chief judge Simon E. Sobeloff wrote in a consolidated case, striking down Virginian tuition grants[16]:

> The label applied to these (private) schools cannot blind courts, or anyone else, to the realities. ... It is of no importance whether grants are made directly to (the private) school or indirectly through the conduit of pupil subventions for restricted use as tuition fees. The involvement of public officials and public funds so essentially characterizes the enterprise in each of the counties that the (private) schools must be regarded as public facilities in which discrimination on racial lines is constitutionally impermissible. (Sobeloff 1964)

White supremacists' efforts to suppress the connection between state and school did not deceive federal courts, as cases such as *Griffin* v. *County School Board of Prince Edward County* reveal (Black 1964).[17] In *Griffin*, the "personal, parental, and race-conscious choice to discriminate was rendered de jure by virtue of state funding, which was used to support the voucher program" (Gooden, Jabbar, and Torres 2016, 525). The Supreme Court found that the use of a voucher to exercise school choice constituted a state violation of the desegregation mandate established by *Brown*.

In *Hall* v. *Helena Parish* (1961), the court said that tuition grant programs were a "transparent artifice" designed to circumvent blacks'

[16] *Griffin* v. *Board of Supervisors of Prince Edward County* and *Pettaway* v. *Board of Supervisors for Surry County*, 339 F 2d 486 (4th Cir. 1964).

[17] *Griffin* v. *County School Board of Prince Edward County*, 377 US 218 (1964).

"constitutional right to attend desegregated public schools" (Wisdom 1961). A US district court found in *South Carolina Board of Education* v. *Brown* (1968) that the South Carolina tuition grants were also created to circumvent constitutional restrictions: "A review of the record, including the historical background of the Act, clearly reveals that the purpose, motive and effect of the Act is to unconstitutionally circumvent the requirement first enunciated in *Brown* v. *Board of Education* ... that the State of South Carolina not discriminate on the basis of race or color in its public educational system" (Per Curiam 1968).[18] In *Poindexter* (1967), the court stated that the state cannot "perform acts indirectly through private persons which it is forbidden to do directly" (Wisdom 1967).

The district court that decided *Hall* v. *Helena Parish* quoted a Supreme Court case, *Miller* v. *City of Milwaukee*,[19] to argue that "[a] result intelligently foreseen and offering the most obvious motive for an act that will bring it about, fairly may be taken to have been a purpose of the act" (Holmes 1927). The district court in these and other tuition grant cases judged the segregation of school children to have been the motive for the passage of the bills. However tortuous the delivery mechanism, the racist motives of the acts' authors rendered the vouchers unconstitutional.

These contested-attenuated policies – in which policy design, but not political communications, attenuated the connection between state and school – proved legally vulnerable because the state's purposes were easily exposed. If policymakers had been more adept at concealing their purposes, they may have found their programs' legal defense easier.

In Mississippi, South Carolina, Alabama, Virginia, and Louisiana, lawsuits ended the segregation vouchers. Congress and the courts became more decisive in embedding civil rights in the decade between 1964 and 1973. As these laws and rulings took effect, the blatant use of publicly financed tuition grant vouchers for white students to escape desegregation was finally defeated. By 1970, segregation tuition grants had been struck down as unconstitutional across the South, though segregated institutions, including private segregated academies, remained (Carr 2012).

More broadly, segregation was legally displaced by the civil rights legislation in the 1960s enacted in response to the demands of the reform movement (Francis 2014; R. P. Young and Burstein 1995). Legal and federally upheld

[18] *South Carolina Board of Education* v. *Brown*, 393 US 222 (1968).

[19] *Miller* v. *City of Milwaukee*, 272 US 713 (1927).

segregation encountered decisive legislative defeat in the 1960s as Congress eventually passed laws against it between 1957 and 1968. Combined with busing programs and new federal funding made available as a condition of desegregating schools, southern states made dramatic strides to integrate schools between 1968 and 1973 (D. King 2017; Clotfelter 2004).

Court orders were also crucial in ending vouchers as tools of segregated schools. In the North, the voucher cause experienced further setbacks during the 1970s. Segregation was mostly not de jure in the North but de facto present, and resistance to school integration was fierce and often violent (Douglas 2005).

Despite support for the idea of vouchers among members of the Office of Economic Opportunity during the Great Society years, the Nixon and Reagan administrations, and academics such as Diane Ravitch and sociologist Christopher Jencks, no major voucher tuition programs were instituted during the 1970s and 1980s (Carl 2011; Ravitch 2001). This was an era in which the race-conscious policy alliance's commitment to activist federal policy to advance racial equality enjoyed national political support, even if voter resentment toward affirmative action and related measures was brewing (Frymer and Skrentny 1998).

Vouchers' Continued Entanglement with Racial Controversies

After the collapse of segregation, the white supremacist and racial egalitarian orders reassembled around a fresh point of contention: whether government can and should ameliorate racial inequalities directly through state action or instead avoid the use of racial categories entirely (D. King and Smith 2005). The former is the core commitment of the race-conscious alliance; the latter that of the color-blind alliance. Color blindness and race consciousness manifest in the "framing of racial issues" and in parties' "professed commitments," whereby elites rhetorically emphasize or diminish racial categories (Table 3.3, row 1). Color blindness and race consciousness also occur in the design and implementation of policy (Table 3.3, row 2) (Hackett and King 2019).

In the period after the triumphs of the civil rights movement, proponents of race-conscious policies tended to utilize explicit racial categories to confront racial inequalities directly through government action (what Justice Sonia Sotomayor calls "race-targeting" measures), whereas color-blind policy designs favor a market-driven "free-choice" approach by individual consumers (Table 3.3). The former are naturally deattenuated because they favor direct state action to remedy racial inequality;

TABLE 3.3. *Two arenas of racial policy alliance contestation: policy framing and design*

	Color blindness	Race consciousness	In *King and Smith*
Rhetorical dimension	No mention of race in policy wording, discussion points, or among elites during bill passage *Example:* Disavowal of racial categories in Republican Party platform	Legislation mentions race, or policy is framed in racial terms during bill passage *Example:* Direct acknowledgment of racial groups in Democratic party platform	"This *framing of racial issues* has produced a polarized politics of disputatious mutual disrespect" (D. King and Smith 2011, 12) "[T]he party has *professed commitments* to color-blind policy approaches" (D. King and Smith 2011, 10)
Design dimension	Policy does not target particular racial groups; individual-based market-oriented mechanisms *Example:* Tax expenditure programs	Direct state action to ameliorate racial inequalities; policy targets particular racial categories *Example:* Affirmative action programs	"Proponents of both *color-blind and race-conscious policies* have drawn the wrong lesson from this history" (D. King and Smith 2011, 11) "*Measures … designed and implemented* with specific goals of racial equality in view" (D. King and Smith 2011, 9)

the latter are typically attenuated, elevating the "color-blind" logic of the marketplace regardless of racialized risk exposure.

All major civil rights organizations, led by the NAACP, oppose vouchers. The sole national organization created to advance vouchers for nonwhite students – the Black Alliance for Educational Options (BAEO) – dissolved in 2017. The race-conscious policy alliance – institutions and organizations devoted to remedying material racial inequality through government action – sets itself against vouchers, in opposition to a color-blind policy alliance that disclaims such race-targeted measures (D. King and Smith 2011; Hackett and King 2019).

Yet despite civil rights leaders' opposition to the voucher cause, the evidence for strong opposition to vouchers among black and Hispanic *citizens* is more mixed. Polls generally find that African American support for vouchers and tax credits exceeds that of other racial groups: 61 percent support in a 2017 Education Next poll (compared with 52 percent for white non-Hispanic respondents), 76 percent support in a 1992 National Catholic Education Association poll, 62 percent support in a 1997 Phi Delta Kappa/Gallup poll (compared with 47 percent among white respondents), 57.3 percent support in a 1997 Joint Center for Political and Economic Studies poll (compared with an evenly divided white response) (Lawton 1992; Coles 1997; D. Hill 1998).

However, exit polls in California and Michigan voucher ballot initiatives showed no difference or lower support for vouchers among blacks than among whites, and other nationwide polls displayed greater skepticism of vouchers by African Americans: for example, 41 percent of African Americans "strongly oppose" vouchers in a 2001 Zogby International poll compared with 32 percent in the whole sample (Reid 2001; Leal 2004). Voucher opinions are highly sensitive to question wording.

Racial Struggles and Voucher Votes

In order to examine the effect of America's racial struggles upon modern voucher votes, I utilize my dataset of 6,693 state legislative votes on the 47 voucher bills passed 2005–17.[20] The dataset contains the universe of

[20] I exclude the Colorado Douglas County school board voucher pilot, launched in 2011 as it is the only program created at the local school district level. All other programs were passed by state legislatures. The 2005–17 period was selected because it incorporates the steep growth of modern voucher programs.

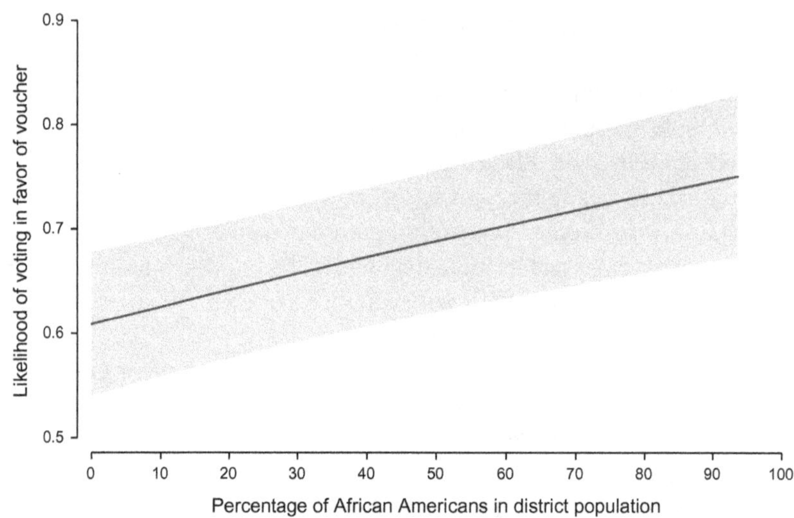

FIGURE 3.6. Racial district characteristics and voucher votes.

votes during this period. Details of my empirical strategy and datasets are listed in the Appendix, and the full table of results with controls is detailed in Table A9.

Controlling for legislator partisanship and a host of other factors, African American legislators are slightly *less* supportive of vouchers than white legislators, but the proportion of African Americans in a legislator's district is *positively* related to their likelihood of voting in favor of a voucher bill (Figure 3.6). This striking datum is reminiscent of the era of segregation vouchers: whiter districts were, and remain, less enthusiastic about vouchers (Catsam 2009; Bonastia 2012; Hackett and King 2019).

The opposition to vouchers from civil rights organizations does not prevent some voucher supporters from advocating for these policies on race-conscious grounds. A voucher opponent in Illinois described these arguments during the 2017 passage of a voucher bill.

> Republicans were saying, as they usually do on these vouchers, like poor black and brown kids ought to ... be able to go to the same good schools as everybody else, right. And it's, I think, a specious argument but it's just like saying "Why do you wanna take away scholarships for poor kids?" That was it. (Montgomery 2018)

Openly, race-conscious arguments like these are more politically acceptable than white supremacist ones, but color-blind arguments are even more powerful. Most voucher programs are defended in color-blind terms, even when those programs are not racially innocent. Today, antidiscrimination norms are powerful, so potential discriminators face pressures to maintain consistency with color blindness (Pager 2007).

Modern, "universal" voucher programs place no income limits on student eligibility and, in some cases, no requirement to have spent time in the public school before taking up a voucher. Race-conscious policy alliance members argue that targeting is required to ensure that children of color benefit and that public money is not distributed to economically advantaged households, who would have sent their children to private schools regardless. When Wisconsin representative Polly Williams and former Milwaukee superintendent Howard Fuller championed vouchers in 2010, they argued that the programs should not be extended to higher income groups but instead should focus only on low-income minorities, a further cooling in race-conscious support for the new vouchers and the surge of color blindness (Marley 2013; Marley and Stein 2011; Bice 2013).

The fight between advocates of compensatory vouchers and those who favor "universal" vouchers mirrors the clash between race-conscious and color-blind forces. It has been sharpened by the recent finding that color-blind voucher statutes provide insufficient protection against racial discrimination in private school admissions (Eckes, Mead, and Ulm 2016). In May 2017, under questioning from House appropriations committee members, US Secretary of Education Betsy DeVos declined to say if the federal government would step in to prevent voucher-receiving private schools from discriminating against students (Resmovits 2017). DeVos argued that decisions should be left to parents, an approach to voucher politics that is quintessentially color-blind in its elevation of individual choice over direct and purposeful state action.

Reducing the traceability of the connection between government and policy administration is characteristic of color-blind policymaking. Individuals make choices in private markets that are officially color-blind. The state is merely a neutral umpire. This attenuated form of governance is the opposite of race-conscious policymaking, which typically involves direct state action to remedy racial disadvantage.

The attenuation defense also appears in other racially charged public policy arenas, such as housing. For example, the White House's 1934 response to an NAACP allegation that the Federal Housing Administration (FHA) was discriminating against African Americans married color-blind rhetoric with an attenuation defense. The FHA defended itself as an agency that "lends no Government money but simply insures mortgage loans made by private financial institutions, such as banks, life insurance companies, etc." (Thurston 2018, 111–12). By asserting that "no Government money" was involved, the FHA could argue that it "simply reflected the impartial logic of supply and demand" (Thurston 2018, 112).

As with the segregation tuition grants, explicitly racial language in the FHA's early regulatory manuals aroused strong opposition and was quickly erased. If the government failed to dissociate itself from racist purposes through attenuated policy delivery mechanisms and attenuating rhetoric, it was vulnerable to newly empowered transformative egalitarian forces. The legal vulnerability of these social policies was proportional to the level of governmental aid or action involved (Thurston 2018).

Although segregation tuition grants were eliminated by court action fifty years ago, vouchers remain vulnerable to the charge that they segregate children by race, as a New York State assemblyman argues:

> If you were to allow so-called religious schools or private schools in any way to become funded with state dollars or federal dollars, I believe there would be more segregation in our society again. Again. You know I still hear people talk about "those people." Ok? "*Those* people." Who are "those people?" Well, it could be African-American, it could be poor, it could be, whatever. But you're going to start segregating the society in two, and I think that's what public schools do, brings everybody together. (Magnarelli 2012)

Even voucher supporters admit that the lingering history of racial controversy makes the politics of vouchers more challenging. In the words of a member of Louisiana's Board of Elementary and Secondary Education, "You make it extremely tricky where you're looking at the haves and the have-nots in terms of race and the fact that people have used the private system as a way to segregate their children" (Boffy 2012).

Reflecting upon the failure of several voucher bills in Illinois between 2009 and 2012, a former Republican representative argues, "In the city of Chicago itself, there was not enough support from the Black Caucus and inner-city Democratic legislators to put it over the top … because I think they believe that this would have cherry-picked. I think they understand their own city; they understand the politics of their city; and they understand who would have got those vouchers" (Eddy 2012). Attenuation may be of limited use here: regardless of the means by which the vouchers were delivered, black policymakers were concerned that the vouchers would go to whites, as they had done in their earliest incarnations in the Jim Crow South.

CONCLUSION

America's racial struggle is one of the three foundational identity struggles: battles between rival coalitions of ideas, institutions, and individuals with deeply held commitments about the role of the state. In the racial struggle, white supremacist forces – for over a century in the ascendant, particularly in the institutions and governing commitments of the South – adhere to a harsh racial hierarchy that elevates "whiteness" over "blackness" and institutionalizes white privilege. Their opponents are racial egalitarians, a coalition of individuals and organizations actively resisting racial hierarchies and seeking to utilize state power to confront racial inequality directly.

As racial egalitarian forces won new commitments from the federal government and judiciary during the civil rights era, white supremacists found that they could not pursue their aims directly because they were liable to be struck down as unconstitutional. In an effort to protect their rigid racial hierarchy, white supremacist regimes in the South turned to tuition grant vouchers. These programs provided public money to individual parents to spend exclusively at private segregated academies. Instead of funding segregation directly, white supremacists funded it indirectly – through the intervention of parents and of "private," arm's-length financial assistance commissions whose job was to administer the voucher payments on behalf of the legislature. But a change in legislative means reflected no change in ends.

Despite their popularity among white parents, the *contested-attenuated* nature of segregationist tuition grants made them vulnerable to legal challenges as the Jim Crow system disintegrated. Although – like their modern color-blind counterparts – white supremacist vouchers utilized an attenuated policy delivery that disclaimed any mention of racial categories, white supremacists proved unable to distance themselves from controversy in their political communications. Remarking upon the distinction between attenuated delivery and *de*attenuating rhetoric, judges struck the programs down as unconstitutional. In their modern incarnations, vouchers are color-blind but have never fully shaken off the racial connotations of their segregationist forebears. After the demise of segregation vouchers, it took many decades for vouchers to be reinvented, and when they did, they faced an additional source of controversy: the *religious struggle* over accommodationism.

Like the racial struggle, this religious struggle is a set of confrontations between forces with deeply held beliefs about the role of the state, controversies that were present at the Founding and have reoccurred throughout the life of the nation. Secularist forces claim the mantle of Thomas Jefferson in arguing that church and state should be kept separate. Their accommodationist rivals believe, by contrast, that the duty of the state is to encourage the fullest flourishing of religious activity. Earl Warren's ascendance to the chief justiceship of the US Supreme Court marked the beginning of the end of the Jim Crow era, but it also marked an acceleration of the turn toward secularism in federal jurisprudence.

As accommodationist policies became legally vulnerable, accommodationists sought to protect religious schools indirectly. Utilizing a legal rationale known as *child benefit theory*, the principle that aid programs benefit the child and not the school, accommodationists defended new voucher programs in court. But they were only partially successful, because the design and communications strategies were weakly attenuated. Chapter 4 shows why such *quasi-direct* voucher programs were vulnerable to legal challenge.

4

The Religious Struggle

Vouchers and the Church–State Question

"OH YEAH, IT WAS WHITE HOT": CHURCH–STATE JURISPRUDENCE IN THE RELIGIOUS STRUGGLE

The second of America's fundamental identity struggles is the combat between two rival religious orders, secularist and accommodationist, with deeply held opposing views about the appropriate relationship between church and state. The secularist order applied the First Amendment to the states for the first time in the Mormon polygamy case *Reynolds* v. *United States* (1878)[1] and enshrined prohibitions of public aid to denominational institutions into forty-three state constitutions (1835–1959). Yet accommodationists won benefits for parochial schools in multiple states during the first half of the twentieth century with legal backing in cases such as *Everson* v. *Board of Education* (1947),[2] a decision concerning publicly-funded bus transportation to Catholic schools.

In the first half of the twentieth century, debates over private school funding generally focused on the direct and indirect benefits to private schools, often highlighting Protestant and Catholic cleavages in local, state, and even national politics. There had long been a fear among Protestants that Catholic immigration and Catholic schools were a threat to Protestant-dominated public schools (Hamburger 2002).

The anti-Catholic American Protective Association opposed Roman Catholic candidates and public servants (Wilson and Drakeman 2003). Protestants and Other Americans United for Separation of Church and

[1] *Reynolds* v. *United States*, 98 US 145 (1878).

[2] *Everson* v. *Board of Education of the Township of Ewing*, 330 US 1 (1947).

State (now simply Americans United) was formed largely for the purpose of bringing legal challenge to funding for Catholic parochial schools. Paul Blanshard, a leader in the organization, warned against the Catholic takeover in *American Freedom and Catholic Power* (Blanshard 1949), arguing that if Catholics ascended to power in America, the Constitution would contain a "Christian Education Amendment," transferring all educational supervision to Rome (Wilson and Drakeman 2003).

When Earl Warren assumed the chief justiceship of the Supreme Court in 1953, the court turned toward separationism in its church–state jurisprudence, seeking to separate public institutions and religious groups – despite the accommodationist approach of the contemporary Congress and growing public religiosity. The court's endorsement of the secular narrative of national identity was heavily contested, both within the court itself and in the nation more generally (Lacorne 2011). In the face of "a storm of protest," the court outlawed (mostly Protestant) devotional Bible reading and (mostly Protestant) prayer in public schools in *Engel* v. *Vitale* (1962) and *Abington School District* v. *Schempp* (1963)[3] (B. Schwartz 1983, 440). It overturned a law prohibiting the teaching of evolution in *Epperson* v. *Arkansas* (1968) and granted conscientious objector status to an avowed agnostic in *United States* v. *Seeger* (1965)[4] (Hammond 2001).

In the following decades, groups proffered objections to several types of public aid to religious schools, including salaries, textbooks and instructional materials (*Lemon* v. *Kurtzman* 1971),[5] tax deductions for tuition paid to parochial schools (*Mueller* v. *Allen*, 1983),[6] and state-paid disability service in a Catholic school (*Zobrest* v. *Catalina Foothills School District*, 1993).[7]

For secularists, this turn toward separationism was overdue, on the grounds that it protected the rights of religious and nonreligious minorities (Feldman 2005; Justice and Macleod 2016). For accommodationists, however, the affiliation of the Warren Court and its successors with the secularist order presented a problem: How to aid religious institutions in their mission without running afoul of the courts?

[3] *Engel* v. *Vitale*, 370 US 421 (1962); *Abington School District* v. *Schempp*, 374 US 203 (1963).

[4] *Epperson* v. *Arkansas*, 393 US 97 (1968); *United States* v. *Seeger*, 380 US 163 (1965).

[5] *Lemon* v. *Kurtzman*, 403 US 602 (1971).

[6] *Mueller* v. *Allen*, 463 US 388 (1983).

[7] *Zobrest* v. *Catalina Foothills School District*, 509 US 1 (1993).

A New York assemblyman acknowledges the problem: "There is a separation of church and state. We can only do so much" (Magnarelli 2012). The secularist order's ascendance continued after Earl Warren stepped down in 1969 and his successor Warren E. Burger took up the chief justiceship (Curry 1981). The first line of Table 4.1 details the necessity of attenuation for accommodationists, as secularist judges ascended to the highest court and other courts around the nation.

In a series of decisions striking down aid programs to children at private religious schools, the Supreme Court and other federal and state courts reasoned that legislatures had unconstitutionally attempted to benefit religious schools. The Supreme Court's reasoning in *Sloan* v. *Lemon*,[8] a challenge to a Pennsylvanian program, is typical.

> In view of the fact that so substantial a majority of the law's designated beneficiaries were affiliated with religious organizations, it could not be assumed that the state legislature would have passed the law to aid only those attending the relatively few nonsectarian schools. (Powell 1973b)

Despite a severability clause – a clause stating that even if parts of the law were declared unconstitutional, the remainder would remain operable – secularists on the nation's highest court determined that the overwhelming predominance of religious schools among private schools eligible for payments illegally entangled the state with religious purposes.

The accommodationists' rejoinder – that *denying* funds to sectarian schools violated the First Amendment's guarantee of the free exercise of religion – cut little ice with increasingly secularist courts. In *Rhode Island Federation of Teachers* v. *Norberg* (1980),[9] the First US Circuit Court of Appeals identified the accommodationist intervenors' argument:

> In summary the intervenors' legal theory is that the excessive funding of public education amounts to an advancement of the religion of Secular Humanism in violation of the establishment clause, infringes upon the free exercise rights of the intervenors since there is no concomitant aid to those who seek sectarian education, and is an abandonment of the governmental neutrality towards religion which the First Amendment commands. (Bownes 1980)

Rejecting the intervenors' Free Exercise argument, the Court of Appeals struck down a Rhode Island statute, reimbursing parents for the cost of private school tuition. Thereafter, accommodationists were forced to find other means of achieving their policy objectives.

[8] *Sloan* v. *Lemon*, 413 US 825 (1973).

[9] *Rhode Island Federation of Teachers* v. *Norberg*, 630 F 2d 850 (1980).

TABLE 4.1. *The value of attenuated governance in the religious struggle*

Order	Aim	Need for attenuation	Means of attenuation	Success of attenuation
Accommodationist order	Support religious schools	First Amendment applied to states, 1947; Warren Court	Child benefit theory defense[10]	Growing success, e.g. Zelman (2001) and Winn (2009)[11]
Secularist order	Achieve secular goals over religious objections	Passage of federal and state Religious Freedom Restoration Acts	State action defense[12]	Succeeded in some cases, e.g. *Village of Bensenville*, 2006[13]
Secularist order	Prevent religious organizations from blocking contraceptive coverage	Passage of federal and state Religious Freedom Restoration Acts	Exemptions from government mandates	Failure to uphold mandate for closely held corporations, e.g. *Hobby Lobby*, 2014[14]

10 Child benefit theory (CBT) is the legal rationale that states money granted to an individual child and not *directly* to the private school at which they spend the money is constitutional in a way that direct grants would not be.

11 *Zelman* v. *Simmons-Harris*, 536 US 639 (2002); *Arizona Christian School Tuition Organization* v. *Winn*, 563 US 125 (2011).

12 State action is a legal rationale invoked by private parties in their defense against lawsuits. The defense is that the private conduct in question is actively supervised by the state, and therefore, the private party reasonably relies upon state action. By repudiating the state action defense, opponents *attenuate* the connection between state policy and private action, arguing that the private conduct was *not* the result of deliberate and intended state policy.

13 *Village of Bensenville* v. *Federal Aviation Administration*, 457 F 3d 52 (2006).

14 *Burwell* v. *Hobby Lobby Stores, Inc.*, 573 US_ (2014).

Historically, Catholics have been ambivalent or hostile to school choice measures such as school vouchers and tax credit programs but enthusiastic about in-kind aid programs such as publicly provided transportation, textbook loans, equipment, and health and food services for children attending private religious schools (Connell 2000; Hackett 2016). This ambivalence might be a function of the Catholic church's worries about voucher regulation, its focus on the family's role in education and concern about dilution of Church mission, but it may be related to Catholics' particular concern for low-income children (Faith and Reason Institute 2000), who cannot take advantage of voucher tuition payments if their parents struggle to afford private school uniform, equipment, and transportation. Catholic church–organized social assistance agencies, prevalent in Northern and Midwestern states to combat poverty, gladly accepted public funds (Weir and Schirmer 2018).

The seminal Supreme Court judgments on the provision of publicly funded services to religious school students – textbook loan cases *Cochran* and *Allen*, the secular teachers case *Lemon*, the transportation case *Everson*, and the auxiliary services case *Zobrest* – concerned Catholic parochial school students. States with large Catholic populations, particularly New Jersey, California, and Nebraska (but also Illinois, Rhode Island, Connecticut, Pennsylvania, and New York), all provided generous accommodation through in-kind aid and support for various social services.

Under a secularist order, accommodationist programs such as state payments for religious hospitals, schools, and services were also vulnerable to being struck down as unconstitutional. It became difficult to pass such policies because policymakers could not risk being seen to aid religious institutions, as the school finance director for the Utah State Department of Education describes:

> There was a bill introduced in our 2012 legislature that got thumped thoroughly … it was the standard of Howard Stevenson's tax credit bill. If you watched the process there he had the bill then he had a revised bill, a substitute, and then a complete substitute changed and it was just a study [*Interviewer: Right, beaten back*.] Oh yeah, it was white hot. (Newton and Kanth 2012)

With the secularist order newly ascendant, support for religious schools became "white hot": legally vulnerable, hotly contested, and liable to overthrow by hostile forces. Avoiding the heat was a strategic imperative for members of the accommodationist order. A Florida lawyer describes the situation: "How deeply involved is the state going to be in funding religious inculcation? I think that's going to spawn a great deal of litigation" (Meyer 2012).

Constitutional Obstacles for the Accommodationist Order

As the secularist order grew in strength – that is, as groups such as Americans United were founded,[15] and secularist justices and judges ascended to courts across the country, striking down school prayer and other religious accommodations – the accommodationist policies' chief vulnerability lay not with the First Amendment challenge but with state constitutions, which are more easily amended by rivals (Dinan 2018). Between 1835 and 1959, forty-three US states had added provisions known as no-aid provisions (NAPs) to their state constitutions that ban public aid to denominational schools (Hackett 2014). Twenty-nine states enacted Compelled Support Clauses, according to which no person can be compelled to support a religious institution without his or her consent.

Many NAPs were introduced in the late nineteenth century in the aftermath of the failed attempt by Senator James Blaine to introduce a federal amendment in 1876 (Figure 4.1). There is lively scholarly debate about the extent to which these NAPs and their failed federal counterpart reflected anti-Catholic animus (Viteritti 1997; Green 1992; Hackett 2014), but it is generally acknowledged that the majority passed

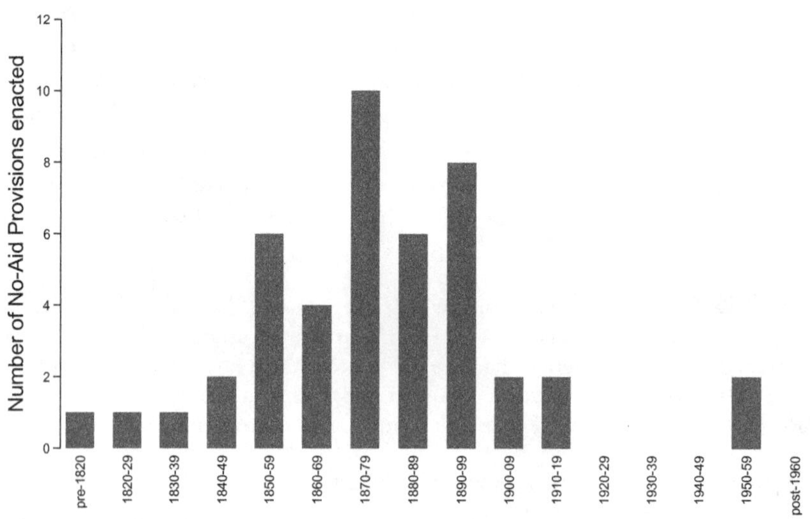

FIGURE 4.1. New no-aid provisions enacted by decade, 1793–2018.

[15] Americans United for Separation of Church and State, a nonprofit advocacy organization, was founded in 1948 as Protestants and Other Americans United for Separation of Church and State. The group is a lynchpin of the secular order.

during a period of widespread anti-Catholicism. States with larger Catholic populations were statistically significantly more likely to pass strongly worded NAPs than those with smaller Catholic populations (Hackett 2014).

Senator Blaine's no-aid effort had the support of President Ulysses S. Grant in his 1875 speech to the Army of Tennessee.

> Let us then begin by guarding against every enemy threatening this perpetuity of free republican institutions.... Encourage free schools and resolve that not one dollar appropriated for their support shall be appropriated to the support of any sectarian schools. Resolve that either the state or the nation, or both combined, shall support institutions of learning sufficient to afford to every child growing up in the land the opportunity of a good common school education, unmixed with sectarian, pagan, or atheistical dogmas. Leave the matter of religion to the family circle, the church, and the private school supported entirely by private contributions. Keep the church and state forever separate. (Grant 1875)

The plain meaning of Grant's words were secularist, and although some supporters of NAPs were motivated by the desire to avoid supporting Catholic institutions in particular (Viteritti 1997), these provisions became bulwarks of the secularist order.

While all state NAPs serve fundamentally the same purpose – to prohibit public funding of denominational educational institutions – the diversity of NAPs in stridency and scope can be measured and analyzed statistically. In the words of the director of public policy and education research for the National Catholic Education Association, "A lot depends on how the state amendment is written. In some cases, it prevents, prohibits, funding in independent schools. It may prohibit direct services. So the wording of the state constitution would kind of determine how much latitude you have in interpreting it" (McDonald 2012). Table 4.2 displays some examples of NAP language.

Court decisions have recognized these differences and have turned upon close distinctions in language. For instance, in *Matthews* v. *Quinton*,[16] the Alaskan Supreme Court found that since the transportation was a "direct benefit" to the nonpublic school, it violated the state's prohibition of aid for the direct benefit of religious institutions (Arend 1961). But in *Honohan* v. *Holt*,[17] an Ohioan Common Pleas Court concluded that "the *indirect* benefits resulting to such school from bus transportation of students to and from school is not 'support' of such 'place of worship'

[16] *Matthews* v. *Quinton*, 362 P 2d 932 (1961).

[17] *Honohan* v. *Holt*, 17 Ohio Misc. 57 (1968).

TABLE 4.2. *Example no-aid provisions in state constitutions*

State	Provision	Adopted	Language
Alabama	Article XIV, §263	1875	"No money raised for the support of the public schools shall be appropriated to or used for the support of any sectarian or denominational school."
California	Article IX, §8	1880	"No public money shall ever be appropriated for the support of any sectarian or denominational school, or any school not under the exclusive control of the officers of the public schools; nor shall any sectarian or denominational doctrine be taught, or instruction thereon be permitted, directly or indirectly, in any of the common schools of this State."
Florida	Article I, §3	1885	"No revenue of the state or any political subdivision or agency thereof shall ever be taken from the public treasury directly or indirectly in aid of any church, sect, or religious denomination or in aid of any sectarian institution."
Missouri	Article I, §7	1875	"No money shall ever be taken from the public treasury, directly or indirectly, in aid of any church, sect or denomination of religion, or in aid of any priest, preacher, minister or teacher thereof."
South Carolina	Article XI, §4	1896	"No money shall be paid from public funds nor shall the credit of the State or any of its political subdivisions be used for the direct benefit of any religious or other private educational institution."
Utah	Article X, §9	1896	"Neither the state of Utah nor its political subdivisions may make any appropriation for the direct support of any school or educational institution controlled by any religious organization."

TABLE 4.3. *Bans on "direct" and "indirect" aid for religious institutions in state constitutions*

"Direct and Indirect"	CA, FL, GA, HI, MI 1970, MO, MT, NY 1894 & 1938, OK
Only "direct"	AK, SC, UT 1986
No mention of "direct" or "indirect"	AL, AZ, AR 1868, CO, DE 1967 & 1897, DC, ID, IL, IN, IA, KS, KY, LA 1879, MA 1855, 1917 & 1974, MI 1835 & 1850, MN, MS 1868 & 1890, NE 1875 & 1976, NV 1864 & 1880, NH, NJ 1844, NM, ND, OH, OR, PA 1874 & 1975, SD, TX, UT 1896, VA, WA, WI 1848, WI 1967 & 1972, WY

within the purview of [the Ohioan No-Aid] constitutional provision" (Leach 1968). A voucher-supporting Ohioan state representative argued, "We're not funding it directly; we're just allowing it to happen.... And that I think is why the funding stream goes that way, not directly in, it goes sort of around" (S. Morgan 2010). Demonstrably, the distinction between *indirect and direct* aid and merely *direct* aid can become consequential.

I code each NAP by five criteria, detailed in Tables A5–A7 in the Appendix. The most important criterion is whether the amendment prohibits direct or indirect aid. *Direct aid* refers to the inclusion of religious schools within the publicly funded school system or, in other words, state funding of religious schools through direct appropriation of taxpayers' money. According to the executive director of the Catholic School Administrators Association of New York State, "we cannot receive anything directly" (Geddis 2012). "It does make it difficult for the kind of direct aid," said an education specialist at the California Catholic Conference (Burnell 2012).

Indirect aid is a more contested concept. It refers to the provision of education-related services by the government for children at private religious schools or to schemes in which families are offered a publicly funded sum to be spent on public or private school tuition. The aid is indirect because it is offered to the parent or child and not directly to the school. Some NAPs explicitly state only that direct aid is prohibited. These amendments are coded as weaker than amendments that simply do not mention the language of directness or indirectness, because of the explicit inclusion of the weaker prohibition (Table 4.3 and Figure 4.2).

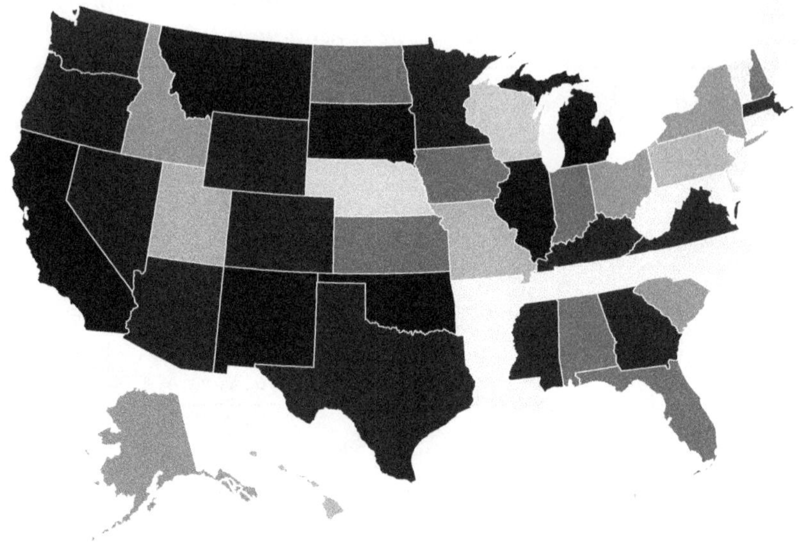

FIGURE 4.2. Modern no-aid provisions by the Hackett strength index, 2019.

The distribution of NAPs across the nation (Figure 4.2) reveals stronger NAPs in the western states, many of which were required to pass such provisions as a condition for their entry to the Union. The darker a state is shaded in Figure 4.2, the stronger its NAP. Today, ten state constitutions (Arkansas, Connecticut, Louisiana, Maine, Maryland, New Jersey, North Carolina, Rhode Island, Vermont, and West Virginia) have no NAP.

Utah is exceptional among western states in the weakness of its NAP, although it has never sought to eliminate it as several other states have done.[18] Unsurprisingly, in Louisiana, one of three states that eliminated their NAP,[19] few policymakers had heard of a state "Blaine Amendment." Of those that had, one described the removal of the NAP as "open[ing] the door" to educational vouchers and tax credits but did not claim that the NAP was central to aid for students at private religious schools (Loar 2012). Many Midwestern respondents, by contrast, cited a strong state Blaine Amendment as a barrier to aid. "Illinois has a pretty strong Blaine Amendment" (Reick 2018). "Blaine Amendments prevent state money going directly to religious education" (Matthiesen 2018).

[18] Only Arkansas, Louisiana, and New Jersey have succeeded in eliminating their no-aid provisions.

[19] The Louisiana no-aid provision was eliminated by the State Constitutional Convention in 1973.

Blaine Barriers?

Scholars are divided as to whether these provisions are real obstacles to the creation of aid programs for children at private religious schools (Viteritti 1997; Fusarelli 2003; Green 2004; Cauthen 2012). Anti-voucher coalitions use NAPs to block voucher plans (Fusarelli 2003). "I think we're all constrained by the constitution" (Magnarelli 2012). "The Blaine Amendment[s] ... are a problem that makes it difficult to skirt around it" (McDonald 2012). Many school choice advocates consider Blaine Amendments to be a remnant of anti-Catholic prejudice and a barrier to school choice initiatives (Dolejsi 2012; Wichmann 2018; T. Jones 2010; Levesque 2012). In a 2018 speech to the Alfred E. Smith Foundation in New York City, Education Secretary Betsy DeVos argued, "These amendments should be assigned to the ash heap of history and this 'last acceptable prejudice' should be stamped out once and for all" (Klein 2018b).

Policymakers and their allies take account of these constitutional prohibitions when crafting bills, as the director of the Cato Institute's Center for Educational Freedom explains:

> I know for a fact that legislators and policy advisers in various states have taken into consideration whether the given state constitution contains a Blaine Amendment to decide whether or not to offer, for instance, a school voucher program. And to the extent that that was not done – as for instance in Arizona with its special needs voucher programs – it was revealed to be a bad idea not to consider it, because the two Arizona programs for special needs students were struck down by the court on essentially Blaine Amendment grounds. (Coulson 2010b)

In Michigan, the only state to have strengthened its NAP twice in successive state constitutions in 1850 and again in 1970, policymakers are wary of its power as a grounds for challenges. The vice-chair of the Michigan Senate Education Committee emphasizes the NAP's role in separating church and state:

> I think there was some fear, when I was first elected that I had a hidden agenda to help the private schools at the expense of public education but I knew that simply wasn't possible. There is a constitutional amendment that says that the state government may not provide aid or direct aid to private education, and whatever efforts the legislature takes it will be ruled unconstitutional and so we have pretty much complete separation between the state legislature, state funding, and private education here in the state of Michigan. (Van Woerkom 2010)

School choice advocates such as the Milton Friedman Foundation list state NAPs in their legislative information booklets as possible barriers to vouchers. For instance, in their guide for legislators, the Institute for Justice and the American Legislative Exchange Council (ALEC)[20] assert that "[a]fter the U.S. Supreme Court eliminated the federal Establishment Clause as a potential barrier to school choice in 2002, opponents were left with state constitutions as their only avenue for attacking school choice programs" (The Institute for Justice and the American Legislative Exchange Council 2007).[21]

The Institute for Justice guide goes on to say, however, that "[n]either voucher nor tax credit programs involve the kinds of special grants to private religious schools that Blaine Amendments sought to prohibit" (The Institute for Justice and the American Legislative Exchange Council 2007). Since the 1930 Supreme Court *Cochran* case involving textbooks for religious school students, judges at both state and federal levels have used *child benefit theory* (CBT) to uphold aid to children at private religious schools, NAPs notwithstanding (Hughes 1930).[22]

CBT is the legal theory that funding provided for the child – and not directly for the school – does not constitute a violation of the separation of church and state because the religious institution benefits only indirectly. On this view direct taxpayer funding of religious school tuition is unconstitutional but providing vouchers, tax credit scholarships, transportation, or other services to *children at those schools* is not. The concept of CBT was first coined by the Louisiana Supreme Court in its 1929 case, *Borden v. Louisiana*,[23] in which the court defended the furnishing of state-funded textbooks to parochial school children in the following terms:

> The schools ... are not the beneficiaries of these appropriations. They obtain nothing from them, nor are they relieved of a single obligation, because of them. The school children and the state alone are the beneficiaries. (W. G. Rogers 1929)

[20] The American Legislative Exchange Council (ALEC) is an organization that creates conservative model legislation for state legislators across the country. ALEC promotes school choice by publishing model voucher policies on its website.

[21] The Institute for Justice is a nonprofit libertarian public interest law firm, and the ALEC is an organization campaigning for limited government and free markets. Both organizations support school choice.

[22] CBT, of course, is not the only grounds on which judges have decided aid cases. The most common legal justifications invoked in such cases include Free Exercise and Establishment (and religious "exclusion," "accommodation," or "advancement") and state requirements to provide "thorough," "adequate," and "efficient" education for all state citizens (and local control rules, "equal protection," competition, and community benefits).

[23] *Borden* v. *Louisiana*, 168 La. 1005 (Louisiana Supreme Court 1929).

The rationale being taken up by other courts, CBT became an important conceptual tool for later school choice activists (Viteritti 1997). Even if the school ultimately banks the money and thereby benefits "incidentally," the benefit to the student is the statute's primary purpose. The connection between state and segregated school is attenuated.

Policymakers take CBT seriously, carefully portraying their policies as benefiting the child rather than the religious school. "There are things that the parochial schools are given because they go to the student not to the school" (Magnarelli 2012). "The money is going to the parent, not to the school and it's constitutional" (Loar 2012). "But that's why the government is not giving schools money, they're giving students money who then go and spend it accordingly" (Matthiesen 2018). A Louisiana state senator elaborates,

> That's the whole philosophy of this, the money is going to the child. The money follows the child and we're not giving a check to St Mary Margaret School, we're giving a check to Mary Smith who's going to St Mary Margaret School. I mean this is ... the intent is not to ... I mean, indirectly, I guess it might, help fund a church school but ... it's not aimed at church schools and there's no language in the law that says we shall fund church schools through this program, it could be a private school. (Appel 2012)

For others – even some advocating in favor of vouchers – the use of CBT to preclude legal challenges is a palpable act of evasion. Thomas B. Fordham Institute professor Chester E. Finn argues that the money aids the school through the parent consumer-citizen, concealing the source and use of state funds.

> Yeah that's the laundering, that's the money laundering is the parental decision. It cannot be the state aiding the school. It is the state aiding the parent, who has freedom of choice and launders the public dollars in whatever direction they wish to do so. (Finn 2010)

The money laundering analogy breaks down when tested in court, however, as successive courts have found CBT a robust rationale for programs that might otherwise entangle the government with a legally contentious purpose: subsidizing religious schools.

I examine the universe of voucher court opinions, the cases heard between 1955 and 2017, in order to track the use of the CBT rationale over time. Figure 4.3 displays trends in the usage of this defense: the cumulative total of judicial rulings utilizing, rejecting, and mentioning or not mentioning CBT. The rationale had existed before any voucher

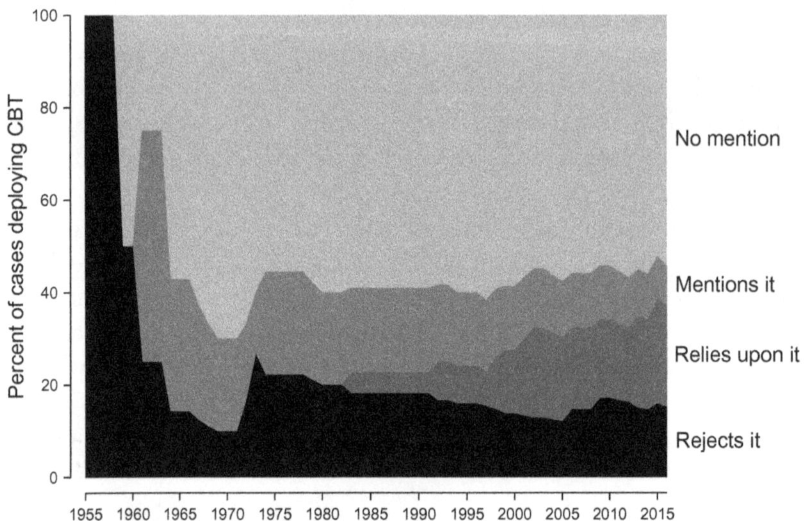

FIGURE 4.3. Trends in usage of child benefit theory, 1955–2017: cumulative total of judicial rulings.

cases were heard, but early courts typically rejected the theory, or merely mentioned it, rather than relying on it to uphold the constitutionality of vouchers. Although voucher cases are decided on a range of grounds, Figure 4.3 shows steady usage of the CBT defense starting with *Mueller* v. *Allen* (1983).[24]

Figure 4.4 breaks down the use of the CBT rationale in terms of whether the court ultimately upheld the voucher as constitutional or struck it down as unconstitutional. More than half of judicial decisions upholding a voucher program as constitutional relied upon the CBT defense. A quarter of the judicial decisions striking down vouchers as unconstitutional did so by explicitly rejecting CBT.

Table 4.4 shows how judges and justices have utilized CBT: relying upon it to support the constitutionality of voucher programs or striking down programs by rejecting it. Although Figures 4.3 and 4.4, and Table 4.4 show that the CBT defense is not always effective, policymakers are confident that judges tend to look favorably upon CBT, and this confidence helps policymakers and bureaucrats to plan for a future for

[24] *Mueller* v. *Allen*, 463 US 388 (1983).

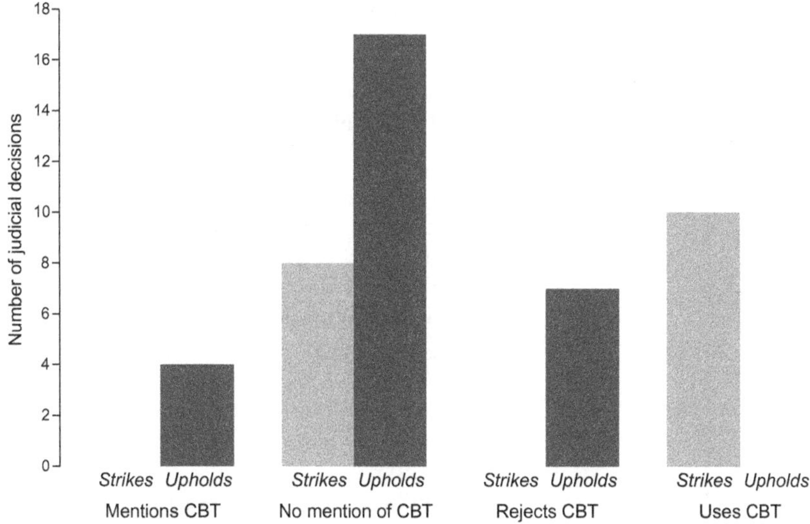

FIGURE 4.4. Use of child benefit theory defense by judicial decision, 1955–2017.

their programs (Boffy 2012; Lancaster 2012; Loar 2012). For example, the deputy superintendent of policy at the Louisiana Department of Education states that their legal team is convinced that the voucher program is constitutional because it does not entangle the state with religious institutions.

> Our attorneys are still very confident in that regard, that ... we are providing a state-funded scholarship, really to the families for them to take and exercise their options, to pay for the education of their child at a school of their choosing. It is not a situation where the state is actively supporting any type of religious teaching. (Bendily 2012)

CBT is a sturdy defense for those supporting voucher programs and a legal hurdle for those opposing them. "They'll [ACLU and Americans United] be challenging [vouchers] in court but they're not going to succeed as long as the actual public dollars are not directly subsidizing" (Finn 2010).

Although CBT is a robust defense for voucher programs, it presents policymakers with a problem of control over the use of state funds. By attenuating the connection between state and school, policymakers avoid entangling the state with legally contentious issues but lose the ability to direct funds to particular sorts of school – as segregationists had done during the dying days of Jim Crow. In a footnote to the

TABLE 4.4. *Examples of child benefit theory defense in court decisions*

Case	Assertion
Court decisions *relying* upon CBT to uphold a program as constitutional	
Luthens v. *Bair*, 788 F Supp 1032 (S.D. Iowa 1992)	"The benefits of the deduction/credit law go to the parents of schoolchildren rather than to the schools. Their 'character' is that of human beings and their 'purpose' is to educate their children. Any financial benefit resulting to the schools is secondary and attenuated."
Jackson v. *Benson*, 578 N.W. 2d 602 (Wis. 1998)	"The amended MPCP, therefore, places on equal footing options of public and private school choice, and vests power in the hands of parents to choose where to direct the funds allocated for their children's benefit."
Kotterman v. *Killian*, 193 Ariz. 273 (Ariz. 1999)	"Safeguards built into the statute ensure that the benefits accruing from this tax credit fall generally to taxpayers making the donation, to families receiving assistance in sending children to schools of their choice, and to the students themselves."
Niehaus v. *Huppenthal*, 310 P 3d 983 (Ariz. Ct Apl 2013)	"The specified object of the ESA is the beneficiary families, not private or sectarian schools."
Louisiana Federation of Teachers, et al. v. *State of Louisiana, et al.*, 118 So. 3d 1033 (La. 2013)	"The direct beneficiaries under the voucher program are the families of eligible students and not the schools selected by the parents for their children to attend."
Court decisions *rejecting* CBT in striking down a program as unconstitutional	
Almond v. *Day*, 89 S.E. 2d 851 (Va. 1955)	"Assuming, but not deciding, the soundness of the view that the private institutions involved receive no direct benefit from the transportation of pupils or the furnishing of textbooks to them, the same cannot be said of provisions for the payment of tuition and institutional fees at such schools. Tuition and institutional fees go directly to the institution and are its very life blood."
Committee for Public Education v. *Nyquist*, 413 US 756 (1973)	"The tuition reimbursement grants, if given directly to sectarian schools, would similarly violate the Establishment Clause, and the fact that they are delivered to the parents, rather than the schools, does not compel a contrary result, as the effect of the aid is unmistakably to provide financial support for nonpublic, sectarian institutions."

Case	Assertion
Cain v. *Horne*, 202 P 3d 1178 (Ariz. 2009)	"These programs transfer state funds directly from the state treasury to private schools. That the checks or warrants first pass through the hands of parents is immaterial."
Taxpayers for Public Education v. *Douglas County School District*, 356 P 3d 833 (Co. 2015)	"The fact remains, however, that the CSP [Choice Scholarship Pilot Program] awards public money to students who may then use that money to pay for a religious education. In so doing, the CSP aids religious institutions."

Hall v. *St Helena Parish* (1961)[25] district court decision, Justice Wisdom remarked upon this dilemma.

The large number of Catholic schools in Louisiana presented the legislature with an insoluble problem. If the tuition grants are "benefits to the child," and not state support of the schools, the legislation is discriminatory on its face in excluding children attending church schools. If the grants amount to state support of schools, support of religious institutions is prohibited by the First Amendment not to speak of the federal constitutional prohibition against state action in supporting segregated schools or the state prohibition against spending public funds for private purposes. (Wisdom 1961)

Ironically, under the CBT rationale, attenuated governance avoids entangling the state with religion precisely by *making benefits available to religious institutions*.

Policymakers act strategically in an attempt to avoid running afoul of the NAP in court, as a voucher opponent explains:

In fact it [NAP] has been applied in court cases, striking down the very first program, the Opportunity Scholarships and on the basis of Article I, Section 3 [the NAP], as lawmakers will debate it. They will strategically try to avoid the question as not wanting to have it applied to the policies they are proposing. (McCarron and Herzog 2012)

Placing the focus on children rather than on the religious institution involves both the rhetorical and policy design dimensions of attenuated governance. The program utilizes an individual consumer-citizen to carry a portion of state funding and avoids granting moneys

[25] *Hall* v. *St Helena Parish School Board*, 197 F Supp 649 (E.D. La. 1961).

directly to institutions (*attenuated delivery*). But deploying CBT is also a rhetorical exercise: a legal rationale diffused across state and federal judiciaries that enables attorneys to argue with confidence that a program does not excessively entangle government with religious purposes (*attenuating rhetoric*).

Since the 1971 *Lemon* v. *Kurtzman* case,[26] judges utilize "the Lemon test," a three-pronged standard aid programs must meet: programs must have a secular purpose, neither advancing nor inhibiting religious practice, and must not result in "excessive governmental entanglement" with religious affairs (O'Connor 1997). This latter standard – the so-called Entanglement Prong – may be met through the avoidance of direct transfers between government and religious organizations (Rehnquist 2002).

Attenuating rhetoric is messaging that distances the government from legally contentious policy goals – in this case, entanglement with religious schools. The executive director of the Californian Catholic Conference reflects upon his organization's messaging around voucher bills:

> It focuses only on the child, regardless of where the child goes to school.... And I think that has a good message for both public and private, and I think there'll be some openness to that, particular as we keep it focused on the child, nothing comes to the school, and it all goes just to the child to help the child... and I think if we can keep that as the dominant tone [then that will be a good thing]. (Dolejsi 2012)

The focus of the California Catholic Conference in advocating for vouchers is to keep the rhetorical focus off the school and on the child instead. Advocates and policymakers know that this attenuating rhetoric helps the program survive and avoid court challenge.

"The Tentacles of the State": Attenuation as Protection for Both Sides

Avoiding entanglement between church and state through an attenuated policy delivery provides more than just legal protection for vouchers. Some religious institutions fear modern voucher programs, because they often contain multiple governmental requirements that religious organizations wish to avoid (Forman 2007). The supreme court of Vermont held in *Campbell* v. *Manchester Board of School District Directors* (1994)[27]: "To allow students to accept tuition reimbursement, religious

[26] *Lemon* v. *Kurtzman*, 403 US 602 (1971).

[27] *Campbell* v. *Manchester Board of School District Directors*, 161 Vt. 441, 641 A 2d 352 (1994).

schools will have to go through the approval process that will increase governmental regulation. Even more governmental regulation is the price for full tuition reimbursement under the current law" (Dooley 1994). A Missouri state senator explains these concerns:

> One of the things that we've worked really hard on is building as many safeguards as we could into [the voucher program], so that the state does not have tentacles and that's difficult…there are parents that want to be free of the tentacles of the state and yet you have legislators that say, "We can't let these schools have taxpayer dollars unless we make them subject to the tentacles of the state." (Emery 2018)

The "tentacles of the state" could include the requirement that voucher students take part in standardized testing or that private schools modify their curricula or submit to state oversight (Manar 2018; J. Morgan 2018). On average, regular voucher programs impose eight state requirements upon private school participants, with Wisconsin imposing more than ten such requirements per program. Table 4.5 provides some examples of the state requirements imposed upon voucher recipients and schools.

By attenuating the connection between state and school, policymakers signal their commitment to religious independence. A Republican on the Illinois Assembly Education Committee expressed this concern about the regulation that comes with the subsidy of religious institutions:

> I've got a lot of [complaints about] my votes against giving money to parochial schools.…Because we have some great Catholic schools in my district and Christian schools as well and they always want to know, why won't you help us? I say, because you want your independence. If you want to follow up all the rules and regulations of a public school then you can have public funds but remember you cannot buy a statue of Mother Theresa with public funds, you just can't do that and they always look at me like, but religion is part of our education and god bless you I understand that, but you can't take public funds for that because not everybody shares your view. How do you think our atheists feel? I don't say that to them. (Mitchell 2012)

Other religious organizations are more open about their connections with state officials. For example, a Californian Catholic Conference leader said that the Conference aims to "build on their [the policymakers'] interest in having a pluralism of educational experience in their communities. And we do that by having our principals… be in dialogue with local officials, and so we want them to appreciate that we're part of their community, that we employ people in their community, we serve people in their community" (Dolejsi 2012).

TABLE 4.5. *Example state requirements for voucher schools*

Program	Requirements of participating schools include...
Arkansas Succeed Scholarship Program for Students with Disabilities	Must gain accreditation; be in business for one year; provide a Certified Public Accountant validated statement of fiscal solvency and insurance coverage; comply with health and safety laws; gain approval from Arkansas Department of Education; employ teachers with no less than a bachelor's degree; comply with federal anti-discrimination provisions
Douglas County Colorado Scholarship Pilot Program	Be accredited by a recognized state or national accrediting organization; demonstrate student achievement and growth results for participating students at least as strong as district public and charter schools; disclose audited financial history; indemnify the district for any loss if the school closes; comply with building codes; conduct criminal background checks; provide information on employment, enrollment, student performance, discipline and conduct, governance, and operations
District of Columbia Opportunity Scholarship Program	No discrimination; comply with district health and safety codes; maintain a valid certificate of occupancy; teachers in core subjects must have a bachelor's degree; must be accredited and comply with district standards; must allow site visits by the administering program entity; administer a nationally norm-referenced test; submit proof of financial sustainability and have financial systems in place
Utah Carson Smith Special Needs Scholarship Program	Must be approved by the state; comply with state health and safety codes; submit an audit and financial report to the state; possess adequate working capital; disclose to parents the special education services provided and their cost; administer annual assessments of students' academic progress and report results; teachers must have bachelor's degrees or multiple years of experience
Wisconsin Parental Choice Program	Meet state nondiscrimination policies; administer state testing to scholarship recipients in fourth, eighth, and tenth grades; receive accreditation; annually submit to the state financial audit; provide state evidence of sound fiscal practices and financial viability; school administrators must undergo financial training and have at least a bachelor's degree from an accredited institution; teachers must have a bachelor's degree from an accredited institution; must provide 1,050 hours of direct pupil instruction in grades 1–6 and 1,137 hours in grades 7–12; provide test score information to the state; meet all health and safety codes

The desire to avoid entangling the government with legally contentious issues of church and state can help explain the geographical and temporal patterns of voucher program passage. For example, Utah's continued reluctance to pass voucher legislation despite unified Republican control can be explained in terms of its history of the church–state controversy. "But this is one of the unique things about Utah and I think it goes to this separation of church and state things that we were talking about. That we're so concerned about it, that we just want to avoid all" (Lockhart 2012). Avoiding controversy over religious matters is of particular interest to Utahns because of the persecution of the Church of Jesus Christ of Latter-day Saints amid suspicion about its political influence. In Chapter 5, I explain the puzzling non-occurrence of vouchers in some conservative states.

Vouchers Rise Again in the 1990s

After the demise of segregation vouchers by 1970, voucher growth was anemic. The key change came in the 1990s when first Wisconsin (1990) and then Ohio (1995) passed major new voucher programs. Wisconsin's program is an important punctuation in the movement from conservative Democrat to overwhelmingly Republican patterns of voucher support. It rested on a "strange bedfellow"[28] alliance launched in the late 1980s by Democratic Wisconsin state representative Polly Williams, the sponsor of the Milwaukee Parental Choice Program (MPCP) legislation. Williams allied with conservatives and the state's Republican governor, Tommy Thompson, to pass Wisconsin's first voucher program in an effort to improve an urban school system wracked with weak results and growing poverty rates (Hess 2004). Although it did not initially include parochial schools, in 1995 the Wisconsin legislature expanded the program to include them.

The same year Ohio inaugurated the first voucher program to incorporate parochial schools from the start. This would be the program who's litigation would lead to the landmark *Zelman* v. *Simmons-Harris* (2002) Supreme Court decision on the constitutionality of school vouchers.

[28] "Strange bedfellows" is a term used to describe alliances between unlikely coalition partners, particularly those with different ideologies and partisan commitments. Strange bedfellow coalitions are not unique to school vouchers. Other such coalitions include alliances between liberal Democrats and fiscal conservatives on prison reform or conservative taxpayer watchdog groups and liberal "sustainable agriculture" groups on the issue of farm subsidies.

Early in his tenure, Republican governor George Voinovich of Ohio made education reform and specifically vouchers a high priority, leveraging his connections with Catholic organizations. As early as October 1991, he signaled his support for a voucher program in a letter to a religious minister concerned about homeschooling (Voinovich 1991b), and he had Ted Sanders, the superintendent of public instruction, lay the groundwork for a voucher program, and established the Governor's Commission on Educational Choice, chaired by businessman David Brennan.

While educational choice was initially pitched as "one more alternative on the smorgasbord of educational reform which must be looked at" (Voinovich 1992), it became clear that this was central to the governor's approach (Voinovich 1993, 1994a; Ohio Business Roundtable 1994). In addition, Voinovich leveraged his relationships with the Catholic church in Ohio, whose parochial schools would be a primary beneficiary of the voucher program. He communicated frequently with the bishop of Cleveland and the archbishop of Cincinnati. At the beginning of the process, Voinovich wrote to the archbishop of Cincinnati, sharing a statement of the US Catholic bishops in support of educational choice. He also indicated that he had discussed this plan with the bishop of Cleveland. Voinovich closed with his vision: "I want to do everything I can do as Governor, consistent with the Constitution, to provide all parents in our state with an opportunity to choose the education they would like to have for their children" (Voinovich 1991a). The archbishop of Cincinnati responded, providing a list of names to serve on the Governor's Committee on Choice (Pilarczyk 1991).

In December 1992, the bishop of Cleveland sent Voinovich detailed information on the state of the Cleveland Catholic schools, asking for support for the financially troubled schools. As the initial legislation was being considered in the summer of 1993, the Catholic Conference of Ohio determined that the conference would "adopt a low profile position on the bill." Members would testify in committee favorably but would strategically refrain from making public appearances or press statements. Yet, the Catholic Conference would activate grassroots parent organizations to "lobby for its passage" (Pilarczyk 1993b).

Catholic networks on school choice were broad. Voinovich's office had an extensive policy lunch with the state Catholic bishops in June 1994, laying out the plans for nonpublic schools and responding to the Catholic Conference's concerns (Needles 1994; Luckhaupt 1994). The president of the Franciscan University of Steubenville wrote to Voinovich in 1993 that school choice and abortion were his two highest state policy priorities (Scanlan 1993). In 1994, the governor sought to meet with every bishop in the state (Voinovich 1994b).

Voinovich increased the state budget allocation for auxiliary services[29] to parochial schools. Yet in a blow to the governor in 1993, the Catholic Conference determined that, on the advice of their legal counsel, they could not support the voucher program as proposed (Pilarczyk 1993a). Voinovich altered the program, and later that year, he asked the Catholic Conference to remain at worst neutral on the voucher legislation. In return, Voinovich would increase the state funding for the auxiliary services of nonpublic schools (Pilarczyk 1994).

The Catholic church vetted the constitutionality of this plan (D. Young 1994), and in 1995, Voinovich included this in his budget. The archbishop of Cincinnati wrote to Voinovich, alerting him that the Catholic Conference "will be asking out people to contact their legislators to support at least these items [auxiliary services] in your budget" (Pilarczyk 1995). After being told that legislators had not heard from constituents, Voinovich asked the Catholic Conference to encourage grassroots support (Voinovich 1995).

The Catholic Conference responded to these requests by writing a letter to local church leaders, explaining that they were attempting to coordinate an "all-out effort involving parents who have children attending Catholic schools" (Catholic Conference of Ohio 1995). Catholic churches even included the grassroots efforts in their local bulletins (Church of St. Gregory the Great 1995). When the grassroots effort was successful, Voinovich wrote to the archbishop of Cincinnati and leader of the Catholic Conference, alerting them of the proposed pilot voucher program in Cleveland and asking to keep up the "full court press in the Senate" (Voinovich 1995).

Quasi-direct Vouchers and the Church–State Question

The voucher programs established under Governors Voinovich and Thompson in Milwaukee and Cleveland took a *quasi-direct* rather than a *contested-attenuated* approach, attenuating the programs' design and communications only weakly. These policies could be more visible because they were not directed to segregationist ends and drew bipartisan support. There was no perceived need to obscure policymakers'

[29] Auxiliary services include medical services such as dental and eye examinations, nurses, and equipment.

purposes when vouchers were available to all qualifying students rather than whites alone.

Moreover, supporters of vouchers at this time did not feel that they "could afford the luxury of intrafamilial squabbles over design features of school choice programs" because their opponents were gathering and voucher supporters "were not ... at the point as a movement where we could pick and choose" between quasi-direct and more attenuated policy delivery (Bolick 2003, 62). Governor Voinovich in Ohio found that the Catholic Conference was slow to support his voucher program in the form originally proposed, despite the Church's financial troubles.

Unlike segregation grants, the voucher programs in Wisconsin (1990) and Ohio (1995) were specifically aimed at remedying racial disadvantages, and schools were required to abide by nondiscrimination regulations. However, they faced new forms of challenge. The overwhelming majority of the vouchers (96 percent in the Ohioan case) were spent at religious schools. For opponents, voucher programs violated the separation of church and state (enshrined in forty state NAPs and the First Amendment) by unconstitutionally aiding religious institutions (Hackett 2014). Opponents characterized the Wisconsin voucher program as a "money laundering scheme" to funnel government funds into religious schools (Bolick 2003, 93).

An Ohioan voucher supporter expressed his sense of this opposition: "There is an anti-religious narrow band in the Democratic Party that are just hostile to things that are supportive of parochial institutions as they relate to government interaction. The idea that any money flows to any institution having anything to do with a church or synagogue is opposed" (T. Jones 2010). Attenuated governance could help here: by funding the individual consumer and not the school directly, the state could attempt to avoid legal confrontation (Hackett 2017).

CBT Is Tested by Quasi-direct Vouchers

The weakly attenuated program design – in which money was granted to the parent rather than to the school directly – offered some protection to vouchers, most famously in the 2001 Supreme Court case *Zelman* v. *Simmons-Harris*.[30] But vouchers remained *quasi-direct* in both design

[30] *Zelman* v. *Simmons-Harris*, 536 US 639 (2002).

and communication. No arm's-length agencies directed public funds to voucher-using parents. The amended MPCP involved the state of Wisconsin sending checks directly to participating private schools, with parents restrictively endorsing the checks (Steinmetz 1998). No private organizations administered the programs. Legislatures appropriated money directly and imposed state requirements directly upon participating schools. In its *amicus* brief in *Zelman*, the American Federation of Teachers (AFT) referred to school choice parents as "inconsequential conduits" in the transmission of aid to religion (Bolick 2003, 93).

Policymakers tended to be open about the need for state support of parochial schools because of the financial costs associated with its removal. If children leave private schools, the public school district is required to find them a place, and each place costs the public school district money. A New York assemblyman is open about this pressure:

> The church is running out of money, the neighborhoods are changing, the support for the [Catholic] Church isn't what it used to be and so we have more and more parochial schools closing. That's a serious threat to the public school system because we cannot afford to take on the, I hate to use the word "burden" but that's what it is, the financial burden and physical plant burden of that many additional kids coming in to the public school system and so I have very actively supported every bill that expands the state support for parochial schools. And I don't find anything wrong with that. It's a matter of survival. The fact that we bus, we bus for all religions, I don't have a problem with it. But we cannot afford to have those schools close. (Miller 2012)

Where policymakers are open about the role of the government in supporting private institutions, vouchers take a *quasi-direct* form. "Because of the urban exodus the majority of the children are there because of the vouchers. And that's actually helping keep those parochial schools open in the urban centers. And they definitely appreciate the fact that that's helping them out" (Spence 2010).

Not only was the design weakly attenuated but there was a vigorous public debate about the government's role in providing such benefits. Voters rejected vouchers in referendums in Maryland (1972), Michigan (1978), Colorado (1992), California (1993), and Washington (1996).[31]

[31] A 1990 referendum in Oregon and a 1998 effort in Colorado on proposed tuition tax credit programs involved the deeply submerged program design being subjected to a visible debate (a *contested-attenuated* scenario). The voters turned both plans down by a two-to-one margin (Menendez 1999).

"Any of the school programs, whether they're a voucher or a tax credit program, have all been enacted solely by the state legislature. Any of them which they tried to do as a ballot initiative have failed, miserably" (McDonald 2012). In *Wirzburger* v. *Galvin* (2005),[32] a challenge to the constitutionality of a state NAP, the First Circuit Court of Appeals stated that "a state initiative process provides a uniquely provocative and effective method of spurring public debate on an issue of importance to the proponents of the proposed initiative" (Torruella 2005).

Florida's 1998 Constitutional Revision Commission proceedings featured numerous anti-voucher interventions (Mills and McLendon 1998). Opposition to vouchers during a 2007 Utah referendum focused on the argument that vouchers would "take resources from the public schools." The opposition prevailed, with 62 percent of the votes (Bolick 2008). This was loud politics. Vouchers had become a matter of nationwide public debate.

During the past three decades of the twentieth century, judges noted that policymakers were often open about the government's role in providing voucher benefits: they used *de*attenuating rhetoric. The court's reasoning in *Sloan* v. *Lemon*[33] is typical in exposing policymakers' intent and using it to strike down programs as unconstitutional. "The State has singled out a class of its citizens for a special economic benefit ... at bottom its intended consequence is to preserve and support religion-oriented institutions" (Powell 1973b).

Like the segregationists before them, authors of vouchers were typically open about their purposes. For example, in a floor debate during consideration of Nebraska's tuition voucher bill, State Senator Terry Carpenter argued in favor of vouchers on the grounds that "if we don't do something for these private schools, they're going to have to close the doors." On another occasion he stated on the floor of the Nebraska legislature that "I would like to find some legal way in order to have the state make a contribution, either in the bill or any other area, in order to use up the unused parts of these private schools." In introducing the voucher bill, Senator E. Thome Johnson argued that his program would increase the student numbers for private schools. Senator Harold Moylan stated, "Now it's not only a thing

[32] *Wirzburger* v. *Galvin*, 412 F 3d 271 (2005).

[33] *Sloan* v. *Lemon*, 413 US 825 (1973).

of keeping these colleges alive, it's the case of financial assessts (*sic.*) to the state" (Spencer 1974).

These public utterances were cited by courts striking down voucher programs. The weakly submerged rhetoric of these fresh voucher programs became legally significant, just as it had for white supremacists during the era of *Brown*. By exposing the intention of the bill's authors to aid private schools, the courts found the statute to be "a patent attempt to sanction by indirection that which the Constitution forbids" (Spencer 1974). Voucher supporters know that courts look unfavorably upon programs that flaunt the role of the government in supporting private, particularly religious, institutions.

> I think that very few people in state legislatures consider the welfare of existing schools, private schools, particularly parochial schools, in enacting legislation, not least of which because doing so is unconstitutional in the United States and the few laws that have been passed that have even a hint of wanting to prop up parochial schools have tended to be struck down by the Supreme Court if they even made it that far. (Coulson 2010b)

In these cases the CBT defense failed. The cause of failure was not the presence of strong NAPs, since voucher programs were struck down in states with weak provisions (Missouri, Nebraska, and Pennsylvania) and even states without any NAP at all (Rhode Island and Tennessee) (Hackett 2014). A better explanation lies in program design and associated rhetoric: many judges found that *quasi-direct* vouchers unconstitutionally entangled the state with religious purposes because they were insufficiently attenuated (see Table 4.4). For example, the Arizona Supreme Court found Arizonan vouchers unconstitutional on the basis of its weakly attenuated program design:

> For all intents and purposes, the voucher programs do precisely what the Aid Clause prohibits. These programs transfer state funds directly from the state treasury to private schools. That the checks or warrants first pass through the hands of parents is immaterial; once a pupil has been accepted into a qualified school under either program, the parents or guardians have no choice; they must endorse the check or warrant to the qualified school. (Ryan 2009)

Of the sixteen voucher cases heard between the demise of the segregation vouchers and the start of the Obama presidency, eleven resulted in the voucher program being judged unconstitutional. Just five, including *Zelman*, upheld vouchers. Being open about the government's role makes voucher programs legally vulnerable because it entangles the government with legally contentious purposes, exposing programs to the charge that they violate the separation of church and state. CBT could help defend vouchers, but their weakly attenuated delivery, combined with policymakers' openness about the role of the government in providing a benefit to the private schools, damaged the programs' chances in court.

CONCLUSION

Secularist forces in America's religious struggle believe that church and state should be separated as completely as possible. Their accommodationist opponents believe the state should encourage religious activity. During the nineteenth century, religious organizations had a major role educating American children, but sectarian disputes about the distribution of public school funds marred the politics of education. One consequence of these controversies was the instantiation of NAPs in forty state constitutions, prohibiting public aid for religious institutions. When secularists ascended to the nation's highest courts during the 1950s and 1960s, accommodationists feared that secularists would use such provisions to strike down publicly funded programs used by children at private religious schools.

In several NAPs, the distinction between "indirect" and "direct" aids for religious institutions is legally consequential. Hence, drawing from an obscure Louisianan case first heard in 1928 (*Borden* v. *Louisiana*),[34] accommodationists crafted arguments for vouchers that emphasized the benefit to the child and not to the religious school itself. President Lyndon Johnson and his legislative allies utilized a similar technique as a means of circumventing Catholic objections to the first major piece of federal education legislation, the Elementary and Secondary Education Act (ESEA) of 1965. ESEA's primary funding mechanism directed benefits to disadvantaged children, rather than schools, so that children attending parochial and other private schools could benefit from federal funds alongside public school students (Davis 1999; P. T. Hill, Cross, and Kilgore 2000).

Accommodationists also sought to protect religious schools from unwelcome government intrusion by attenuating the connection between government and school, yet modern vouchers typically impose regulations upon participating schools. When Governors Thompson and

[34] *Borden* v. *Louisiana*, 168 La. 1005 (Louisiana Supreme Court 1929).

Voinovich reinvigorated the voucher cause in the 1990s, voucher supporters felt they had little choice of voucher design but needed to find political support wherever they could, including through strange bedfellow alliances of Republicans and urban Democrats. Catholic leaders suspicious of government regulation and concerned about low-income children were persuaded by the Republican governors to join the voucher cause.

Immediately, the Midwestern voucher programs faced secularist challenges in court. Although the programs in Milwaukee, Wisconsin, and Cleveland, Ohio, survived legal challenge, most famously in *Zelman* v. *Simmons-Harris*, many other *quasi-direct* vouchers were struck down as unconstitutional in state and federal courts during the latter part of the twentieth century. Their weakly attenuated policy design and weakly attenuating rhetoric made them vulnerable to the secularist charge that they unconstitutionally aided religious institutions and entangled the state with religious purposes.

Just as the voucher supporters were reeling from secularist challenge, they were also called upon to defend the programs against attacks by communitarians. In America's foundational identity struggles, the *public–private struggle* pits individualist forces – committed to the idea that individuals should be protected from an overweening state – against communitarian forces seeking to build civic institutions for the collective good. Led by unions and public school interests, opponents of vouchers allege that the programs unconstitutionally defund public schools. Attenuated governance can help individualists to defend vouchers against this charge, because it enables policymakers and advocates to distance the government from legally and politically controversial policy goals: the diminishment of public education – prohibited by state constitutions – and the demolition of teacher unions. Chapter 5 details the fight between communitarian and individualist orders and the role attenuation plays in efforts to defend the programs against attack.

5

The Public–Private Struggle

Union Opposition and the Educational Establishment

"IT'S THE SLOW DISMANTLING OF THE PUBLIC SYSTEM AS WE KNOW IT"

Teacher unions, public school superintendents, and school board associations oppose school vouchers. Since voucher programs transfer public resources from a heavily unionized sector of the workforce – neighborhood public school teaching – to one of the least unionized – private school educators – teacher unions oppose such programs while Republicans and conservatives pledge to expand them. Individuals and organizations vary in their commitment to the principle of public education – the "one best system" (Tyack 1974) – a commitment that economists term a "taste for education" (Schueler and West 2016). Communitarians in *America's public–private struggle* are firmly committed to public education as a transmitter of civic culture; individualists are not.

Members of the individualist order identify public schools as bastions of communitarian values. Public schools are seen as "the most socialized industry in the world," nurturing "community values, many of which are inimical to a free society" (MacLean 2017, 196). Individualists wish to end the "government monopoly" of public schooling (Friedman 1955). For individualists, public education is an imposition of settlements made long ago as constraints on modern decision-makers' range of action. Their fight is an effort to dislodge an entrenched, politically powerful institution – these "monuments of progressive state building" (Skowronek and Orren 2016, 32). As private sector unions have diminished, unionized public sector workers represent an even greater share of the labor movement – with teacher unions among the most prominent.

Unions and superintendents often argue that the money spent on vouchers drains the public school system of desperately needed funds. Like the subsidy of religious or racially segregated institutions in America's racial and religious struggles, the communitarian order's argument focuses on the source of the funds and the ultimate purpose to which the money is put. Unlike the former cases, the supposition that voucher programs are zero-sum in nature – a win for private schools entails a loss for public ones – is the key. Policy burdens, as well as policy benefits, affect the ability of individuals and groups to organize and participate in democratic contests (Jacobs and Mettler 2018). Sociologist Peter W. Cookson describes vouchers as a "struggle for the soul of American education" (Cookson 1994). The stakes are high.

Voucher proponents face a challenge: countering the argument that their programs undermine public education. "Our country has a two hundred and some odd tradition of the public school system. It's engrained in the American ideal that there will be public schools" (Wichmann 2012). "It's a mindset that says, 'If you think something different ought to be done then you're an enemy of public education' and that's a difficult mindset to break" (Emery 2018). In the communitarian view, public education is a vital civic institution that binds communities together. Vouchers threaten this system by elevating an individualist regard for consumer choice and reducing the public money available for public institutions, as a public school superintendent association leader argues:

> It's the slow dismantling of the public system as we know it. Some would say; that's wonderful, that's great. There are others who'd say ... what has made this country strong for centuries is a viable public education: institutions where everybody is treated the same and that's the great equalizer. That is what has made our country different than other countries similar to yours [UK]. That's the difference where every child has an equal opportunity. It doesn't matter what church you attend. It doesn't matter where you live. It doesn't matter the means that's available to you, everybody's equal. Everybody has a chance, an equal chance, and you won't have that here. (Montford 2012)

Any perceived threat to public schools provokes fierce opposition, as both voucher supporters and opponents attest. "It [my voucher bill] actually would have increased education funding and left more money per pupil in our public system for every student that walked out to a private entity ...

but the thirty-second commercials or fifteen-second commercials simply said 'this bill will destroy public education'" (Sumsion 2012). "You're pulling that money from there over to the private school and you're milking that whole school and there'll be nothing left" (Bangert 2018). "The biggest thing is the public schools want everybody in a public school. I mean 'How dare anybody not go to a public school?' and they're afraid that it might, you know, siphon money away from them" (Koenig 2018).

The president of the Illinois Federation of Teachers echoes a common criticism of vouchers when he states that his organization does *not* "believe public tax dollars should be used to fund private school tuition" (Montgomery 2018). By utilizing *attenuated policy delivery* and *attenuating rhetoric*, members of the individualist order hope to deemphasize the subsidy of private schooling that arouses such controversy. An indirect policy form can be defended as private, rather than state, action in order to forestall the criticism that vouchers drain the public school system of needed funds (row 1 of Table 5.1).

Constitutional Challenge in the Public–Private Struggle

As with the charges that vouchers violate the separation of church and state, or support segregation, the argument that vouchers drain public education of money has both political and legal significance. Since 1973 it has been established precedent that state legislatures – not the federal government – are ultimately responsible for educating their citizens (Powell 1973a). The federal Constitution never mentions education, but *state* constitutions contain a host of positive educational rights and mandates, constitutionally entrenched during the nineteenth century at the behest of the common school movement (Zackin 2013). Many state constitutions require that legislatures provide a "free," "common," "public," "thorough," "efficient," and "uniform" education for all and that money be appropriated for the purposes of education.

For example, Montana's 1972 constitution guarantees all citizens "equality of educational opportunity" through a "system of free quality public elementary and secondary schools."[1] Florida's 1968 constitution requires the legislature to provide "[a] uniform, efficient, safe, secure and high-quality system of free public schools that allows students to

[1] The Montana constitution's 1889 predecessor similarly charged the legislative assembly of Montana with the duty to "establish and maintain a general, uniform and thorough system of public, free, common schools" (Montana 1889).

TABLE 5.1. *The value of attenuated governance in the public–private struggle*

Order	Aim	Need for attenuation	Means of attenuation	Success of attenuation
Individualistic order	Reduce the amount spent on public education	Growth in federal funding for education after the Elementary and Secondary Education Act of 1965	Redeploy public money to private providers; solicit private funds for education initiatives	Substantial growth of tax expenditures but traditional spending also continues to grow
Communitarian order	Increase control over private schools	Increase in private schooling; Every Student Succeeds Act reduces federal leverage	Require third parties to regulate schools and voucher holders	Regulations vary greatly by state; limited success in some states
Individualistic order	Decrease union strength	Rise of public sector unions, 1950s–70s	Promote freedom of choice for parents to choose weakly- or un-unionized private and charter schools	Decrease in public and private sector union membership
Communitarian order	Grow the social welfare apparatus of the state; increase redistribution	Conservative state retrenchment during and after the Reagan presidency	Use tax expenditures; "private" funds to increase the state contribution invisibly; "choice-based rationing" of welfare benefits	Substantial growth of tax expenditures but problem of control and equity

obtain a high-quality education."[2] Georgia's 1982 constitution imposes a "primary obligation" upon the state of Georgia to provide an "adequate public education."[3] Indiana's 1851 constitution, still in operation, asserts that "[t]he income [of the Common School Fund] shall be inviolably appropriated to the support of Common Schools, and to no other purpose whatever."

Opponents often invoke these provisions when they allege in court that voucher programs are unconstitutional (Rowe 2016; Pariente 2006). Figure 5.1 displays the education provision language in all fifty state constitutions. The vertical axis shows a count of the number of constitutions (education section) containing each adjective. Most constitutions contain more than one such adjective.

The education provisions in Figure 5.1 often form the basis of judicial decisions about the constitutionality of voucher programs. For example, *Taxpayers for Public Education* v. *Douglas County School*

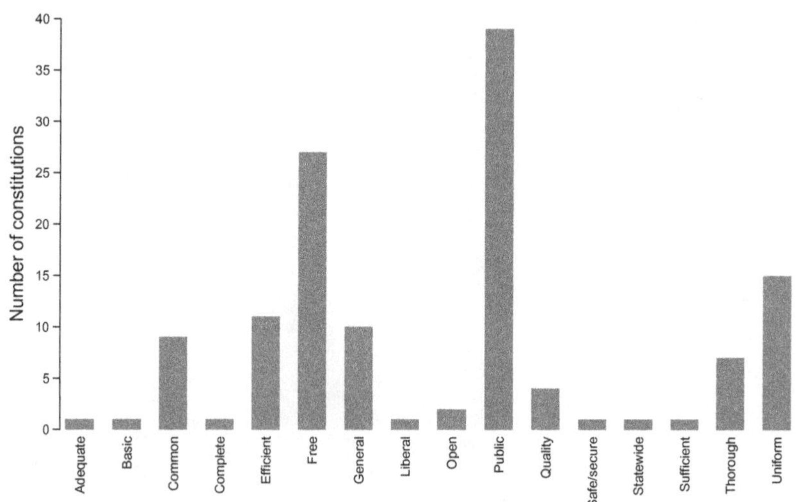

FIGURE 5.1. Education provision language in fifty state constitutions.

[2] The first Florida constitution, promulgated in 1838, provided that the state education fund "shall be inviolably appropriated to the use of Schools and Seminaries of learning respectively, and to no other purpose" (Florida 1838).

[3] The Georgia constitution's predecessors, stretching back to the constitution of 1868, had variously called for an "adequate education," a "thorough system of general education," a "thorough system of common schools" (Georgia 1868, 1877, 1945).

District (2015)[4] turned in part upon the Colorado state constitution's requirement that the state provide a "thorough and uniform" system of public schools. Opponents of the Milwaukee Parental Choice Program argued in *Davis* v. *Grover* (1992)[5] that "by offering a 'character of instruction' that is different from the one found under the mandate of sec. 121.02, the participating private schools violate the uniformity clause [of the Wisconsin constitution]" (Callow 1992).

In *Louisiana Federation of Teachers, et al.* v. *State of Louisiana, et al.* (2013),[6] the Louisiana Supreme Court struck down the state's voucher programs on the grounds that "[l]egislative instruments SCR 99 and Act 2 undeniably divert state MFP funds from public to non-public schools" (Weimer 2013). In *Bush* v. *Holmes* (2006),[7] the Florida Supreme Court held that the state's voucher program

> contravenes [the education] provision because it allows some children to receive a publicly funded education through an alternative system of private schools that are not subject to the uniformity requirements of the public school system. The diversion of money not only reduces public funds for a public education but also uses public funds to provide an alternative education in private schools that are not subject to the "uniformity" requirements for public schools. (Pariente 2006)

The language of state education provisions provides constitutional rationales for members of the communitarian order to challenge vouchers.

The executive director of Foundation for Florida's Future, a pro-voucher group, argues that a Florida ballot initiative to remove the no-aid provision (NAP) Amendment 8 would not be so consequential for vouchers' future as persistence of uniformity language in the Florida state constitution.[8]

> I will tell you that even if Amendment 8 passes you will not see more school choice in Florida because... the Florida Supreme Court's decision in ruling vouchers unconstitutional was not because of the Blaine provision, it was because of the uniformity provision... pursuing Amendment 8 does not fix the voucher issue. (Levesque 2012)

4 *Taxpayers for Public Education* v. *Douglas County School District*, 356 P 3d 833 (Colo. App. 2015).

5 *Davis* v. *Grover*, 166 Wis. 2d 501 (1992).

6 *Louisiana Federation of Teachers, et al.* v. *State of Louisiana, et al.*, 118 So. 3d 1033 (La. 2013).

7 *Bush* v. *Holmes*, 919 So. 2d 392 (2006).

8 The Eighth Amendment – the 2012 Florida Religious Freedom Amendment to remove the NAP language in the Florida State Constitution and replace it with antidiscrimination language – failed by 55.5 to 44.5 percent.

Although the First District Court of Appeal ruled that the Florida Opportunity Scholarship was unconstitutional under the state NAP, the Florida Supreme Court in *Bush* v. *Holmes* did not reach the separation of church and state issue.[9] Accordingly voucher and tax credit aid in Florida is affected more by considerations of educational uniformity, equity, and adequacy than by separation of church and state issues.

Vouchers and the Public School Establishment

Unions and superintendents also contend that vouchers are a means of indirectly undermining their institutional clout by transferring resources to private schools with significantly lower rates of unionization. In addition to vouchers, the conservative model legislation powerhouse American Legislative Exchange Council (ALEC) also promotes policies such as legislation making it more difficult for unions to deduct dues automatically from workers' paychecks, which tend to demobilize public sector unions and their liberal allies, using "policy feedback as a political weapon" (Hertel-Fernandez 2018, 368). But this allegation does not have equal resonance among members of both parties and geographies. As teacher unions have become more closely associated with the Democratic Party, this allegation tends to spur Democratic but not Republican mobilization and opposition. Many Republicans are indifferent to, or celebrate, the demise of the teacher unions as a political force. Yet rural Republicans may ally with Democrats to support "the educational establishment" where they face electoral pressures to do so.

Controversy over the support of private schools does not emanate solely from the communitarian side of America's public–private struggles. A third source of voucher controversy on the culture axis is the *individualist* argument that providing more government support for private schools will actually *grow*, rather than shrink, the size of government (see row 2, Table 5.1). This perspective was articulated forcefully by Secretary of Education Betsy DeVos in a speech in New York City in May 2018:

> A top-down solution emanating from Washington would only grow government…a new federal office to oversee your private schools and your scholarship organizations. An office staffed with more unelected and unaccountable bureaucrats tasked to make decisions families should be free to make for

[9] *Bush* v. *Holmes*, 886 So. 2d 340, 366 (Fla. 1st DCA 2004); *Bush* v. *Holmes*, 919 So. 2d 392 (2006).

> themselves. Just imagine for a moment how that might impact you under an administration hostile to your faith! So, when it comes to education, no solution – not even ones we like – should be dictated by Washington, D.C. (Klein 2018a)

For individualists, the concern with state support for private schools is not that such support would drain funds from community institutions but that it would increase the supervisory capacity of government. An attenuated governance arrangement can help communitarians here, at least publicly: by distancing the government from the supervision of private schools through policy design and communications, voucher supporters can plausibly claim to shrink, rather than grow, the supervisory capacity of the state that individualists decry (Chubb and Moe 1990).

The Growth of Antivoucher Sentiment among Unionists

Surprising though it may seem to the modern observer, teacher unions have in the past been less opposed to private school funding arrangements than they have since become. Despite President Franklin D. Roosevelt's lukewarm support for federal aid to education, unions supported federal-aid plans after the war that could accommodate nonpublic as well as public schools (M. Lieberman 2000).

The National Education Association (NEA) was firmly opposed to the idea of funding Catholic parochial schools, but the American Federation of Teachers (AFT) advocated for some discretion in the allocation of funds, in urban areas particularly, because it saw its public school teachers as partners with parochial schools in bearing the burdens of education (Murphy 1990). After the *Everson* v. *Board of Education* decision in 1947,[10] in which the court found publicly funded transportation for parochial school students constitutional, the AFT remained riven by disagreements on the private school funding issue.

Revolted by the segregation vouchers of the South but wavering over liberal proposals for tax credit tuition vouchers during the years following the Great Society, unions began to coalesce around an antivoucher position in the second half of the twentieth century. The NEA first recorded its opposition to vouchers in 1970, programs it said "could lead to racial, economic, and social isolation of children and weaken or destroy the public school system" (Cibulka 2000, 155). After Democratic candidate George McGovern advanced a tax credit voucher proposal in his failed 1972 campaign, a United Federation of Teachers (UFT)

[10] *Everson* v. *Board of Education of the Township of Ewing*, 330 US 1 (1947).

member referendum voted against endorsing him by 58 to 42 percent (Kahlenberg 2007). The UFT's Albert Shanker reacted with fury when Senators Daniel Patrick Moynihan (D-NY) and Robert Packwood (R-OR) advanced a bipartisan federal tax credit voucher bill in 1978.

Although some unionists (including Shanker) flirted with voucher proposals aimed at low-income minority children during the latter half of the twentieth century, most were opposed. The NEA repeatedly passed resolutions denouncing Republican president Ronald Reagan's plans for federal tuition tax credits during the 1980s, spent thousands of dollars to help defeat voter voucher referendums during the 1990s, and established the antivoucher Center for the Preservation of Public Education in 1993 (Cibulka 2000).

Unions started to switch from the nonpartisan approach to politics that had dominated during the years immediately following the Second World War toward political interventions on behalf of the Democratic Party alone. In Midwestern states, this switch toward Democrats was accelerated by Republicans' increasing focus on school vouchers under Governors George Voinovich and Tommy Thompson (Umhoefer 2016). In early 1992, the Ohio Federation of Teachers wrote to Governor Voinovich regarding its "concern" about the administration looking at the voucher issue, declaring that this "very divisive issue … could explode any chance at building a statewide consensus and 'shared vision'" (Ohio Federation of Teachers 1992). Growing antivoucher sentiment among unionists notwithstanding, even at the beginning of the twenty-first century, scholars could imagine a situation in which the unions might support government assistance to private schooling as part of a push for more educational funding overall (M. Lieberman 2000). That would soon change.

By the 2010s unions had emerged as the most implacable opponents of vouchers (Dorfman 2016; Worden and Hardy 2011; Smith Richards 2012). They litigated voucher cases and rallied opponents of school choice measures at state houses across the nation (Wall 2012a; Illescas 2013; Denny 2011). The executive director of the Catholic School Administrators Association of New York State named union opposition as a barrier to voucher legislation. "So we did go down that route [a voucher bill] for a while but we backed off because it never gets us very far except a big fight from the teachers unions who will plug millions of dollars into stopping anything that comes our way" (Geddis 2012).

The deadlocked 2016 union dues case *Friedrichs* v. *California Teachers Association*[11] dramatized the links between labor laws, unions, and vouchers. Chief plaintiff Rebecca Friedrichs ascribed her decision to challenge mandatory union agency fees to a dispute with her union on the voucher issue (Brown 2015). She felt forced to conform to her union's position of voucher opposition, against her personal views. When *Friedrichs* was litigated, many amicus briefs filed in favor of the plaintiff came from organizations active on questions of school choice, including the Cato Institute, the Goldwater Institute, the Friedman Foundation, and the Pacific Legal Foundation (Per Curiam 2016a; Denniston 2016).

The voucher cause is bound up with the fate of unions in three arenas of communitarian–individualist conflict: first, an indirect challenge to teacher union power embodied in the transfer of money to private schools; second, an overlap between groups engaged with questions of school choice and those concerned with reducing union power in American politics; and third, the growth of partisan polarization that has pushed voucher advocacy toward the Republican Party and union support toward the Democratic Party. "The Democratic Party ... is largely funded by these teachers unions. They're just a huge, huge force in their campaign contributions" (Quinn 2010). In the 2016 election cycle, the AFT and NEA were ranked ninth and eleventh, respectively, in the top organizational donors, giving almost 100 percent of their donations to Democrats and liberals (Open Secrets 2018). Rapid voucher expansion has sharpened union disputes. In states such as Wisconsin, Louisiana, and Indiana, Republicans reduced union bargaining rights even as they passed school voucher programs (Wall 2012a, 2012c; Carr and Barrow 2008).

The teacher union association with the Democratic Party, already virtually complete, was further solidified by the antiunion rhetoric of a 2016 Republican field overwhelmingly supportive of private school choice (Ollstein 2015). Unions responded with anger to the appointment of Betsy DeVos as the secretary of education, in part because she could be expected to promote voucher policies (Sawchuk 2017). Even reform-unionist[12] AFT president Randi Weingarten condemned vouchers as injurious to public education, drawing connections between the modern voucher movement and its segregation grant precursors (Toppo 2017).

[11] *Friedrichs* v. *California Teachers Association*, 578 US _ (2016).

[12] "Reform-unionism" is the idea that teacher unions should collaborate with management in the process of reforming schools (Peterson, Henderson, and West 2014).

On the voucher supporter side, unions were denounced as shamefully self-interested obstacles to much-needed reforms (Alpert 2012; Quaratiello 2013). The taxpayer-funded benefits enjoyed by members of teacher unions drew particular opprobrium given widening gaps between public and private sector employee benefits. Unions had become integral to both sides in the voucher battle. They were the main organizing forces fighting vouchers and also a powerful symbol for pro-voucher forces to combat in America's public–private struggle.

"Who Will Win? Our Children or the Powerful Teacher's Union?"

The position of unions within education politics has always been fiercely contested. "Public school employee unions are politically partisan and polarizing institutions" (Coulson 2010b, 155). Teacher union power is politicized. School voucher supporters portray unions as formidable opponents of reform. They are a superb foil. Ever since Republican presidential candidate Bob Dole lambasted teacher unions as an obstacle to school choice in his party nomination acceptance speech in 1994, rhetorical attacks upon unions have become commonplace (Cibulka 2000; Uetricht 2014). Secretary of Education Rod Paige famously described the NEA as a "terrorist organization" (Pear 2004; Koppich 2005). Secretary of Education Betsy DeVos said, "I know that those sycophants of 'the system' have kept legislators here from enacting a common-sense program that would open options to thousands of kids in need" (Klein 2018a).

Defending his 2012 voucher initiative, Governor Bobby Jindal (R-LA) condemned the teacher union as an "entity that is working hard every day" to make sure parents do not have the opportunity to remove their children from failing schools (Alpert 2012). Governor Bob McDonnell (R-VA) argued that Democratic voucher opponents in the state senate "decided to side with special-interest groups and unions" (Meola 2011). New Hampshire Republican majority leader Peter Silva contended that the only reason Democratic governor John Lynch vetoed the 2012 New Hampshire voucher bill was "that he feels he has to protect his teacher union buddies and Democrat education bureaucrats from competition" (Landrigan 2012).

For conservative supporters of vouchers, "unions are a problem" (J. Clark 2010). "The education cabal" are seen as powerful opponents (Appel 2012; Boffy 2012; Ezell 2012; S. Morgan 2010; Van Woerkom 2010; Roeber 2018).

> Most Democrats and some Republicans are afraid of the teachers unions and the teachers unions are politically very powerful.... They take huge sums of money to use for political purposes and they control most of the state legislatures in the country. I mean control. They control Congress to a significantly lesser extent but in most state legislatures the teachers union may be responsible for a majority of campaign contributions to a majority of members. That's how powerful they are. (M. Schwartz 2010)

Many pro-voucher advocates see their donations as a necessary counterbalance to the large contributions teacher unions have made in state politics over the years (Bunch 2011; Wall 2012a; Coulson 2010b). FreedomWorks[13] mailers attacking both Republican and Democrat voucher opponents in Pennsylvania asked voters rhetorically, "Who will win? Our children or the powerful teacher's union?" StudentsFirst-sponsored mailers identified unions as voucher opponents who have "contributed a fortune" to legislative allies (Tabachnik 2011). Powerful teacher unions are the primary villain in the pro-voucher narrative. They are accused of siphoning money for teacher benefits at the expense of classroom resources and protecting inadequate teachers who do damage to children's education (Richards and Crowe 2013).

Antiunion language is emotive, even in scholarly work. "The NEA and AFT sabotage reform and hold students, parents, teachers, and taxpayers hostage to bureaucracy" (M. Lieberman 1997). Unions are "reform blockers" (Moe 2003). "About 90% of American children now go to so-called public schools, which are not really public at all but simply private fiefs, primarily of the administrators and the union officials" (Friedman 1997, 342). The core of voucher supporters' critique of unions is not only that they are opposed to vouchers but also that the unions are strong enough to defeat voucher programs.

Richard Kahlenberg attributed the sluggish growth of vouchers after *Zelman*[14] to the efforts of Albert Shanker and the modern teacher union movement. He argued that Shanker – president of the AFT[15] from 1964 to 1997 – had kept vouchers at bay by forging "the single most powerful political obstacle to school vouchers": strong teacher unions (Kahlenberg 2007, 390). Shanker's overtures to conservatives built

[13] FreedomWorks is a conservative, libertarian pro-voucher advocacy group based in Washington, DC.

[14] *Zelman* v. *Simmons-Harris*, 536 US 639 (2002).

[15] Previously the United Federation of Teachers (UFT).

bipartisan relationships that made it easier to keep vouchers off the table during negotiations. In addition, Kahlenberg declared, the unions had preserved the most important argument in favor of public education: the assimilation of students of different backgrounds into a common American culture.

A decade after Kahlenberg advanced them, these three propositions – union strength, bipartisanship, and public support for assimilation – are on far shakier ground. Unions, reduced in size and passionately opposed to vouchers, face an ideologically polarized political landscape. They also confront six more Right to Work states[16] and a more voucherized education system. By 2007 there were nineteen voucher programs in existence. Ten years later there were fifty-eight. In 2015 I estimate that 665,759 students used some form of voucher (see Appendix). The number is growing.

Teacher Union Weakness?

Among teacher unions, membership as a proportion of the total public school teacher workforce declined by seven percentage points between 1996 and 2012 according to the Current Population Survey. The AFT's membership rose slightly between 2002 and 2014 (Weingarten 2014). But the NEA experienced a calamitous drop in membership, losing more than 100,000 members over the two-year period from 2010 (Toppo 2012; Sawchuk 2017). Since member dues fund union operations, this corresponds to an 18 percent budget shrinkage.

Temporarily reprieved by Supreme Court stalemate in *Friedrichs*, a restored Supreme Court conservative majority struck down the constitutionality of agency fees[17] in *Janus* v. *AFSCME* (2018),[18] as unions had long anticipated (Sawchuk 2017; Semuels 2016; Brown 2015). School voucher proposals have the potential to reduce the power of teacher unions because private school teachers are much harder to unionize than

[16] Right to Work states have enshrined in law the principle that no person can be compelled to join a union, or pay union dues, as a condition of employment. It eliminates the closed shop. Indiana, Michigan, Wisconsin, West Virginia, Kentucky, and Missouri became Right to Work states after 2007.

[17] Agency fees were fees levied by unions upon nonunion members of their bargaining unit to pay for costs related to the union's collective bargaining activities but not for political activities such as lobbying.

[18] *Janus* v. *American Federation of State, County, and Municipal Employees, Council 31, No 16-1466*, 585 US _ (2018).

TABLE 5.2. *Unionization of private and public school teachers and workers, 1996–2012*

	Teachers		Nonteacher workers		
	Public	Private	Public	Private	All
Union membership (%)	65	28	36	9	15
Number of observations	47,779	8,752	228,895	1,200,395	1,485,821

Source: Bureau of Labor Statistics, September 2014.

public school teachers (M. Lieberman 2000; Moe 2006). These differences are reflected in unionization rate disparities in private and public schools (Table 5.2).

Over the sixteen-year period to 2012, Table 5.2 shows that private school teachers had on average less than half the rate of unionization of public school teachers (28 versus 65 percent). If school voucher programs bolster the private school sector (a widely accepted proposition) or deplete public sector funds (a hotly contested proposition), then teacher unions may be right to view vouchers as an existential threat. Any reform that reallocates resources from the public to the private sector has the capacity to threaten union power (Fusarelli 2003).

Some school choice proponents explicitly present their reforms as a corrective to union influence. President Trump pitched his administration's school voucher plans as an effort to bust the "education monopoly" of government schools (Burke 2016). "If the future holds a solution to the problem of union power," argues voucher supporter and scholar Terry Moe, "it will probably develop as a by-product of the school-choice movement.... Competition spells trouble for unions. It undermines their organizational strength – and with it, their political power" (Moe 2006, 135).

Cross-national evidence suggests that voucher programs pass when union power retreats. The Pinochet government in Chile dissolved its teacher unions entirely before launching a voucher system (Jeynes 2014; Gauri 1999), although hostility toward societal institutions is typical of fascist, military, and communist governments, so the causal linkage may not be straightforward. Some scholars attribute the successful passage of the only federal school voucher program – the Washington DC Opportunity Scholarship Program – to the fact that the bill's major opponents, the local teachers' union, "had fallen into disarray" (Hsu 2006).

But others find that, during the period 1992–2013, the strength of teacher unions in a state did *not* impact the passage of voucher laws (Finger 2018). The relationship between union power, public school districts, and private school choice reforms is contingent and contested.

How Unions and Superintendents Oppose Vouchers

Public school employees and their representatives – teacher unions, school superintendents, and school board associations – oppose vouchers by lobbying, advocating, and funding antivoucher candidates in campaigns (Eddy 2012; Morrison 2012; Kamphaus 2012; Sumsion 2012; Melton 2012). Their opposition makes it more challenging to pass voucher bills, because "education has very strong lobbyists" (Roeber 2018). A regular voucher bill sponsor in Missouri notes that public school interests' opposition stalls voucher bills on financial grounds:

> I do have trouble getting a positive fiscal note. I have trouble getting DESE (Department of Elementary and Secondary Education) to give me numbers that would portray that. Even though, like in the State of Florida saved millions of dollars with one of their school choice programs…But they can, when they do a fiscal note, they can only take information from a government entity. So, they're only going to go to the Missouri Department of Education, or the school districts in the State, who are going to be against my Bill! (Koenig 2018)

Voucher programs are vulnerable to the charge that they drain taxpayer funds from the public schooling system and deploy money that could be used elsewhere. This particular opposition to vouchers is widespread, as both Republican and Democratic interviewees attest. An Illinois Republican explains his "No" vote on vouchers in the following terms:

> That's where I think most of the objections came from. Virtually everyone was in agreement with the education reform package overall except for the tax credit scholarships. My recollection of the folks who spoke on the House floor, those folks who are very strong public education advocates probably felt this is a way to dilute public education and take support away from public education. (Harris 2018)

Opposition to the transfer of public dollars to the private sector is much stronger among Democrats than among Republicans. A Missouri Democrat explains her opposition to vouchers: "We're strong supporters of the institution of public education and…we have a foundation formula that is not always fully funded. We don't want to see those dollars go to non-public, often private and parochial schools" (Schupp 2018).

Attenuation Helps Proponents Avoid the "Defunding" Criticism

Florida lawyer Ronald Meyer argues that funding *quasi-direct* vouchers tends to provoke litigation. "I think as they keep trying to grow this operation and make it bigger and take more and more resources away from public schools to fund these, I think that's just forcing a broader challenge again" (Meyer 2012).

Using attenuated policy delivery and attenuating rhetoric helps proponents of vouchers assert that the program will not use "public" dollars, as a Missouri Republican representative and tax credit proponent argues:

> So like the NEA, National Education Association, MSTA, Missouri State Teachers Association, the bills like mine that have these tax credits scholarships, they don't like it because we will collect less taxes. Now they automatically say all that money that's lost is going to come directly out of the education ledger. Bullshit! This year we're increasing spending on public education, K-12 education by $84 million, alright. The up to $17 million of taxes that our state might collect less of if my bill passed is not going to touch the $84 million that we are sending to our public schools. It's not going to happen. But that's what they claim, that's their scare tactic, is that public schools will not have any money if any of these school choice options pass. (Matthiesen 2018)

His Republican Senate colleagues are also keen to counter the impression that vouchers use public dollars.

> There's that threat of, "Well, you're going to be taking money away from the public schools" and really depending on how you look at that, that really isn't true, because funding per student actually goes up when you do most of these choice ventures, because you don't take all the money away, usually it's a percentage of it and so the per student funding actually goes up, but that argument seems to get no weight. (Emery 2018)

With tax credit vouchers, the question of whether funding such schemes is truly a zero-sum game – as teacher unions and superintendents argue – is murkier than it is for quasi-direct vouchers or tuition grants described in Chapters 3 and 4. The issue hinges in part upon the validity of tax expenditure analysis. For tax expenditure analysts, the tax expenditure is equivalent to direct spending (Surrey 1970; Adler 1993). In the revisionist literature on the welfare state, scholars tend to hew to this line: counting tax expenditures as government spending implies that tax expenditures grow the state (Mettler 2009; Howard 2007). Monica Prasad provides a *reductio ad absurdum* argument against this line of thought on the grounds that *cutting* taxes cannot increase the size of the state or a 100 percent tax cut would be a maximal state (Prasad 2016).

If tax expenditures are indeed equivalent to spending, then the government has chosen to spend its money on private institutions rather than public ones. It is a simple step from there to infer that, unless the budget increases in size, money will need to be recouped elsewhere as the director of legislative affairs for Florida School Boards Association argues:

> This is the epitome of a self-licking ice cream cone. We reduce the amount that corporations have to pay to our state, we live in a state that doesn't have a personal income tax and so, we reduce the corporate income tax overall and then, we excuse them from paying it to us, in addition to that. Hundreds of millions of dollars a year, the state doesn't collect and then, it becomes easier and easier and easier to say "oh my gosh, we're gonna have to cut public education, we just don't have the money." (Melton 2012)

When funds are limited, fights over the uses of public dollars intensify (Saladino 2012). If, on the other hand, tax expenditures are *not* equivalent to direct spending, then it is easier to argue alongside Republican supporters of vouchers that there is no trade-off between the two. Attenuated governance, which leverages tax expenditures and deemphasizes the government role, can help policymakers fend off the criticism that they are funding private schools in opposition to the interests of the public schools.

Twenty years ago, tax expenditure analysis seemed all-encompassing and self-evidently true to scholars working in the field. Scholars attributed little significance to any divergence from the tax expenditure line: "Conservatives' opposition to the concept of tax expenditures is dismissed here mostly because it is a minority view *with little support from academic experts and little effect on government practice*" (Howard 1997, 4) [italics added]. The fact that policymakers frequently reject tax expenditure analysis in order to downplay the costs of voucher programs suggests that this "minority view" may be growing in popularity.

The supporters of voucher programs counter the argument that they seek to defund the public school system by stressing the value of the programs for *public* schools and teachers. In Illinois, for example, the policymaker brief utilized by the Archdiocese of Chicago in its advocacy for the Invest in Kids Act placed the public school establishment at the heart of its appeal (Figure 5.2).

Throughout, this brochure emphasizes the advantages the legislation would bring to the public schools. Support for Teachers and Support for Public Schools are the first two objectives. Tax credit voucher

Support the Invest in Kids Act

Support for Teachers

Capped at $250 per teacher, the Teacher Tax Credit gives relief to teachers who so often buy classroom materials and supplies out of their own pocket.

Support for Public Schools

Corporate and individual donations to public schools for education technology, music, arts and sports programs; district or public school foundations; and nonprofit organizations that provide education-related supplemental services are eligible for tax credits. This is capped at $50 million.

School Infrastructure

This tax credit is capped at $50 million for corporate and individual donations to public schools for facilities costs. These funds will help students by providing safe well-maintained buildings.

Scholarships

Capped at $100 million, this tax credit for donations to nonprofit scholarship organizations allows more students to receive scholarships to attend out-of-district public schools and quality private schools.

Tuition Expenses

The maximum amount of tax deductions that parents can claim for public school fees and private school tuition will increase from $500 and will now be capped at $750.

District	Public schools, foundations, and non-profit organizations	Scholarship organizations
1	$19.3 million	$50.4 million
2	$14.3 million	$25.2 million
3	$7.1 million	$9.8 million
4	$4.4 million	$7.3 million
5	$4.9 million	$7.3 million

FIGURE 5.2. Invest in Kids Act brochure, 2015–16.

scholarships are tucked away under the fourth item, Scholarships, and the Tuition Expenses section states that parents can claim *public* school fees too.

The Invest in Kids Act provided not only tax credit scholarships and $750 of tuition expenses but also tax credits for teachers to purchase classroom supplies (Support for Teachers) for corporate and individual donations to public schools for equipment and arts and sports programs (Support for Public Schools), and for facilities costs (School Infrastructure). In addition to emphasizing the benefits to public schools, placing tax credits and vouchers for tuition payments alongside other forms of expenditure and tax relief can help to reduce potential opposition by providing alternative talking points and room for bipartisan compromise. By deemphasizing the role of the government in potentially defunding public schools in favor of private ones, voucher proponents seek to defuse the communitarian critique.

Texas and Missouri: The "Education Establishment" Fights Back

Elsewhere, the communitarian critique, and the institutional power of the communitarian order, can help explain voucher failures. Some Republican states have conspicuously failed to pass vouchers or tax credit scholarships of any sort, including states such as Missouri with long-standing Republican control. The most puzzling case of this kind is Texas: a conservative state without vouchers, bounded to the North and the East by enthusiastic voucher adopters, Oklahoma, Louisiana, and Arkansas.

Texan state legislators have voted on school voucher bills at least a dozen times since the modern wave of voucher passage first began in 2010.[19] Despite unified Republican control throughout this period and a resurgent Republican right wing (Kincaid 2016), none of these bills reached the governor's desk because the Texan lower house has consistently voted down such legislation. Strange bedfellow alliances of rural Republican legislators and Democratic members continually unite to kill voucher bills. Many rural districts are wary of private school choice programs on the grounds that they defund and damage public education (a major source of well-paying jobs in some districts), allying with teacher unions in an unusually bipartisan fashion.

Supporters and opponents who rally around the Texan voucher cause are chiefly Texan, not out-of-state organizations. The two state teachers' unions are joined by other state-level opponents, including Pastors for Texas Children, Raise Your Hand Texas, Texans for Homeschool Freedom, Texas Association of School Boards, and Texas

[19] Voucher plans had been introduced in successive legislative sessions of the Texas state legislature as far back as 1991 but failed despite the support of Governors George Bush and Rick Perry (Fusarelli 2003, 88). During the 1990s Texan voucher plans typically fizzled out in the upper, rather than the lower, house.

Rural Education Association. Voucher sympathizers have to deal not only with union opposition but also with religious and homeschooling organizations. These strange bedfellow alliances, with their multipronged attack strategies, are key to understanding the repeated failure of vouchers in the Lone Star state and other rural states.

Core members of the individualist order – homeschoolers concerned about the government regulation that might come with publicly funded vouchers – split from the pro-voucher Texas Homeschool Coalition in 2017 to form the antivoucher group Texans for Homeschool Freedom. The Coalition for Public Schools (CPS), an umbrella organization – including four teacher unions – created solely to oppose choice measures, has helped defeat voucher bills since its founding in 1995 (Fusarelli 2003, 77).[20] Rural organizations rallied in opposition to the bill on the grounds that it could reduce funding for rural public schools. Progress Texas, a liberal political action committee, even released a video claiming vouchers could drain money for high school football.

The threat to public school sports teams is significant for rural legislators. "The high school sports team is the entertainment for and the pride for the whole area. So the Friday night football game becomes the binding force that brings the community together" (Bahr 2018). Public school superintendents attend the football games (Roeber 2018). "It's more about this is the hub of their community, this is where they come for community gatherings. Their school sports teams are a source of pride. Then it's the one gathering place where you can fit everybody in the community if you have community events. So to undermine that or to dilute that is a threat and they see that as a threat" (Burnett 2018). One legislator described the dynamic tongue in cheek: "I finally came to the understanding, the real reason why it's opposed, aside from obviously the superintendents don't want to lose their jobs, is that the communities don't want to lose their mascots" (Bahr 2018).

Across the country, rural legislators are suspicious of voucher initiatives. Contemplating the failures of vouchers in Illinois between 2009 and 2012, a Republican representative identified rural legislators as reluctant. "If you look at the Republicans that didn't vote for it [voucher bill], most of them lived in rural areas of the state.

[20] Several of the organizations acting in opposition to the voucher bill in their own right are also members of CPS, including the Texas AFT, the Texan Association of School Boards, the Texas State Teachers Association, the Association of Texas Professional Educators, and Pastors for Texas Children.

The bill was a Chicago-only bill" (Eddy 2012). In Louisiana, reflecting on Republican governor Bobby Jindal's expansion of school vouchers statewide from their initial base in New Orleans, a Democratic state senator and voucher opponent detected hypocrisy among rural and suburban legislators:

> The interesting thing with the state-wide voucher program is almost all of those rural school systems were completely against it ... when Hitler invaded Austria the logic was "well if we give him Austria he'll stop." The logic of rural school boards was "if we give the governor New Orleans for his vouchers, he gets to check it off on his national agenda and he'll leave the rest of us alone." In actuality it was just really the start of his war against all schools in regarding vouchers ... all these different groups they were like "just give him New Orleans, if we give him New Orleans he'll be happy." But it was like "no, no, no it is coming for all of you next." Then lo and behold this last session everyone got it and when you look at a lot of the testimony, a lot of the votes you had people that literally went to the floor, to the wall, lobbied to get vouchers in New Orleans who when the vouchers were coming to their area completely lost their minds. They were like "these things are terrible." (Morrell 2012)

For legislators in poorly populated rural areas, the threat to public education is magnified because of the importance of public schools as employers.

> In rural areas in our state, many times the schools that exist in a rural area may be the largest employer in a particular community and certainly it has an effect on the identity of a community. The so-called public school arrangement has a tremendous effect on the community and so those rural legislators are very concerned with representing their people obviously, they are elected by the people that sent them here and so those rural communities listen pretty heavily to their superintendents. (Stacy 2018)

"These rural Republicans literally think they're gonna lose an election if they vote for school choice," said a Republican voucher proponent in frustration (Koenig 2018). His rural Republican counterpart argues that support or opposition to vouchers "depends on the geography lots of times" and that opposition to vouchers (which he shares) is led by superintendents and administrators: "Ed heads. A lot of them are the traditional ed heads that don't want to change" (Libla 2018). Hence, where "teachers' unions, school boards, administrators' unions ... have worked together very well" (J. Morgan 2018), as in Texas and Missouri, the voucher cause makes limited headway.

The Baptist group Pastors for Texas Children clashed with the Texas Catholic Conference on the appropriate way to promote social justice. While the Texas Catholic Conference sees "potential" in vouchers, Pastors for Texas Children maintain that public education is "a basic provision of the social contract" (Swaby 2017). Voucher supporters face an unusually diverse but well-organized opposition, rooted in Texas's rural, Protestant, individualistic culture as much as its traditionalistic or communitarian elements (Elazar 1970; Wuthnow 2014).

Teacher unions and their communitarian allies are central to the voucher opposition in rural areas, arguing that voucher programs would defund important civic institutions whose importance is magnified in less-populated districts. When they are able to ally with individualists suspicious of federal and state interference, as in states such as Texas and Missouri, they are often able to block voucher initiatives. Conservative, pro-voucher, federal advocacy organizations, such as the Friedman Foundation, the American Federation for Children, EdChoice, Heritage Foundation, Center for Education Freedom, Heartland Institute, and the Institute for Justice, face formidable local opposition. Led by communitarian teacher unions, antivoucher strange bedfellow alliances unite to block voucher bills in unlikely places.

Effects of Unionization on State Legislator Votes for and against Vouchers

Determining the effect of unions upon state legislators' likelihood of voting for or against voucher bills is complicated by the fact that there is no scholarly consensus as to the best way to measure the independent variable. Many previous studies of the influence of teacher unions on state education policies use problematic measures that fail to provide a true measure of direct political influence (Hartney and Flavin 2011). Union size does not necessarily equate to influence (Tomlins 1985; Toppo 2012; Finger 2018). Legislation and regulations that restrict or assist union activities vary widely across states (Winkler, Scull, and Zeehandelaar 2012). Teacher unions can gain leverage even in Right to Work states through ratcheting up campaign contributions to candidates for state office (Hartney and Flavin 2011).

Moreover, the strength of a union in a particular state can be supplemented by national union organization and funding, as Cato Institute's Center for Educational Freedom director Andrew Coulson points out:

> Even if you identify a state as having internally not a very strong union lobby ... you can easily be mistaken as to the extent to which teachers unions as national organizations can have an influence on policy and in particular I would draw attention to the case of Utah, which was a state viewed as having

a relatively weak teachers organization but the national teachers organizations poured three and a half or so million dollars into that state…to fight a school voucher program…And so they poured millions of dollars from the national organization's coffers into that state on the basis of the belief that if vouchers were successful in Utah it would be a, you know, domino that might start knocking over other states. So any successful school choice program in any state is a perceived threat to the unions so they will direct national union reserves to fight a school choice program even in a state that might not have internally a very strong union organization. (Coulson 2010a)

One point of agreement is that union strength is multiply instantiated. Hence, I collect several different measures of union influence: the laws that govern union activity (Right to Work status, the probation of agency fees, and the nature of collective bargaining), contributions by teachers unions to state-level campaign candidates during the period immediately prior to rapid voucher expansion (1998–2006), the level of overall unionization in each state, and the percentage of the workforce in government employment in each state legislative district.

In order to examine the effect of unions on legislator votes, I utilize my dataset of 6,693 state legislative votes on the forty-seven voucher bills passed during 2005–17.[21] The dataset contains the universe of votes during this period and a further 1,158 votes on dead bills (including Texas's recent failed efforts) yielding a total of 7,851 voucher votes.

Table A8 in the Appendix contains a list of all bill numbers and governing regulations. There is a potential selection issue here, given that hundreds of school choice bills are introduced in state legislative sessions every year but do not receive votes. The fact that the votes collected on failed vouchers came from all regions of the country, and from states both with and without existing voucher programs, should help forestall selection concerns. Any observed connections apply across a broad range of states.

To examine the effect of unions and the public school establishment on voucher votes, I model state legislators' votes using multilevel logistic regression in terms of their partisan affiliation, district ideology, private school enrollment, district government employees, educational expenditure, unionization rates, and Right to Work status, inter alia. The regression output is displayed in Table A9 in the Appendix. The results show that voucher votes have become polarized and that some measures of union strength seem to influence legislator votes. For example,

[21] See Appendix for full details.

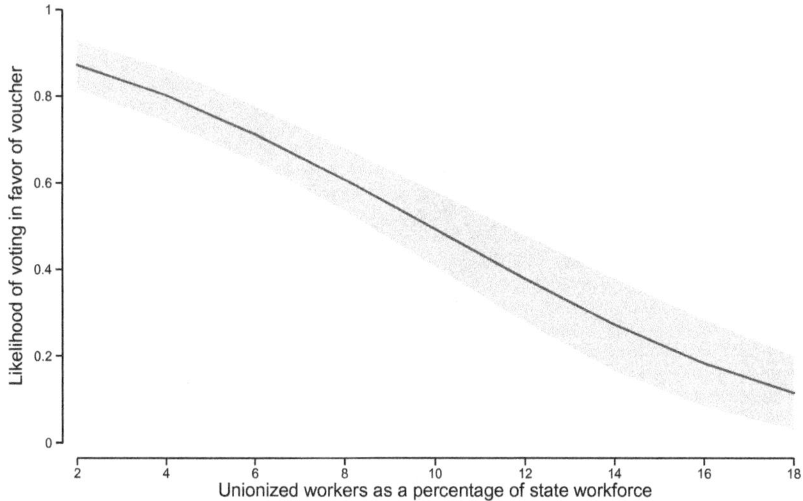

FIGURE 5.3. Relationship between unionization and voucher votes.

controlling for a range of other factors,[22] the percentage of state workers who are members of unions has a statistically significant negative relationship upon the likelihood that a state policymaker will vote in favor of a voucher (Figure 5.3).

As Figure 5.3 shows, unionization and union political influence impact a legislator's likelihood of voting for a voucher bill. Legislators in states with a high degree of unionization are statistically significantly less likely to vote for vouchers than those in states with a lower degree of overall unionization. This pattern is consistent with unions' strong opposition to vouchers (Moe 2014; Cibulka 2000; M. Lieberman 2000). These connections underline the relationship between unionization and voucher votes.

In individual districts, legislators with a higher proportion of government workers – which have a greater degree of unionization than the private sector – are less likely to cast a pro-voucher vote than those with fewer government workers in their district, although this relationship is statistically weaker than that between unionization and voucher votes (Figure 5.4).

[22] For a full list of independent and control variables, and the regression output, see Table A9 in the Appendix.

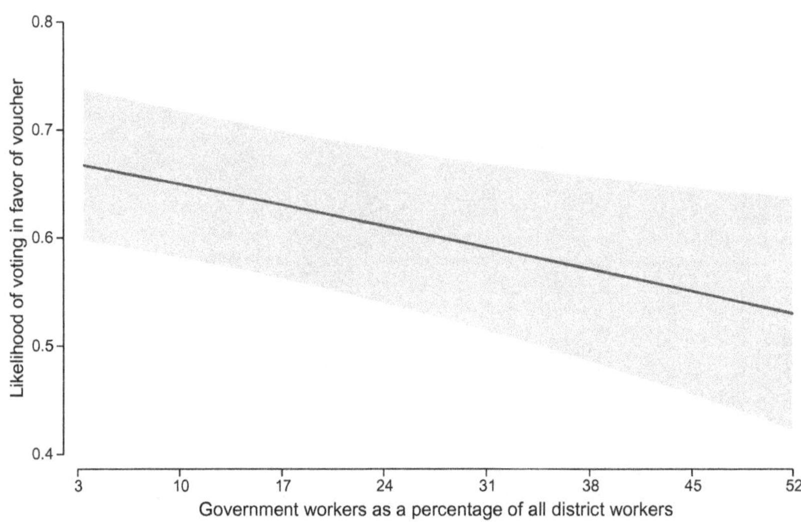

FIGURE 5.4. Relationship between government workforce by district and voucher votes.

As expected, the controls show that Republicans, whites, men, and legislators with conservative districts and in low-spending states are more likely to vote in favor of vouchers.[23] But Figure 5.5 displays complexity respecting union influence. There is a strong connection between being a Right to Work state and a state legislator's likelihood of voting in favor of a voucher bill, but it is a negative connection. Legislators in Right to Work states are statistically significantly less likely to cast a pro-voucher vote than legislators in non-Right to Work states (Figure 5.5).

States such as Indiana and Wisconsin became school choice hotspots before they became Right to Work states (in 2012 and 2015, respectively). This finding may reflect the fact that *indirect* antiunion measures, such as vouchers, are an easier political sell than *direct* antiunion measures, such as Right to Work. If the ultimate aim is to reduce Democratic Party's strength by defunding public sector unions, but vigorous opposition is expected, then vouchers (which indirectly affect union density) may be

[23] The proportion of African Americans in a legislator's district is *positively* related to their likelihood of voting in favor of a voucher bill. This striking datum is reminiscent of the era of segregation vouchers: whiter districts were, and remain, less enthusiastic about vouchers (Bonastia 2012).

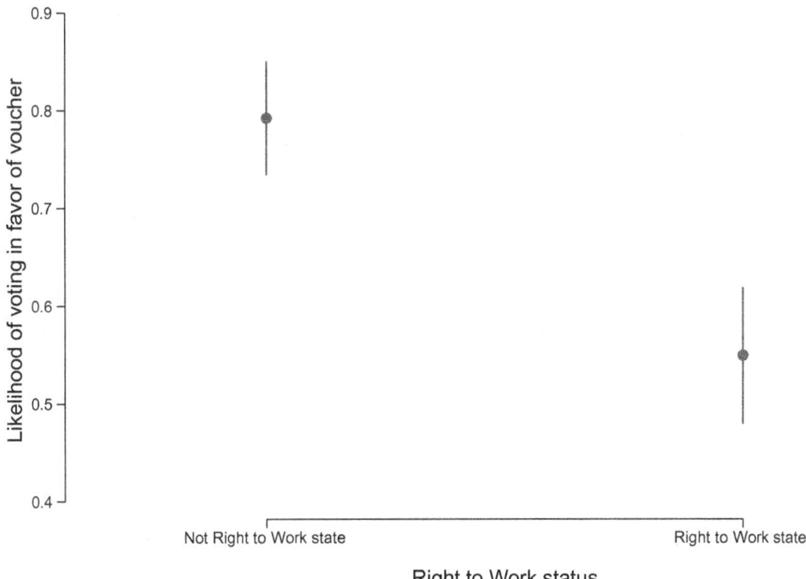

FIGURE 5.5. Right to Work status and voucher votes.

an easier political sell than measures (such as Right to Work) that are obviously targeted at reducing union power. Thus, vouchers are likely to precede Right to Work. In the Indiana and Wisconsin cases, voucher bills formed part of a conservative, antiunion, political thrust that culminated in the passage of Right to Work legislation.

"The Legislature Was Doing Indirectly What It Is Forbidden to Do Directly"

Individualist forces seeking to destroy the political power of unions must act strategically because they face the communitarian charge – still powerful – that they secretly wish to undermine public education and the rights of labor. Right to Work legislation is one rhetorical masterstroke. As litigants in the union agency-fee case *Janus* v. *AFSCME* (2018) argued, Right to Work legislation can be framed in terms of individual liberty, in which the diminishment of unions is a mere side effect.

Another crucial means by which individualist forces seek to undermine their opponents is through voucher schemes, because private schools have much lower rates of unionization than public ones. When litigated, these voucher cases often turn upon the extent to which government can be held responsible for a controversial policy outcome: funding private schools and defunding public ones. Quasi-direct vouchers are more vulnerable to the charge that they divert public money than doubly distanced tax credits. Hence, funding consumer-citizens directly is a more legally perilous path than administering a complex tax credit.

For example, on January 5, 2006, the Florida Supreme Court struck down a voucher program as unconstitutional in *Bush* v. *Holmes*.[24] In a 5–2 triumph for the communitarian order, the majority condemned vouchers on the grounds that they divert money from public schools, a view asserted by public school interests and teacher unions. "The diversion of money not only reduces public funds for a public education but also uses public funds to provide an alternative education in private schools that are not subject to the 'uniformity' requirements for public schools" (Pariente 2006).

The attorney general argued in defense of the program that the voucher "is not an appropriation *directly to* the institutions which the eligible children may attend, but is an appropriation to the parents or guardians of such children, is primarily for the benefit of such children, and only incidentally for the benefit of the selected private schools" (Pariente 2006). But the Tallahassee court stood firm, holding that the relevant constitutional sections were intended to prohibit both direct *and indirect* aid to private institutions. The quasi-direct voucher form was insufficient to attenuate the connection between public money and private institutions.

Nine years later the Alabama Supreme Court upheld a state tax credit voucher as constitutional in *Magee* v. *Boyd* on March 2, 2015.[25] Its 8–1 decision elevated the individualist claim that parental choice is paramount and that nonpublic institutions have a role to play in educating children according to their individual needs. In so arguing, the court countered the lower (circuit) court's determination that the tax credit legislation improperly appropriated public funds to a "charitable or educational institution not under the control of the state." Given the residual strength of the communitarian order's commitment to public education, this was a dangerous charge.

Help for the Montgomery court came from the design of the voucher at issue. Instead of appropriating money directly, legislators had funded

[24] *Bush* v. *Holmes*, 919 So. 2d 392 (2006).

[25] *Magee* v. *Boyd*, 175 So. 3d 79 (2015).

the vouchers through tax credits. Before rendering its opinion, the state's top court first quoted the hostile lower court:

> The circuit court concluded that because the intent of the appropriation was to pay tuition for eligible students to attend private schools in that parents receive the tax refunds only in reimbursement of money they have spent for tuition, the legislature was doing indirectly what it is forbidden to do directly. The circuit court determined that because the Section 9 tax credit for donations to scholarship-granting organizations reimburses such donations in full, there is no private contribution, but simply a redirection of funds from the public fisc to scholarship-granting organizations. (Bolin 2015)

In a victory for individualist forces, the Alabama court rejected this reasoning. Drawing upon a well-established body of reason giving, which had been given federal clearance in the US Supreme Court's 2011 *Winn* decision,[26] the court held that "traditional definitions of 'appropriations' do not extend to include tax credits" (Bolin 2015).

CONCLUSION

The question of union power is the question of partisan advantage, as Right to Work laws and agency fee restrictions drain the financial resources and reduce the political clout of the Democratic Party's core supporters (Faricy 2015). Weakened already by bruising civil rights litigation in the latter half of the twentieth century, the accelerating decline of labor power undermines one of the constitutive pillars of the Democratic Party (Frymer 2008). This issue polarization is unparalleled. Although union power has always been contested, many members of the modern K–12 school choice movement marry financial support for anti-union measures with exceptionally powerful accusations against unions. In turn, unions invoke a consistently antiprivate school choice agenda unprecedented in their history. The power of unions within voucher debates matters politically amid polarized *public–private struggles* for the future of public schools and the role of the state in providing educational services.

Individualists in America's public–private struggle believe that individuals should be made free from an overbearing state, whereas their communitarian opponents think government should build and sustain civic institutions for the collective good. Growing partisan polarization

[26] *Arizona Christian School Tuition Organization* v. *Winn*, 563 US 125 (2011).

aligns secularists, racial egalitarians, and communitarians with the Democratic Party and opposing accommodationists, whites, color-blind forces, and individualists within the Republican Party.

Yet it is the communitarian critique of vouchers – that they transfer money from public to private schools – that can help explain the surprising absence of voucher programs in conservative states controlled by Republican administrations, such as Texas, Michigan, and Missouri. There, "strange bedfellow" alliances of Democrats and rural Republican legislators prevent these state legislatures from passing voucher legislation, because public school interests play an outsized role in rural districts. The polarized alignment of individualists within the Republican Party and communitarians within the Democratic Party is not complete.

Both *contested-attenuated* and *quasi-direct* vouchers have been attacked on the grounds that they entangle the state with some illegitimate purpose (segregation, religious school funding, or damaging public education). This entanglement could be evidenced in court not only in program design but also in communications by policymakers about the government's role in providing a policy benefit. Making the hidden state "visible" on either dimension is risky.

When Republicans gained control of an unprecedented number of state legislatures after 2010, they and their allies switched tack, passing *doubly distanced* tax credit scholarships in larger numbers. These policies, in which both policy design and communications were deeply attenuated, have experienced dramatic successes. *Doubly distanced* tax credit policies were (and are) more likely to be passed into law, less likely to be challenged in court, and less likely to be struck down as unconstitutional than their *quasi-direct* and *contested-attenuated* cousins. In the next chapter, policymakers and advocates explain, in their own words, why they chose attenuated policy designs and how such designs enable them to avoid legal challenges. I show statistically that these patterns persist across time and space.

6

Tax Credit Scholarships in an Era of Republican Dominance

DOUBLY DISTANCED TAX CREDITS IN AN ERA OF REPUBLICAN DOMINANCE

By the late 2000s, several decades' worth of judicial decisions and referendum results provided policymakers and advocates with information about the most legally acceptable policy designs and communications strategies. Voucher proponents wanted not only to pass school choice programs but also to protect them from subsequent challenges. The responses of judges, rival organizations, and the general public helped policymakers to learn about how to create conditions for future success.

Policymakers need to think about the downstream political consequences of their chosen policy designs so that "politics is not merely about what is possible but also about creating an environment that is conducive to further policy developments in the desired direction" (Campbell 2011, 971). Failure of voter referendums during the 1990s and early 2000s prompted a switch to state legislatures rather than direct balloting. Voucher proponents believed, justifiably, that "initiatives by nature are uphill battles" (Bolick 2003, 153).[1] Quieting the politics of vouchers drew it closer to the classic submerged state politics described by Mettler, Howard, and others (Bedrick, Butcher, and Bolick 2016).

[1] Bolick's statement is true of voucher initiatives – perhaps because voucher questions are sensitive to question wording, as I discuss later in this chapter – but the extent to which it is true *in general* varies by initiative type (legislative or popular referendums, or ballot initiatives), form (length and complexity of language), and subject, inter alia (Gamble 1997; Boudreau and MacKenzie 2014).

The new tax credit voucher scholarship, a policy form that multiplied during this period, is deeply attenuated in both design and communications. These *doubly distanced* programs are funded by deducting taxation from donations to third-party "scholarship tuition organizations" (STOs), which administer the vouchers to parents.

> Let me tell you what we do in Florida, okay? That's pretty clear there; you cannot take money from the state treasury to support an institution there, right? Vouchers, you know what we do in Florida? We say to corporations over here that you don't have to pay your corporate income tax; you just put the money over here, and then we'll take this money and provide vouchers. (Montford 2012)

The rapid growth of voucher programs after 2010 involved the spread of the tax credit form. Although regular vouchers continued to pass, the majority of programs after 2010 took a tax credit form. Why? Policymakers learned that *doubly distanced* policies were better insulated from future challenge on communitarian, secularist, or racial egalitarian grounds. "Supporters feel it [passage of a tax credit scholarship] may be easier than enacting vouchers that are issued by the government" (Associated Press 2011). "Now they're working on a tax credit I think, because it's not ... it's a little easier for people if ... the money goes to the people and ... yes more of a parent trace" (Kamphaus 2012).

Policymakers design certain tax credit and voucher programs to avoid judicial challenge, for instance, by deducting tax from donations to STOs that grant scholarships rather than awarding scholarships directly. The delivery of aid programs by attenuated rather than direct methods makes them politically stronger and more difficult to abolish, as Mettler explains in the case of health and tax policy, but this delivery mode also makes them legally stronger.

They are more resistant to successful legal challenge because their design makes them easier to defend on the basis of child benefit theory (CBT) and the entanglement test. The money does not go to the school directly but through an STO that provides scholarships for the children or through tax deductions for parents who spend the money on their children's education. For example, even in Illinois, which has a very strong no-aid provision (NAP) (Hackett 2014, 511), six state courts found the Illinois Tax Credits for Education Expenses constitutional in two lawsuits (*Toney* v. *Bower* 2001; *Griffith* v. *Bower* 2001).[2]

[2] *Toney* v. *Bower,* 744 N.E. 2d 351 (Ill. App. 4th Dist. 2001); *Griffith* v. *Bower,* 747 N.E. 2d 423 (Ill. App. 5th Dist. 2001).

The grounds for the decision were that the credit allows parents to keep more of their own money to spend on the education of their children as they see fit, through "true private choice," and does not involve the (direct) expenditure of government money (Berg 2003; Underkuffler 2004).

Policymakers and advocates acting in support of voucher programs realized the value of the tax credit form early on. Clint Bolick, Institute for Justice advocate, says that his organization chose to defend the Arizonan income tax credit for contributions to private school scholarships precisely because he realized the potential for a robust *attenuation* defense:

> We decided to take our first stand on the nature of tax credits, which in our view were not "public funds" at all, because the money belonged to the taxpayers and never came under the state's control. It was a long-shot argument, but if successful it would establish an enormously useful precedent. (Bolick 2003, 119)

In an early victory, the Arizona Supreme Court upheld the tax credit as constitutional on January 26, 1999 (Kramer 1999), citing approvingly the *Mueller* v. *Allen* decision that "aid was provided on a neutral basis with any financial benefit to private schools sufficiently attenuated" (Zlaket 1999).[3] Although the Arizonan judges rejected Bolick's efforts to distinguish tax credits and vouchers, they did argue that the tax credit design *attenuated* the connection between government and religious school. The attenuation precedent would become very useful over the next twenty years.

Examination of the five state voucher and tax credit programs passed in the major 2011–12 choice wave and litigated in 2013–15 – in Arizona, Colorado, Indiana, Louisiana, and New Hampshire – reveals that NAPs are strikingly poor barriers to the creation of vouchers. The chief reason NAPs fail is that policymakers adopt indirect delivery channels *intentionally*, in order to insulate them from legal challenge. For example, Arizona's Empowerment Scholarship Account was passed by the state legislature in response to the 2009 *Cain* decision that a state voucher program was unconstitutional (Grado 2011).

Similar efforts to submerge and attenuate voucher programs were debated publicly by legislatures in Indiana, Louisiana, and New Hampshire and in Douglas County school board meetings in Colorado

[3] *Mueller* v. *Allen*, 463 US 388 (1983).

TABLE 6.1. *Examples of judicial reliance on the indirect–direct distinction*

Case	Assertion
Kosydar v. *Wolman*, 353 F Supp 744, 761 (S.D. Ohio 1972)	"The three writers in the majority [in *Walz* v. *Tax Commission of the City of New York* (1970)] all commented on the relative passivity of tax exemptions as opposed to direct money subsidies.... While ... direct monetary subsidies are more direct and entanglement-intensive than are exemptions, tax credits are more direct than income tax exclusions or deductions."
Kotterman v. *Killian*, 972 P 2d 606, 193 Ariz. 272 (Ariz. 1999)	"While the plain language of the provisions now under consideration indicates that the framers opposed direct public funding of religion, including sectarian schools, we see no evidence of a similar concern for indirect benefits."
Meredith v. *Pence*, 984 N.E. 2d 1213 (Ind. 2013)	"Any benefit to religious or theological institutions in the above examples, though potentially substantial, is ancillary and indirect."
Magee v. *Boyd*, 175 So. 3d 79 (Al. 2015)	"Traditional definitions of 'appropriations' do not extend to include tax credits."
McCall v. *Scott*, 199 So. 3d 359 (Fla. 1st DCA 2016)	"Indeed, the legislative actions challenged in this case, the authorization of tax credits under the FTCSP and the payment of private funds to private schools via scholarships authorized under the FTCSP, involve no appropriation from the public treasury. The program is funded through voluntary, private donations by individual and corporate taxpayers."

(Illescas 2011; Barrow 2011; Timmins 2012; Evans-Brown 2013; Landrigan 2014). Table 6.1 shows that when the programs are litigated, judges rely on the distinction between direct and indirect expenditures (Thompson 2013; Dickson 2013; Dalianis 2014; Rice 2015). This reliance may be a function of the use of the rationale in amicus briefs and the precedent set by Clint Bolick and his allies.

For tax expenditure analysts, tax expenditures should be evaluated under the same constitutional standards as direct spending programs (Adler 1993). Opponents of tax credit vouchers tend to agree (Montgomery 2018). One Democratic state senator spells out the tax expenditure line.

> If you owe me 100 and I give you a credit of 75, I've just given you $75, so that is the money that I am supposed to receive, that's $75 million that was supposed to come into the Public Treasury that is now not coming into the Public Treasury because I, the state of Illinois, have granted you a tax credit. (Koehler 2018)

Other Democratic opponents of vouchers argue that tax credits are simply a "scam." "Even if it's a tax credit, that's still using tax payer dollars and that violates the constitution" (J. Morgan 2018). Even some Republican school choice proponents have misgivings about the attenuated design: "If we're gonna be serious and consistent about our willingness to fund alternative forms of education or different types of education, then we need to do it out of money that we have appropriated, rather than through some gimmick, which I see this as being" (Reick 2018).

For opponents, the purpose of tax credits is to aid religious schools, albeit in an attenuated fashion.

> No, but you could argue that it isn't [supporting religion] because we do these in separate pots and that is true, which I suspect is partly why the courts have been willing to uphold some of these tax credit things. But to me it's just a scam that in any reasonable way would be seen to be support for private schools, parochial schools. (Flynn Currie 2018)

Their opponents argue that direct and indirect expenditures are importantly different (C. Weaver 2018; McConchie 2018). "Despite the conventional wisdom that tax exemption is tantamount to a subsidy, religious tax exemptions do not violate the Establishment Clause ban on direct aid to religion" (E. King 1998, 973). The distinction between tax expenditure analysts and their opponents corresponds to the partisan divide, as in this exchange – reported in the *Arizona Capitol Times* in 2017 and quoted by Anne Schneider and Helen Ingram:

> Democratic minority leader: "Tax credits are simply giving away tax money."
>
> Republican majority leader: "Whose money is it?" "Not taxing something is not the same thing as giving it away," he said. "Giving it away suggests we own it." He continued. "They own it and then we force it from them, yes, to provide services for various things. But there's a very important distinction." (Fischer 2017)

Attenuated governance can help mask the role of the government in the provision of a particular policy benefit. Tax credits seem to place responsibility for education and other services primarily with donors and nonprofit delivery systems, while the public responsibilities of government and elected leaders play only a shadowy supporting role (Schneider and Ingram 2019). These policy designs disguise the role of the state.

"We Have to Bypass": Why Policymakers Choose Doubly Distanced Policies

Policymakers choose attenuated delivery *deliberately* to avoid challenges. For example, the Illinois sponsors of tax credit legislation passed in 2017 chose the more attenuated form rather than a regular voucher "because the voucher design undoubtedly would be unconstitutional in Illinois" (Manar 2018). "It was the Speaker's view and leadership's view that this was a more palatable way of doing it" (Guzzardi 2018). "A voucher program would have been too far. It wouldn't have passed" (Koehler 2018).

Efforts to pass a voucher in Missouri also took a tax credit form because, in the words of its supporters:

> It's our opinion that in order to be constitutional – and not potentially lose this in a court situation – that we need to keep the money outside of the state budget, and the only way we know to do that is with tax credits. And that has been adjudicated before, and the courts have recognized that if the money never enters the state coffers then it's never state dollars, and therefore it doesn't become subject to the Blaine Amendment, and so that's the reason we're ... working at it from the tax credit side. (Emery 2018)
>
> Missouri has a particularly tough [constitutional prohibition], so that's why we have to bypass, we can't give money from general revenue, because if they are using it at a Catholic school then that's forbidden. So, doing it this way the money never hits general revenue. You decide who's going to collect it, usually 501(c) groups[4] are the ones that oversee it and they hand out these scholarships. (Roeber 2018)

Advocates also press the advantages of doubly distanced policies. For Cardinal Blase Cupich, who worked with legislators in support of the Illinois tax credit scholarship in 2017, the program took an attenuated form because

> [w]e wanted to do something that would not be challenged by those who say that public funds cannot go to sectarian organizations or religious organizations. Many states have the Blaine amendment which does not allow that kind of

[4] Groups known under the Internal Revenue Service's 501(c)(3) code are charitable organizations eligible to receive tax-deductible contributions in accordance with Code Section 170 (Internal Revenue Service 2017).

funding for religious schools. What this piece of legislation does is it...the money doesn't go directly to the schools. (Cupich 2018)

Attenuating the connection between the consumer-citizen and the state helps policymakers increase the chances of program passage. Even opponents of such legislation recognize the success of these tactics. "They thought that it made it a little bit more distant from the wording in the Constitution. I think that's why they did it that way....They said they thought it really wasn't using tax payer dollars for private education" (J. Morgan 2018).

Additionally, as I have explained in Chapter 4, utilizing an attenuated policy delivery – tax expenditures, STOs, and arm's-length administration – helps reassure private schools that they will not be subject to the "tentacles of the state."

Well it doesn't specifically say that the state will never try to tell them how to operate. But the money you have that buffer, the money goes to the charity, the charity gives the money to the kids and that's it, the only role of government is to issue the tax credits. (Matthiesen 2018)

By quieting concerns about religious Free Exercise as well as establishment, attenuated policy delivery gains legal and political advantages.

"The Scholarship Tuition Organizations Are a Different Animal"

The politics of doubly distanced tax credits is quieter than that of quasi-direct vouchers because these policies are more attenuated. Mettler and others have shown that the general public knows little about policies delivered by third parties and funded through tax expenditures and that it is difficult to mobilize in opposition to such policies as a result (Mettler 2010). The executive director of the Louisiana Conference of Catholic Bishops describes the difference between quasi-direct and doubly distanced policies:

I remember telling one of the guys at the teachers union I said "you guys are putting all your attention on vouchers" because you know vouchers in the education is like abortion, it's one of those hot, hot topics. Really hot topics. All focus is on the vouchers and I said "you know you probably gotta have you know 5,000 kids maybe in this program and you got 700,000 kids overall in the state to go to public school"...but the scholarship tuition organizations are a different animal. In Florida they passed that legislation ten years ago and they've gone from like 7,000 to 27,000 in the space of ten years. So the government needs to get focused over here but in the long term I think this is where you may see more of an impact and that legislation went below the radar. I think because politically the unions knew that vouchers were bad and could rob their base and get everybody out there but [with tax credits] you know ... what is this stuff? (Loar 2012)

The complexity of doubly distanced tax credits enables policymakers to expand the programs' scope without fanfare, avoiding arousing controversy about race, religion, or public school funding.

By quieting the politics of vouchers – switching to a legislative rather than a direct voter ballot route – legislators attempted to reduce the likelihood of intensive contestation. The director of legislative affairs for the Florida School Boards Association considers the legislative route to be more difficult to challenge. "Whenever the legislature puts a proposal for a constitutional amendment, it doesn't get vetted the same way as a citizen initiative might be. And so really your only recourse to challenge it, is to go to court" (Melton 2012).

Doubly distanced tax credit policies have a further advantage over their *quasi-direct* cousins: not only are they passed through legislation, rather than the loud scrutiny of ballot initiatives, but their tax credit nature also allows sponsors of such bills to select among several different legislative routes to find the one most conducive to the passage of legislation (J. Morgan 2018). "Venue shopping" is a venerable political art (Baumgartner and Jones 1993). A Republican senator in Missouri describes his strategic efforts to enact a voucher by utilizing taxation, rather than education committees:

I was able to pass it through the House by not going through Education, but since it was a tax credits scholarship program, I went through Ways and Means, and the Ways and Means Committee was much more favorable towards it. And so that's how I went around that way, and then I was able to pass it through the House, but then it went to the Education Committee where it died in the Senate [*laughter*]. (Koenig 2018)

By placing the tax credit voucher with the powerful taxation committee rather than with the education committee, proponents of vouchers may hope to bypass the contentious politics of private schooling. The politics of tax breaks is less contentious than direct social welfare policies in part because such programs tend to have less clear "origins stories" than regular public programs (Hacker 2016). They are created in a wide variety of different ways: attached as small portions of much larger tax bills, negotiated between unions and management, or established by regulatory activities of agencies, court decisions, or private organizations' interpretations of ambiguous laws (Hacker 2016).

In Illinois the major tax credit scholarship program enacted in 2017 did not receive any committee hearings but was attached to a school funding overhaul at a later stage in the legislative process (Manar 2018; McConchie 2018; Sharkey 2018). Even its Republican supporters were taken by surprise. "It came out of whole cloth and... we are looking at each other like where the hell did that come from?" (Durkin and Reick 2018). A Democratic state senator criticized the low profile of the tax credit scholarship design process:

> This was the first time the State of Illinois has put public dollars into private schools and we had no discussion on it. It went to the House, I think on Monday morning, and came to the Senate on the Tuesday. There were no Hearings, there was nothing. It was a deal that the Governor had made with folks on the bill and I just said "It's wrong," you know, for us to make a major policy change without having public debate and public input. (Koehler 2018)

The process by which this tax credit scholarship became law was much quieter (and ultimately more successful) than the messy voucher ballot initiatives of the 1990s.

Learning from Other States about Doubly Distanced Policies

Awareness of success in other states pushes policymakers to deploy doubly distanced policies by demonstrating models of legislation that could pass constitutional muster.

> They really did think this was a way that they could do it that was not going to raise huge constitutional questions. And they had some evidence for that because there had been some court testing of some of these other programs and the courts had said it's okay because you're not funding the program directly. (Flynn Currie 2018)

Advocates across the nation utilize models of successful practice to refine their legislation, aided by national school choice advocacy organizations such as the Thomas B. Fordham Institute, the Cato Institute's Center for Educational Freedom, and the American Legislative Exchange Council's (ALEC) database of model school choice legislation (Burnell 2012; McDonald 2012; Wichmann 2012; Sumsion 2012; Bahr 2018; Emery 2018).

Advocates observe the advantages of *doubly distanced* tax credit forms in other states when considering their own legislative options, drawing particularly from school choice centers, including Florida, Pennsylvania, Arizona, and Wisconsin. "I mean between Pennsylvania and Arizona and then Florida's, there's an awful lot of Florida's that on the SGO side is very attractive" (Burnell 2012). "We've introduced a different bill this year that would provide a tax credit not to families who sent their kids to private schools but to people who wanted to donate to scholarship organizations, like the Pennsylvania and Florida organizations" (Wichmann 2012).

In California, efforts to aid Catholic schools also tend to take an attenuated form because of the constitutional difficulties facing *quasi-direct* vouchers. "Currently there's a lot of interest in our Catholic community ... in the tax policy around tax credits and the very use of taxes ... anyway, that is ... your Arizona, Pennsylvania kind of tax credit model, which was judged by the Supreme Court to be constitutional. We are a Blaine state so we have to constantly be conscious of that, and so we can't step on things" (Dolejsi 2012). Advocates are aware of, and utilize, policy models available in other states.

The recent rapid growth of tax credit vouchers can be attributed to Republican victories in 2010 and learning about successful repulsion of court challenges in other states. Wary of legal challenges or voter push-back, legislators increasingly craft *doubly distanced* programs.

"Public Education Should Be about Public Money Going to Educate a Child and Not about an Institution"

In the fight for vouchers, says Clint Bolick, voucher litigator for the Goldwater Institute, "another tactic, subtle but important, was rhetoric" (Bolick 2003, 37). Tax credit scholarships are not only *attenuated by design and delivery* but also subject to attenuating *rhetoric*: politicians emphasize the role of private market actors and downplay the role of the state in the provision of benefits to private schools. "We needed to get the focus off of the schools, our schools or any school, and onto the kids and what they needed" (Wichmann 2018). "I think I heard more about the arguments of how this would help the individual students ... and I think that that, politically, was a much more sellable argument" (Koehler 2018). "Public education should be about public money going to educate a child and not about an institution" (Koenig 2018).

The rhetorical attenuation of vouchers involves verbally obscuring the role of the government in providing a benefit to a school. Instead, supporters rhetorically emphasize the benefit to the child (Guzzardi 2018).

> It's never, ever, ever, ever cast, let's be clear on framing, it's never cast as aid to denominational schools. Never, ever, ever. It is aiding needy kids to get to a decent alternative to their dreadful public school. That is, or it's aiding disabled kids to get to a school that will meet their needs. It is never framed as denominational schooling. (Finn 2010)

Part of this attenuation process involves careful decisions about labeling. For example, during a "low-key" 2011 Oklahoman legislative debate, the sponsor of a successful tax credit bill said that his program was not "a voucher system" but rather "a scholarship program allowing individuals and businesses to support a program that would create scholarship funds to give children attending schools that are failing an option to access better schools, including private institutions" (McGuigan and Martin 2011). "'School choice' is the more PC [politically correct] term for many of these things, including vouchers" (Melton 2012). "Vouchers in their original thinking was the term that didn't have a negative connotation. What do you call it? A euphemism: 'educational scholarships.' … Policymaker[s] use that and they want to avoid the other one" (McCarron and Herzog 2012).

Advocates quickly learn to avoid the "voucher" terminology. "You know what? I called it the vouchers for the first two months until someone said, let me tell you, you don't call it vouchers" (Lancaster 2012). "Don't say 'voucher scheme'!" (Boffy 2012). "'Voucher' is a loaded word" (Sharkey 2018). When vouchers were initiated in Ohio, businessman supporter David Brennan insisted that Ohio House Education Committee chair Michael Fox uses the term "scholarship" rather than "voucher." Jim Carl uncovers Fox's rationale: according to Fox, "when you ask, do you support vouchers, people don't know what you're talking about or they don't like it. … If you use the word scholarship, everyone supports scholarships." (Carl 2011, 170).

Opponents find the "scholarship" terminology misleading. "He didn't call it a voucher bill but it really was, you know he called it a scholarship fund but a duck's a duck; if it walks like a duck, quacks like a duck then it's a voucher duck" (Newton and Kanth 2012). "No to me it's all a fig leaf, I mean, the reality is we are using public money to support private education" (Flynn Currie 2018). Even supporters of vouchers, such as the Republican minority leader in the Illinois house, find that the terminology confuses people.

The voucher just becomes a third rail but it is a tax credit. It's an indirect voucher, it's a voucher to a certain extent. But I think … "voucher" … has a connotation that some people get confused with. If the idea is a tax credit from donors who are going to make an investment as opposed to the State giving the money away. (Durkin and Reick 2018)

The substitution of the term "scholarships" for "vouchers" extends to extensive voucher-using states such as Louisiana – where public debate over the 2008 tax credit bill was "relatively muted" (Barrow 2008; Carr 2009; Appel 2012) – and Florida: "We don't say vouchers, we say 'education scholarships' [*laughter*] many of our adversaries in the area of increasing parental choice use the term 'vouchers.' But in policy we have always used the term 'educational scholarship'" (McCarron and Herzog 2012). The rhetorical attenuation of the connection between state and services is a matter of strategy: avoiding the politically loaded "voucher" label reduces the degree of controversy such policies engender because public opinion varies with survey question wording (Newport and Carroll 2001; McMurray 2003; Ray 2004; Prothero 2018).

For tax credit scholarship advocates, "it's mostly framing" (Wichmann 2018). "Vouchers is almost like a dirty word" (Matthiesen 2018). "That's almost a dirty word! It's a dirty word" (Roeber 2018). Voucher and tax credit scholarships achieve the same goal, but the tax credit is more politically palatable.

These words take on these meanings and get just visceral reactions from people and "vouchers" is one of those words and so you gotta get away from that. And is the policy better? I don't necessarily think so, but it's a way to achieve a goal, a similar goal. (Wichmann 2018)

[DURKIN] "You are saying it's not a voucher but what it is, it's a tax credit against donations."
[REICK] "It's a backdoor voucher."
[DURKIN] "It is, it's a backdoor voucher." (Durkin and Reick 2018)

Proponents employ an attenuating rhetoric because the "voucher" label implies too close a relationship between state and private schools.

Obviously, the word "voucher" is a great buzz word to kill any school choice measure. I have sponsored education state account, tax credit scholarship bills in the past. I've filed one this year which has gone absolutely nowhere. But the word voucher is used because there's like: "well you're taking our tax dollars and you're giving it to this evil organization that's not us." (Bahr 2018)

Tax credit voucher supporters deemphasize the role of public money in supporting the markets of the hidden state. For instance, the executive director of the pro-tax credit group Cornerstone Action argued that New Hampshire's 2012 program was "not derived from taxpayer funds and is, in fact, a charitable program working to the benefit of our most vulnerable families in the Granite State" (Leubsdorf 2013).[5]

A Republican tax credit supporter in Missouri draws a sharp distinction between vouchers and tax credits by deemphasizing the role of the government:

> Now here's the difference between a tax credit scholarship bill and a voucher. Because vouchers is almost like a dirty word. A voucher is when you take state money and you give directly to a private school or a family state money to spend on education, that's a voucher program. A tax credit scholarship program is a private citizen or a corporation donates to a charity, they get a partial tax credit so thus reducing the amount of taxes they pay and that charity works with a student and helps them pay. That money goes to the school or it goes to the parent who then forwards it to the school and that is different. Money has never been received by the state because it's a tax credit. (Matthiesen 2018)

The battle between supporters and opponents of tax credit legislation is a battle between attenuated and direct rhetoric: the former rhetorically obscures the role of the state in providing a particular benefit, and the latter reveals it. The 2018 Illinois Democratic Party gubernatorial candidate J. B. Pritzker promised to eliminate the 2017 tax credit scholarship program as part of his campaign platform. A Republican state senator described the battles between two competing frames:

> I think that it is going to be a bit of a war of words in regards to the fact that it is already being framed that Pritzker wants to eliminate the ability of poor children to escape failing schools and he is just framing it as state support for private schools when we have underfunded schools as it is. (McConchie 2018)

The tax credit scholarships' attenuated delivery makes it easier for its supporters to engage in attenuating rhetoric: keeping the focus on the child to avoid entangling the state with private schools.

Sponsors of tax credit legislation typically confine themselves to the themes of parental choice, equal opportunities, and charitable giving.

[5] Charitable giving is widely admired in the United States, and Americans give much more than other Western countries: 1.44 percent of GDP (gross domestic product), almost double that of nearest competitors New Zealand and Canada on 0.79 and 0.77 percent, respectively (Charities Aid Foundation 2016).

Unlike the originators of *contested-attenuated* or *quasi-direct* vouchers of the twentieth century, they do not mention the benefits for the private schools (Guzzardi 2018; Manar 2018; Burnett 2018). Instead, they emphasize the role of private actors interceding between state and school (Schupp 2018). A typical example is Senator Bill Stanley's editorial justification for his 2012 Virginian tax credit legislation: "The school choice law encourages private contributions from both businesses and individuals to approved not-for-profit scholarship organizations, giving business and individual taxpayers limited credits against their Virginia income taxes" (Stanley 2012).

Modern arguments for school vouchers also tend to be color-blind, at least on the surface. Legislators advertise vouchers as an educational option for children in low-income households without mentioning race explicitly but implying that children of color are the target population (O'Brien 1996). Modern case law, state statutes, and voucher-supporting politicians typically frame vouchers as a race-neutral way to address educational inequities, but this does not mean that voucher debates are innocent of the race (Gooden, Jabbar, and Torres 2016).

In the context of America's modern racial hierarchies and intensified racial and ideological polarization, color-blind claims for vouchers may be promoted as impartial, but few voters or lawmakers can fail to grasp their racial implications. For Cardinal Cupich:

> This was an argument *not* to keep our Catholic schools open, not to fund religious education, but to give parents who are struggling to raise their children in an environment that is biased against them because of the historical legacy, particularly of racism and slavery in the United States, and we're talking a lot here about African-American kids, many of whom are Catholic, to give those parents an opportunity to make the most important [choice] that they make for their children, and that is where they're going to go to school. I think that turned some people to look at this differently. (Cupich 2018)

Instead of focusing on the religious school, arguments for vouchers focus on individual parents and their exercise of independent choice. Although Chapter 3 showed that major civil rights organizations such as the National Association for the Advancement of Colored People (NAACP) remain firmly opposed to vouchers, this argument from independent choice resonates with groups such as the Black Alliance for Educational Options. Policymakers have learned that utilizing *attenuating rhetoric* and *attenuated policy delivery* helps insulate such programs from legal challenges.

Republicans and Conservatives Grow the Hidden State

Republican administrations tend to engage enthusiastically in growing the welfare state through tax expenditures, although the distribution of benefits to such policies is typically regressive (Faricy 2015, 2016). How partisan are the politics of voucher programs and their tax credit variants? I subject my legislator data to multilevel logistic regression, modeling state legislators' votes in terms of their individual, district-level, and state or program-level characteristics. The full results detailed in Table A9 in the Appendix illustrate the extent to which voucher votes reflect growing partisan polarization. Even controlling for a variety of variables, Republican Party membership is strongly predictive of a pro-voucher vote (Figure 6.1).

The conservatism of an individual legislator's district is also correlated with voucher votes (Figure 6.2). All else equal, representatives of more conservative districts, as measured by the multi-level regression and post-stratification (MRP) model estimate of public opinion at district level calculated for every district by the American Ideology Project (Tausanovitch and Warshaw 2013),[6] are more likely to vote in favor of voucher bills. The

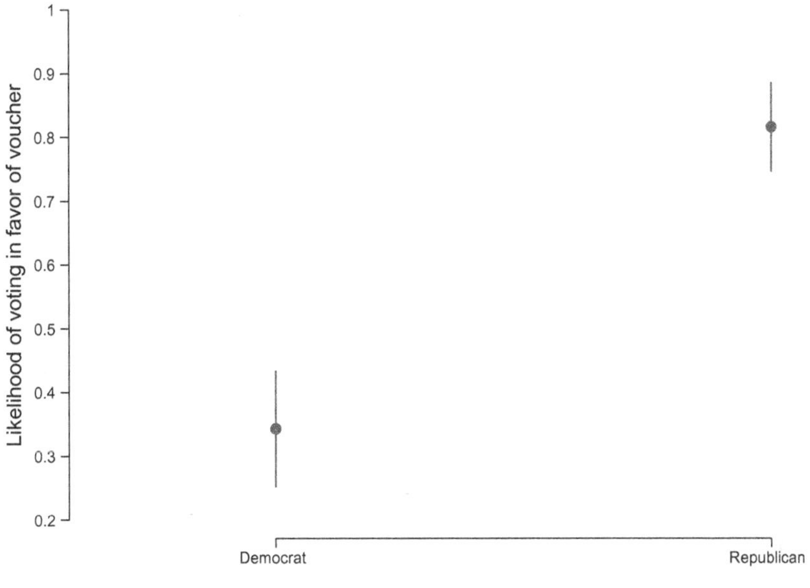

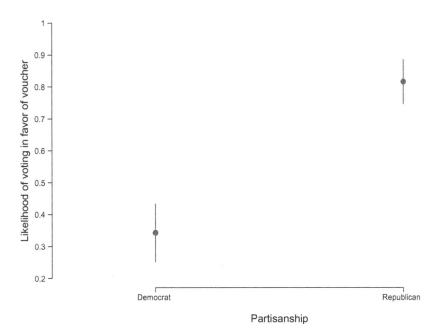

FIGURE 6.1. Relationship between partisanship and voucher votes.

[6] MRP scores are estimates of mean policy preferences for geographical areas, derived using multilevel regression with poststratification.

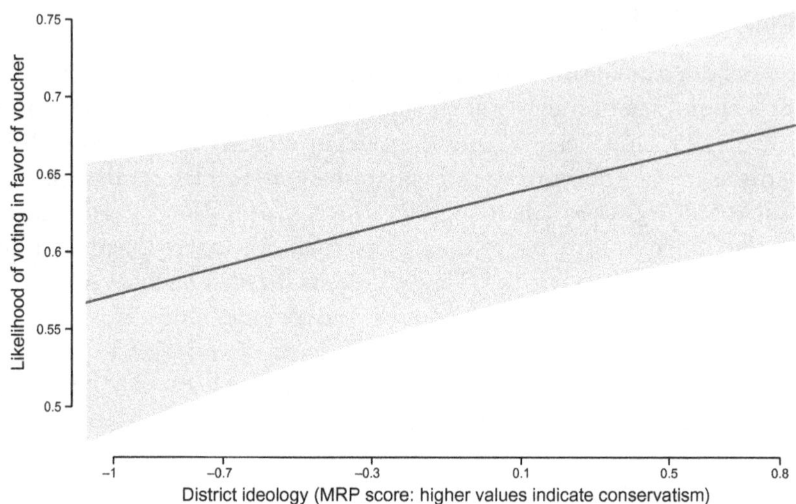

FIGURE 6.2. Relationship between district ideology and voucher votes.

relationship is less clear-cut than it is for partisan affiliation, but Figure 6.2 displays a positive association.

The strength of the finding for the statistical significance of legislator partisanship indicates that the politics of the hidden state is Republican, at least when it comes to vouchers. This finding is consistent with the discovery that it is Republican legislators who produce higher ratios of indirect to direct social spending (Faricy 2011). Even if the politics of some tax expenditures is bipartisan, partisanship is strongly related to individual legislators' votes on voucher bills.

A New York Catholic schools' administrator said that "we have better luck when the Republicans are in control" (Geddis 2012). Her Illinoisan Catholic Conference counterpart separately agreed, with some caveats: "This is not universally true. We have some very strong supporters in the Democratic Party but it has seemed more and more … that the Republican Party is more open to this idea of educational freedom" (Wichmann 2012). "Republicans tend to be in favor of vouchers and Democrats tend not to be" (Maisel 2012). The head of a national school choice advocacy organization, and deputy chief of staff to former Florida governor Jeb Bush, put the case more fully:

It's a Republican promoted issue so if you have a state that has a Republican legislature and a Republican governor, you're more likely to see voucher program than in a state that has Democrat governor or Democrat legislature or even a mix.

So for example in New Mexico, there's a Republican governor and a Republican education commissioner but a Democrat legislature so they'll never get a voucher through the legislature for the governor to sign.... The Republican Party tends to believe and support competition and choice and the Democrat Party tends to support more of the ... teachers' union ... philosophy of "funds to public schools and vouchers hurt public schools" or they're not supportive. In Florida the reason why you have Democrat lawmakers who support it now, it's because they now have constituents, they now have moms and dads and voters that will vote for them or vote against them if they don't support school choice.... But in most states it's a political party issue as to why some states have it and some states don't. (Levesque 2012)

In May 2012 Levesque offered the bold "guarantee" that "when a Republican governor wins in North Carolina they will pass their first voucher" (Levesque 2012). Sure enough, Republican Pat McCrory won the governorship in November 2012, and the Republican-controlled legislature enacted two voucher programs in 2013.[7]

A Catholic Conference leader in California said, "If you're in a strongly controlled, currently Democratic state, your public employees' unions will have an enormous amount of clout and they're not favorable to the public funds going to be used for anything other than public education," but he also went on to say that certain moderate Democrats support the programs: "Where you see more mixture in the legislature, more parity between Republicans and Democrats, or a little more moderate Democratic influence, you have that reality [more aid]" (Dolejsi 2012).

Tax credits and vouchers fit Republican preferences for "limited government" because they are explicitly aimed at creating a competitive educational marketplace. Deeply attenuated tax credits are also more numerous than weakly attenuated vouchers. Their success relative to vouchers can be explained by the fact that tax credits are both market orientated and delivered through tax expenditures rather than direct lump-sum payment to parents. They are easier to pass in state legislatures and more resilient in the face of challenges.

Although Democratic constituencies tend to be more affected by tax credit and voucher programs because such constituencies are more urban, poor, racial minorities, and/or Catholic, with few exceptions, these programs pass only when Republicans have control of the

[7] The programs in question were the Opportunity Scholarships program and the Special Education Scholarship Grants for Children with Disabilities Program.

state offices. Unlike the white supremacist tuition grants detailed in Chapter 3, these programs do not directly impact the economic interests of these (on average less-needy) Republican constituents, but they do satisfy an ideological need to substitute private for public provision. Republicans engage in attenuated governance to safeguard individualistic, accommodationist policies against communitarian and secularist critique. The next section shows that this tactic works.

Doubly Distanced Tax Credits: A Test

My argument that more attenuated forms of voucher are subject to fewer legal challenges, and are more likely to survive challenges brought than less attenuated policy delivery, is confirmed in the data on judicial decisions in voucher cases over the past sixty years (Figure 6.3).

Figure 6.3 shows that tax credit programs are far less likely to be challenged than regular vouchers, and if they are challenged, they are less likely than vouchers to be struck down as unconstitutional. Fewer than three in ten tax credit programs have been taken to court, whereas the average voucher program is *more likely than not* to be challenged in court. Just 43 percent of voucher challenges resulted in the program being upheld as constitutional, but two-thirds of tax credit challenges had that outcome (Figure 6.3).

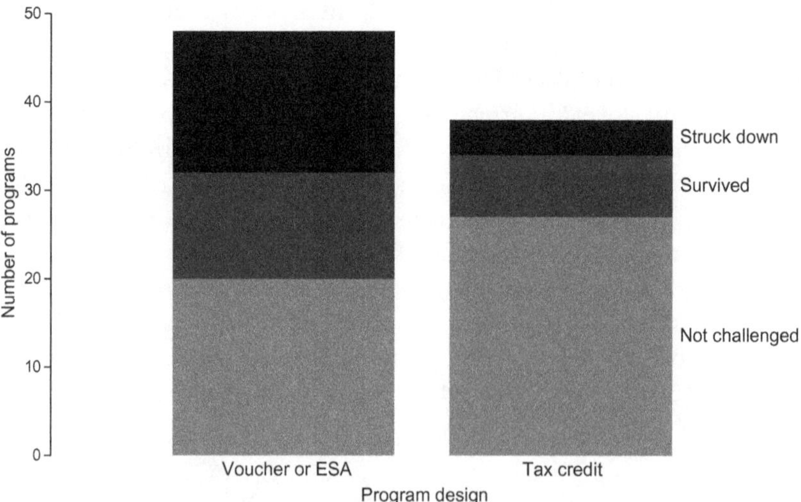

FIGURE 6.3. Challenge and survival rates by voucher program type, 1955–2017.

"Where assistance to religious institutions is indirect and attenuated, i.e. private individuals choose where the funds will go, the Justices have generally been reluctant to find a constitutional impediment" (Zlaket 1999). The US Supreme Court's reasoning in *Mueller* v. *Allen* (1983)[8] is an early example of this reasoning: "The Establishment Clause's historic purposes do not encompass the sort of attenuated financial benefit that eventually flows to parochial schools from the neutrally available tax benefit at issue" (Rehnquist 1983), because the state does not provide benefits to religious institutions directly.

Drawing upon the universe of judicial votes in forty-six voucher cases (1955–2017), and 236 individual votes, I examine the vulnerability of these programs by recording each judge's decision about the constitutionality of the voucher program at issue. An opinion or concurrence upholding vouchers, or a dissent from a decision striking down a voucher program, is coded 1 (supportive of vouchers). An opinion or concurrence striking down vouchers, or a dissent from a decision upholding a voucher program, is coded 0 (opposed to vouchers). The full logistic regression results, with standard errors clustered by court, is available in Table A11 in the Appendix.

As with legislators passing voucher programs, a judge's partisan affiliation is strongly predictive of his or her vote on voucher constitutionality. Republican (or Republican-appointed) judges are statistically significantly more likely than Democratic (or Democratic-appointed) judges to vote to uphold a voucher program (Figure 6.4).

White judges are more favorably disposed to vouchers than nonwhites and Western judges much less favorably disposed to vouchers than southerners. These effects are statistically distinguishable from the effect of policy attenuation. Tax credit vouchers are statistically significantly more likely to be upheld as constitutional than regular vouchers (Figure 6.5). In other words, the more attenuated the connection between state and service, the more likely it is that the program will be judged constitutional.

Judges frequently acknowledge the importance of attenuated policy delivery in their opinions. The Arizona Supreme Court's determination in *Kotterman* v. *Killian*[9] (1999) is typical:

The state does not involve itself in the distribution of funds or in monitoring their application. Its role is entirely passive. Taxpayers who choose to participate may deduct the amount of an STO contribution on their tax returns.

[8] *Mueller* v. *Allen*, 463 US 388 (1983).

[9] *Kotterman* v. *Killian*, 972 P 2d 606, 193 Ariz. 272 (Ariz. 1999).

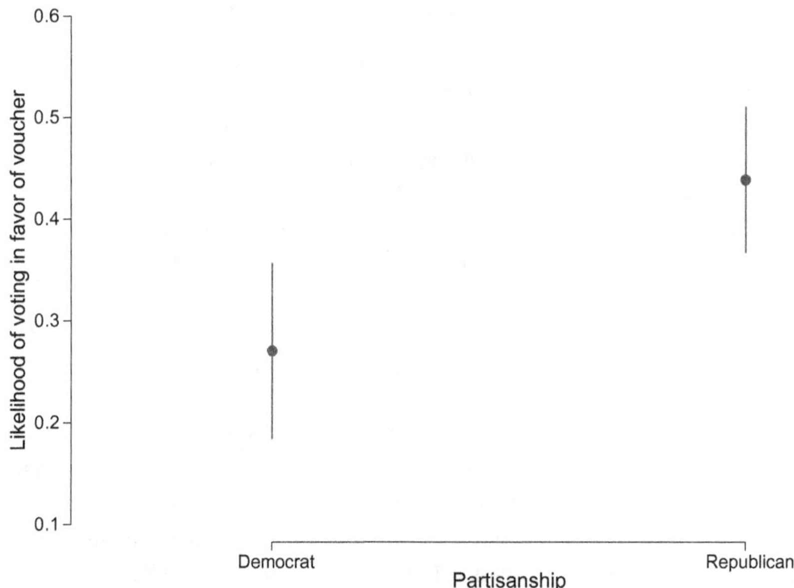

FIGURE 6.4. Judicial partisan affiliation and votes on voucher constitutionality.

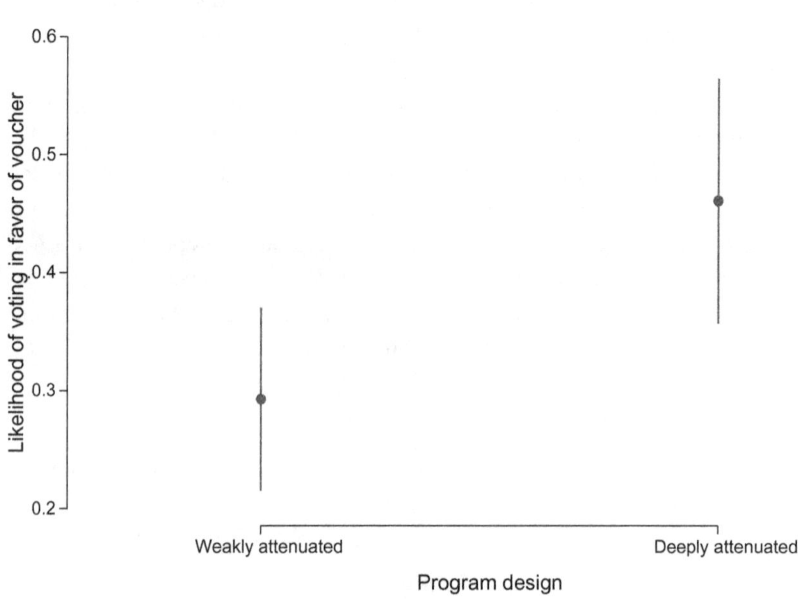

FIGURE 6.5. Program design and judicial votes on voucher constitutionality.

> The STO operates free of government interference beyond ensuring that it qualifies for §501(c)(3) tax-exempt status and complies with state requirements. *Any perceived state connection to private religious schools is indirect and attenuated.* (Zlaket 1999) [italics added]

By attenuating the connection between state and ultimate beneficiary, tax credit voucher scholarships become legally stronger.

How Does Attenuated Program Design Work?

For the general public, scholars have shown that the low traceability of tax expenditures – the fact that not all citizens accept that tax breaks are functionally equivalent to spending – makes the public more supportive of such expenditures than if they had full information about costs (Haselswerdt and Bartels 2015). But what is the mechanism by which the attenuated policy delivery affects judges' decisions? After all, judges do *not* lack information about the costs and benefits of such programs, so they are unlikely to be confused about their nature and scope. Judges, and policymaking elites more generally, have no difficulty understanding the concept of tax expenditures or contemplating the possibility that tax breaks might form a major component of government spending of the American welfare state (Howard 1997; Faricy 2015).

The general public's relative lack of information about submerged policies affects citizens' voting decisions and political engagement (Mettler 2009) but should not affect judicial decisions as to the constitutionality of such programs because these decisions take place in the informationally rich environment of the courts. The answer lies in the *attenuation* of the connection between government and beneficiary via the intervention of private organizations or the tax system.

By distancing the government from legally contentious policy goals, attenuation affects judicial decision-making in three overlapping ways: providing an argument for the constitutionality of aid programs that is utilized by interest groups, embodied in precedent, and consistent with at least some reasonable interpretations of constitutional truth and intent. Elucidating an attenuation mechanism does not require scholars to adjudicate between attitudinal, legal, and strategic models of judicial decision-making but merely to assume that some combination of policy preferences, institutional constraints, and concern for the law as written influences judges' decisions.

Many supportive amicus briefings in aid cases argue that the connection between government and religious institution is weakened by the intervention of private organizations and individual choice. The Alliance Defending Freedom, Cornerstone Institute, and Liberty Institute's joint amicus brief in the 2014 *Duncan* v. *New Hampshire* tax credit scholarship case[10] is typical:

> It is illogical to conclude that [the No-Aid Provision] provides any bar to the state enacting a neutral program like this one to tax credits to private businesses for voluntarily donating to scholarship organizations, which in turn select families to receive scholarships, which in turn select the private school for which they will use the scholarship money to attend. (Compitello, Baylor, and Hacker 2013)

The brief stresses the attenuated chain of private decision-makers intervening between the state and private schools – private businesses, scholarship organizations, and families – such that the program does not benefit any religious institution directly.

As Chapter 4 shows, CBT holds that parental choice attenuates the state–school connection to render aid programs constitutional. Interest groups argue that the additional attenuation of this connection by means of scholarship-granting organizations, private businesses, contracts with private providers, and the tax system further shields aid programs from the challenge. CBT is widely cited in amicus briefs by voucher and tax-credit scholarship supporters (Mellor 2013; Keller 2013).

Interest groups such as the Institute for Justice, Alliance Defending Freedom, Goldwater Institute, Cato Institute, and others mobilize in support of submerged programs because they favor private parental choice and seek to weaken or attenuate the connection between government and education (Lips and Butcher 2015; Institute for Justice 2016; Bedrick, Butcher, and Bolick 2016). Judges supportive of aid can utilize such arguments (Thompson 2013; Dickson 2013; Dalianis 2014); wavering judges may be persuaded by them, and judges opposed to aid often need to counter such arguments if they are to strike a program down (Ronayne 2014; Smith 2014).

Moreover, regardless of judges' political views and interest group mobilization, courts confront precedent. Submerged policies have been defended successfully over a long period by means of an attenuated policy delivery. The idea that public action should be treated differently to private action is a long-standing (albeit fiercely contested) legal principle applied across many policy areas and in constitutional and international law (Maier 1982; Kay 1993).

[10] *Duncan* v. *State of New Hampshire*, 102 A 3d 913 (N.H. 2014).

Judges and advocates have recognized the variable visibility of different aid programs for children at private religious schools, and although the variation has never been formalized as such, court decisions often turn upon the level of attenuation of the program (C. Thomas 2000; Zlaket 1999; Baldwin 1960; Barham 1970). In the 2011 US Supreme Court case *Arizona Christian School Tuition Organization* v. *Winn*, for example, the court's 5–4 decision that the plaintiffs did not have standing to sue rested in part upon the distinction between tax credits and government expenditure.[11] The majority argued:

> Private citizens create private STOs; STOs choose beneficiary schools; and taxpayers then contribute to STOs. Any injury the objectors may suffer are not fairly traceable to the government. (Kennedy 2011)

In dissent, Justice Kagan argued that "cash grants and targeted tax breaks are means of accomplishing the same government objective – to provide financial support to select individuals or organizations.... Appropriations and tax subsidies are readily interchangeable; what is a cash grant today can be a tax break tomorrow" (E. Kagan 2011).

The *Winn* decision broke with a previous Supreme Court decision, *Flast* v. *Cohen* (1968),[12] in which taxpayers *were* found to have standing in their complaint against the use of federal funds "to finance instruction and the purchase of educational materials for use in religious and sectarian schools, in violation of the Establishment and Free Exercise Clauses of the First Amendment" (Warren 1968). The *Winn* justices argued that taxpayers had standing in *Flast* but not in *Winn* because the former involved unconstitutional government taxing and spending, whereas the latter did not. Aid that is provided by means of a more attenuated policy delivery is more easily defended in court.

Three Alternative Accounts

In claiming that hidden forms of policy delivery and obscure communications strategies make more attenuated policies legally stronger than less attenuated policies, I rule out three alternative arguments: *existing conflict, program age,* and *distributional effects.*

[11] *Arizona Christian School Tuition Organization* v. *Winn,* 563 US 125 (2011). The 5–4 decision divided predictably along partisan lines, with the four liberal justices in the minority.

[12] *Flast* v. *Cohen,* 392 US 83 (1968).

Existing conflict

One argument is that the relationship between attenuation and susceptibility to legal challenge is wholly endogenous: settled areas of law, such as tax exemptions, are more attenuated precisely because they lack existing legal conflict. Contentious policies like vouchers are less attenuated simply by virtue of their being more contentious in law, rather than because of the design of the policy itself.

This argument would redefine the submerged state in terms of the degree of existing conflict, decoupling it from policy design and raising methodological problems: how to establish the boundaries of the concept amid fluctuations in policy salience and legal contention between regions and governments and over time. Policies could be sufficiently contentious to qualify as part of the submerged state at one time but not at another, or in one jurisdiction but not another. Such an argument does not explain *why* more attenuated policies are legally stronger because it lacks a causal mechanism by which legal conflict and attenuation interact.

The hypothesized direction of causality, detailed in Chapter 2, is that attenuation influences the likelihood of successful legal challenge, but policymakers may also take into account the likelihood of legal challenge when designing attenuated policies. For example, Arizona's attenuated Empowerment Scholarship Account was passed by the state legislature in response to the 2009 *Cain* v. *Horne* decision[13] that a voucher program was unconstitutional. Attenuating the links between government and religious schools by incorporating a greater degree of parental choice and the intervention of the tax system, tax credit designs are attractive to policymakers seeking to insulate their programs from legal dispute.

The process of insulating programs from legal dispute may *itself* be less contentious than creating less attenuated policies but not necessarily: for example, a new tax credit scholarship program in a state that had not previously offered one is likely to generate more debate than another state's fourth or fifth additional voucher program. I assert that legal outcomes are affected more by policy design than by the political contentiousness of the policymaking process.

[13] *Cain* v. *Horne*, 202 P 3d 1178 (Ariz. 2009).

Program Age

Another argument is that older policies are more settled legally than newer ones, so legal contentiousness is a function of the age of the program rather than its attenuated policy delivery. Settled legal issues attract fewer legal challenges. However, as Table A12 in the Appendix shows, the age of a program supporting private schools is not correlated with successful court challenge. Voucher programs have been subject to legal challenge for more than sixty years, and long-standing transportation policies in West Virginia and Kentucky have been struck down as unconstitutional more than fifty years after they were created. Newer tax-credit scholarships have been subjected to legal challenges, but these have been generally unsuccessful. If program age rather than an attenuated policy delivery was the causally relevant factor for legal challenges, then newer programs would be more likely to be challenged, and challenged successfully, than older programs. There is no evidence that this is the case.[14]

Distributional Effects

A third argument is that legal challenge is a function of the characteristics of the beneficiary population rather than attenuated program design. If tax breaks tend to target wealthier whites while vouchers target poorer nonwhite populations, one might expect the latter to be successfully challenged more often. We know that race and class affect access to courts and that race-conscious policies directly remedying material racial inequalities are less popular than "color-blind" policies (Sandefur 2008; D. King and Smith 2011).

But the argument that a program's distributional effects, rather than its attenuated policy delivery, is responsible for legal challenges fails to account for the fact that school vouchers and tax-credit scholarships target demographically similar populations: color-blind in design, most vouchers and tax credit scholarships are aimed at low- and medium-income families, with incomes up to 150–200 percent of the federal poverty line (Friedman Foundation for Educational Choice 2016).

There is no evidence that vouchers and tax credits differ systematically in enrollment of students by ethnicity or social class, and some evidence that black, Hispanic, and low-income parents prefer the more attenuated policy to the less attenuated one, as Chapter 3 shows (Cato Institute 2016).

[14] Table A12 in the Appendix displays descriptive statistics on the relationship between program age and legal challenges for all forms of aid to private schools, including transportation, textbook loans, and voucher programs.

Although voucher and tax credit scholarships enroll similar low- and medium-income groups, legally they are very different: the latter attenuating the connection between government and private school by means of the tax system and scholarship granting organizations.

CONCLUSION

The sluggish growth of vouchers into the first decade of the twenty-first century prompted voucher supporters to reevaluate their strategy. Ballot initiatives proved fruitless, owing to mobilization by public school interests, (wording-dependent) public opposition, and the greater potency of initiative campaigns that reject, rather than accept, initiative propositions (Magleby 2001; T. Rogers and Middleton 2012). Except in Milwaukee and Cleveland, the racial justice argument for vouchers made only limited headway compared to the "values" claim that they enable parents to send their children to schools that reflect the family's values (Forman 2007). Major civil rights organizations lead opposition to vouchers, programs which were utilized for several decades by white supremacists and struck down as unconstitutional by judges committed to racial egalitarianism (Chapter 3).

Accommodationists face a judiciary hostile to state subsidy of religious institutions (Chapter 4), and individualists confront a strange bedfellow alliance of rural Republicans and Democrats committed to the communitarian institution of the public school (Chapter 5). Policymakers and advocates know that subsidizing private education is legally controversial. Hence, they seek to distance the government from controversy by selecting communication strategies and policy designs that publicly *attenuate* the connection between the state and policy outputs.

Attenuation is a powerful strategy for rival forces in America's foundational struggles because it enables policymakers to achieve their goals obliquely. The link between state and legally controversial policy outputs is plausibly deniable in crucial venues of policy contestation, such as statehouses and courts, *provided* that elites follow the attenuation strategy consistently. White supremacist efforts to preserve segregation failed because judges uncovered the disjuncture between attenuated design and *de*-attenuating rhetoric, exposing the voucher programs' racist purposes and effects. Similarly, accommodationist efforts to subsidize religious institutions ran afoul of NAPs in state constitutions because connections between state and religious school were only weakly attenuated.

As controversy over the Affordable Care Act roiled President Obama's first midterm elections in 2010, Republicans gained unified control of twenty states and embarked upon a vigorous program of visible spending retrenchment, Right to Work legislation, and voucher expansion. By funding the vouchers through tax expenditures, having private organizations administer the programs, and obfuscating the role of the state (and of the taxpayer) in public communications, elites succeeded in insulating their programs from a successful legal challenge.

The *doubly distanced* nature of tax credit scholarships provides political and legal stability. Service providers feel they can "count on the credits for years to come because they are less controversial." Tax credits have wide take-up among both Catholic and non-Catholic parents: "Absolutely. [The Illinois Educational Expense Tax Credit] is saving our parents about seventy-five million dollars a year" (Wichmann 2012). According to Mike Lindell, chief of the Sagamore Institute scholarship granting organization, "Everyone believes tax credits are fairly stable and here to stay. That's not the case with vouchers" (Wall 2012b).

Public policymaking, more generally, is subject to positive feedback effects downstream (Campbell 2011). In other words, even if it is challenging to pass a new program into law, once a program is passed, it is often difficult to repeal because it will have acquired a constituency with a stake in its continuation. Removing benefits is hard because voters are averse to losses. These feedback effects are greater for indirect forms of governance because those with the greatest stake in the continuation of tax expenditures tend to be wealthier, better informed, and better organized than the average voter and are therefore best placed to lobby against repeal efforts (Mettler 2009; Faricy 2015). Yet an even more important source of positive feedback effects is case law: rationales articulated by voucher supporters and embedded in precedent, which insulate the programs from *legal*, as well as political, attack. Judicial rulemaking is fundamentally conditioned by the sequencing and resolution of previous legal disputes (Stone Sweet 2002). Drawing a sharp distinction between direct and indirect forms of policy delivery, and obfuscating the role of the state in the provision of policy benefits, elites deploy *attenuated governance* to preserve their programs for the future.

The passage, growth, and legal durability of *doubly distanced* tax credit scholarships since 2010 have also given legal cover for policymakers and advocates to experiment with new forms of voucher program: education savings accounts (ESAs). ESAs are typically less attenuated in policy delivery than tax credit scholarships – being funded by direct public appropriation without intermediary administration – but they are rhetorically attenuated: policymakers downplay the role of the government in providing the benefit while emphasizing that of the market. Focusing on the wide range of benefits to which ESA money can be put is one way to downplay the subsidy of private K–12 education. And as with many other forms of voucher, ESAs targeting sympathetic constituencies – such as disabled children or military families – are most favorably viewed by the general public. Republicans, in particular, favor military families with modern ESA programs.

As I show in the next chapter, the success of individualist, color-blind, and accommodationist forces under Republican leadership – especially their ability to set the terms governing future political engagements by redistricting constituencies, passing conservative policy, and appointing sympathetic judges and justices – has meant that they have less need for attenuation than they did a decade ago. If they anticipate a sympathetic hearing for their preferred policies, there is no longer a need to distance the state from particular policy outputs. Instead, it is increasingly their communitarian, race-conscious, and secularist rivals in America's *foundational struggles* who must turn to attenuation strategies.

7

Education Savings Accounts and Controversies Beyond

DISTANCED-DIRECT EDUCATION SAVINGS ACCOUNTS AND BEYOND

As voucher supporters seek to build upon their startling recent successes, they draw upon considerable accumulated learning about the most successful political tactics to ensure policy passage, survival, and growth. This chapter considers the newest of these strategies. The latest form of vouchers, first passed in 2011, comprise the education savings account (ESA) programs. ESAs offer a sum of public money to parents to spend on educational services, including private school tuition. ESAs are similar to other individual savings accounts – for health expenses, college savings, and pensions – insofar as they are typically introduced by conservative proponents of what President George W. Bush termed "the ownership society" and emphasize personal responsibility over public programs (Faricy 2015).

Unlike *doubly distanced* tax credit scholarships, most ESAs are *distanced-direct*: the policy design is relatively straightforward, but politicians engage in distancing rhetoric that obscures the role of the government in providing the policy output. The ESA policy design employs few additional mechanisms of attenuation beyond the parent consumer-citizen. There is no tax expenditure or arm's-length administrative office. But ESAs are typically presented in a rhetorically attenuated fashion by their supporters, emphasizing the private market and downplaying benefits to the private schools themselves.

The Trump administration's FY2018 budget, which included federal grant money to pay for school vouchers, exhibited a similar distanced-direct dynamic: rhetorical attenuation without much design attenuation.

A Department of Education spokesperson stated, "[T]o be clear, there is no federal voucher program. The [private school voucher] grant program would support states who apply for funding to develop school choice programs, and those States' plans must adhere to Federal law" (Ujifusa 2017). This arm's-length form of governance is increasingly characteristic of voucher politics.

The Koch brothers and their conservative allies in government and academia consider individual savings accounts to be an excellent first step in the phasing out of government involvement with welfare services more broadly (Skocpol and Hertel-Fernandez 2016). Individualists see government welfare programs such as Social Security, Medicare, and Medicaid as an impediment to economic liberty and the "normal" functioning of labor markets, so they would prefer such programs to be converted into individual savings accounts (MacLean 2017).

Individual savings accounts became attractive policies in light of the passage of the Tax Cuts and Jobs Act by Congress in 2017. This federal legislation enables families to save in a tax-advantaged way for private K–12 school expenses, including religious schools. The new benefit works in the same way as the familiar Section 529 accounts for college expenses, potentially paying considerable sums in tax expenditures for parents in the highest tax brackets. The Missouri sponsor of a state-level version of this bill describes her efforts:

> Mine was truly an education savings account. The other tax credit programs are falsely called "education savings accounts." Simply, probably to try to make them a little bit more palatable initially, to get some attention to them. (Swan 2018)

Leveraging federal interest and enabling legislation, the perceived flexibility of individual savings accounts, and the public's familiarity with 529 accounts, state-level ESAs are politically attractive propositions.

Attenuation through Broadening

One aspect of this rhetorical attenuation is an emphasis on the broad range of educational services included within ESA coverage (Koenig 2018). Although private school tuition forms the largest expenditure, parents also use ESA funds for other educational purposes. Clint Bolick, attorney for the pro-voucher Goldwater Institute, argues that "what makes the legislation legal is that parents need not spend it on private or parochial schools. Instead, they can use it to get tutors or online education for their students who do not attend public schools, and even buy certain specific services directly from public schools" (Fischer 2013a). Emphasizing alternative uses for ESAs helps reduce the focus on the state's private tuition payment.

Legislators recognize the strategic value of broadening the range of services paid for through ESAs. Vouchers are an easier sell when the most politically contentious element – the tuition payment – is accompanied by a range of other services. A Republican representative from Illinois describes her efforts to expand the range of services paid for through the state's existing tax credit scholarship:

> I thought this was very easy. ... [Y]ou're just enhancing the types of things that qualify it for because right now it is a very narrow provision that qualifies it. It's just tuition and fees and the fees have to be of a certain nature and you can't use that for athletic fees and you can't use other stuff right. It's got to be like a chemistry fee for a chemistry class right. So, this would enhance the whole child experience. (Ives 2018)

A Republican senator from Missouri describes the value of ESAs in the following terms: "I think ESAs are most flexible. Because they can be used for home-schooling; they can be used for private school tuition; it can be used for pretty much any kind of educational expense. Where a direct voucher is, or the traditional tax credit scholarship programs go directly to a school, so you lose a little bit of flexibility" (Koenig 2018).

Policymakers and advocates in states such as New York and California that have never passed a voucher bill, judge programs encompassing a broad range of services as offering their best chance of passage. The executive director of the Catholic School Administrators Association of New York State describes the process of redesigning voucher programs in hopes of achieving enough votes to pass legislation:

> We've worked on it in various forms. This one seems to be the most palatable to everyone. We're hoping that that will be an easier sell than a straight voucher, because this state is very much against vouchers. ... It's not a tuition, because we originally started with tuition tax credits, which looked too much like vouchers, so we went to switcher donations to public and private schools.[1] ... [T]hey go to scholarship funds or even ... the art program in a public school could be the beneficiary as long as they're not for profit. (Geddis 2012)

Broadening the scope of a voucher program to include public schools is a form of attenuation because it obscures the role of the government in providing a benefit to *private schools* in particular.

[1] Switcher donations are donations to tax credit voucher programs that support public school students switching to private school.

The director of the California Catholic Conference acknowledges the political value of legislation with a broader remit in comparison to legislation with a narrow focus on private and parochial schools:

> I think they're better because they care for all children. ... There are those with political hats "you need this to pass that." It's actually not where the Bishops are coming from. They care for all kids and we need added resources and how are we going to do this. And we don't think that one should be benefited over the other. (Burnell 2012)

As the director points out, states such as Florida passed voucher legislation that deals only with private school tuition expenses. But in blue states such as New York and California, where the voucher cause faces difficulties, supporters sometimes advocate for *attenuated delivery* that obscures the role of the government in aiding private institutions, not through tax credit mechanisms but by incorporating *public* school expenses into an extended list of eligible items.

This effort to rhetorically attenuate the connection between state and school through widening the program remit was even discussed during the 1990s by advocates working on behalf of the voucher cause. The chief litigator for the Goldwater Institute remembers, "I argued for the broadest possible range of educational choices, suggesting that suburban public schools be added to the mix. I characterized that option as purchasing constitutional 'insurance,' especially on the neutrality side of the ledger. But adding suburban public schools was not politically viable" (Bolick 2003, 70). Legislators have subsequently learned about the political value of attenuation through remit broadening.

Narrowing for Palatability

Another way policymakers attempt to improve the prospects of legislation passage is to take the opposite tack: rather than broadening the remit of the program, they narrow it. By focusing attention on smaller and perhaps more "deserving" segments of the school-age population, such as disabled or poor students, advocates hope to smooth the way for voucher legislation passage. "That's a political thing I believe. Even the teachers unions and other opponents of vouchers have trouble mobilizing a huge amount of public support for opposing the needs of disabled children or trapping children in failing schools" (Finn 2010).

Targeting sympathetic constituencies is a tactic well known to scholars of policy feedback and social construction. In their study of Arizonan legislation, Anne Schneider and Helen Ingram argue that pieces of ESA tax credit legislation "often are cleverly crafted to appear to provide benefits to sympathetically-viewed dependent populations by providing a dollar-for-dollar tax reduction for donations to nonprofits providing services to dependents even as the embedded message is one that undercuts the idea that government is responsible for providing public services to disadvantaged people" (Schneider and Ingram 2019). Well-regarded but politically weak constituencies, which Schneider and Ingram term "dependents," are often the objects of such legislation.

Like Schneider and Ingram, the director of government relations for the New York State School Boards Association sees this focus on disabled children as a ruse deployed strategically by policymakers:

> Now I think they're trying to [pass] special education [vouchers] and ... say "we know that the naked language of the constitution doesn't allow it but if we can get an emotional enough reaction out of the legislature maybe they'll look the other way and do it." (Little 2012)

Utah – which like Missouri, Michigan, and Texas has proved remarkably resistant to voucher and tax credit programs for a red state – nevertheless retains a small voucher program for disabled students. "There's more of a feeling that it's an okay thing" (Newton and Kanth 2012). In Illinois, "the metrics were more lower income folks" (Ives 2018). In Missouri, policymakers target sympathetic constituencies in their efforts to enact an ESA. "Yeah, I think they've done foster kids, they've done military families" (Roeber 2018). "Senator Koenig's proposals have focused on special needs, which is even a smaller population of course, and one of the reasons there is because some of the states that have been successful have started that way and it's easier to pass" (Emery 2018).

Policymakers are correct in their assessment that the general public deems vulnerable voucher recipients to be more deserving of the benefits than others. A choice-based conjoint experiment launched in January 2018 through Amazon's Mechanical Turk[2] (n = 1,000) reveals statistically significant differences between potential voucher target groups in their perceived "deservingness" to receive benefits.

[2] Mechanical Turk (MTurk) is a crowdsourcing service provided by Amazon that enables service requesters to reach thousands of people who are willing to complete tasks online for a small amount of money. The service is widely used in scholarly work (Buhrmester, Kwang, and Gosling 2011), although MTurk has been criticized for its potential to exploit poor populations in less-developed countries (Bohannon 2016). This survey experiment recruited only American subjects and offered more than the federal minimum wage in return for responses to a short survey.

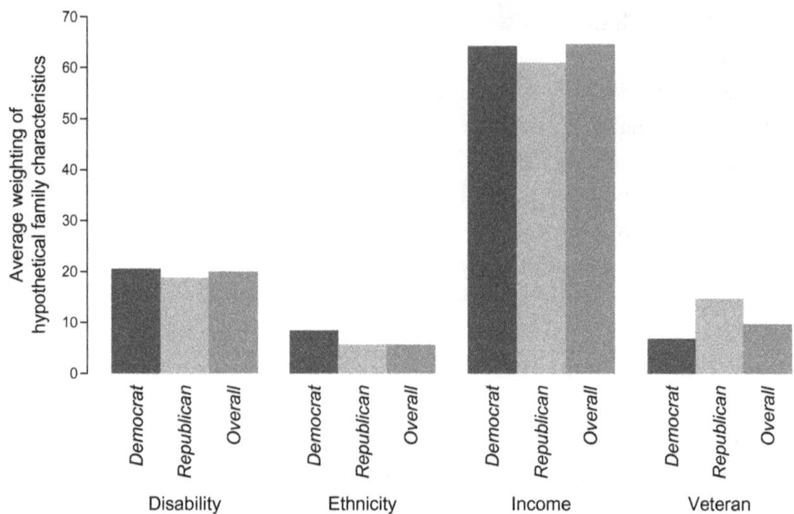

FIGURE 7.1. Importance of hypothetical family characteristics in perceived deservingness to receive a voucher, by respondent partisanship.

Respondents were invited to choose between two hypothetical families to receive a voucher benefit. The hypothetical families varied randomly by income,[3] ethnicity,[4] and veteran and disability status.[5] Figure 7.1 displays the average weighting respondents gave to each characteristic of hypothetical families, scored out of 100.

Respondents saw poor and very poor families as more deserving to receive a voucher than average or wealthy families. Respondents also perceived families with a disabled child or a veteran parent as more deserving of a voucher. Republican respondents attached much more importance to veteran status in determining who deserves a voucher. They placed twice as much weight on the veteran status of the parent as Democrats did (Figure 7.1).

As expected, respondents who are themselves veterans placed more weight on the veteran status as a determinant of deservingness than non-veterans do. Accordingly, many Republican ESA efforts target military bases. In 2018 Representative Jim Banks (R-IN) introduced legislation

[3] Four categories: very poor, poor, average income, and wealthy.
[4] Four categories: African American, Asian, Hispanic, and white.
[5] Two categories: parent is/is not a veteran; two categories: child is/is not disabled.

in Congress to create ESAs for military families using federal Impact Aid (Klein 2018b; Ujifusa 2018). Arizona extends its ESAs to children of service members as well as those living on Native American reservations, in foster care or with disabilities (Christie 2018).

Race also matters. Unlike Republicans, Democratic respondents paid attention to ethnicity, deeming African American and Hispanic families as more deserving of a voucher than white or Asian families. Nonwhite respondents placed more weight on race as a determinant of deservingness than whites do. Although both whites and nonwhites found African American families more deserving of a voucher than white families, the effect was more pronounced for nonwhite respondents. No voucher program explicitly targets by race, but vouchers have never been racially neutral (Hackett and King 2019).

For example, the Black Alliance for Educational Options (BAEO) created television advertisements in advance of the famous *Zelman* v. *Simmons-Harris* Supreme Court decision[6] in 2002 in an effort to sway public opinion and improve the chances of vouchers prevailing in the court. The ads featured poignant stories about individual black families who could use the voucher for private education. BAEO's ally Clint Bolick saw this tactic as a masterstroke. "The ads were unmatchable by the other side – they could spend the money (and they did), but they simply couldn't overcome the message" (Bolick 2003, 157–58).

Targeting poor, black "underdog" clients was an early strategy of the pro-voucher public interest law firm, Institute for Justice (IJ). Taking on such sympathetic clients helped IJ to avoid the assumptions, often voiced in court and in the media, that "conservative lawyers were just fronts for big business" (Teles 2008, 239). In the 2017 debates about the expansion of Arizona's ESA program, Schneider and Ingram argue that policymakers utilized deceptive claims to help the program pass:

> Instead, these scholarships actually cost the state and are used mainly by middle class and upper middle class families as the voucher/scholarship only pays about half the annual tuition costs in a private or religious school. (Schneider and Ingram 2019)

Regardless of the veracity of such claims, targeting a sympathetic constituency helps a program gain political support for passage. In this way,

[6] *Zelman* v. *Simmons-Harris*, 536 US 639 (2002).

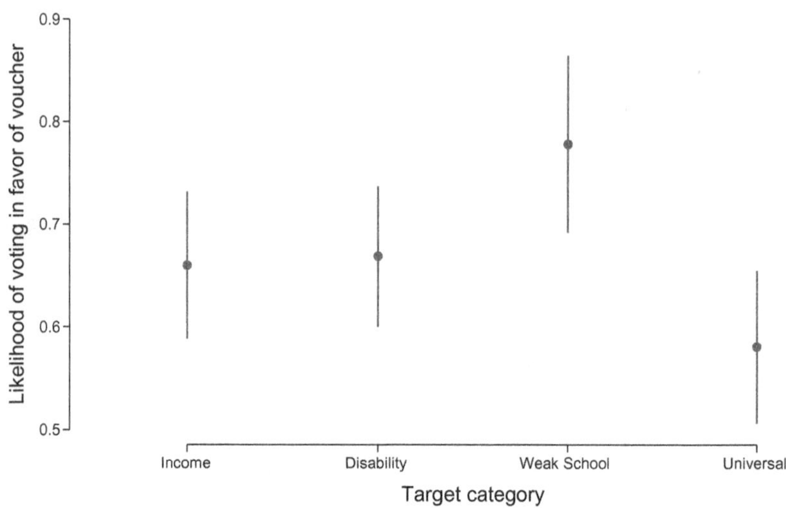

FIGURE 7.2. Voucher votes by program target category.

policymakers anticipate downstream policy feedback and build into their legislation the means of controlling it.

Multilevel logistic regression analysis of my dataset of state legislators' votes reveals that targeted vouchers are more likely to gain votes than untargeted ones (Figure 7.2). Figure 7.2 shows that legislators are more likely to vote in favor of bills targeting disabled children, low-income children, and particularly students in failing schools – perhaps more sympathetic constituencies – than universal, untargeted programs. The full results, with a range of controls, are detailed in Table A9 in the Appendix.

Narrowing the target category of a policy not only focuses attention on sympathetic constituencies but can also assuage fears that the program will have wider, damaging consequences. The persistence of the communitarian commitment to the public school system described in Chapter 5 makes it difficult to challenge that system directly. But by targeting a small subsection of the school population, a program is more likely to survive judicial review. In *Davis* v. *Grover* (1992),[7] the Wisconsin Supreme Court reasoned:

> The program is not an abandonment of the public school system. Rather, the MPCP [Milwaukee Parental Choice Program] would affect at most only 1

[7] *Davis* v. *Grover* 166 Wis. 2d 501 (1992).

> percent of the students in the MPS [Milwaukee Public Schools], giving the program a very small window of opportunity to test the effectiveness of an alternative to the MPS. (Callow 1992)

The court saw the MPCP as "experimental" and hence less threatening to the communitarian regard for public education than its opponents alleged. It upheld the legislation as constitutional.

Targeting a narrow constituency can help sustain legislative achievements politically as well as legally. The vice president of the Chicago Teachers Union explained the challenge posed to his organization by the targeted tax credit scholarship passed by the Illinois legislature in 2017:

> I mean one of the difficulties with this is that it's not a huge amount of money right now in terms of the overall size of the state budget or the size of education spending in the state. It's a bill that has a built in constituency, the people who do pay money to send their kids to a parochial school or other kinds of private schools like it. And I mean I think that's part of the calculus and part of what makes it dangerous is that it's in poetical sense it's sort of like built to kind of fit in, and once it's there getting rid of it angers its constituency; leaving it there doesn't really. (Sharkey 2018)

Mettler explains the tenaciousness of the submerged state in terms of informational asymmetries between a relatively limited set of beneficiaries and the general public. Targeting has the same effect: the smaller constituency that benefits from the bill is easily mobilized to defend it, whereas it is difficult to explain the nature, cost, and scope of the program to the broader class of taxpayers who pay for it.

As with other submerged policies, vouchers have powerful supporting constituencies. Any attempt to alter, reduce, or eliminate these programs is fraught with difficulty because of the path-dependent accumulation of local bureaucratic supporters and advocates. Abolishing a voucher program bears concentrated costs for the financial viability of private schools and local public schools and only diffuse benefits for the broader class of taxpayers. Hence, like all submerged policies, vouchers are subject to positive feedback dynamics that make change difficult.

The Legal Advantages of ESAs

Rhetorically accentuating the role of private interests has legal benefits. When considering the constitutionality of the Nevadan ESA, the state supreme court found the program to be constitutionally acceptable because the "public" funds could be considered "private." "Once the public funds are deposited into an education savings account, the funds are no longer 'public funds' but are instead the private funds of the individual parent who established the account" (Hardesty 2016). Similarly, the Arizona Supreme Court found its state ESA constitutional on the grounds that "[a]ny aid to religious schools would be the result of the genuine and independent private choice of parents" (Corella 2013).

ESA funds can be considered by the courts to be "private" rather than "public," but opponents see the programs as a means by which government conceals its role in subsidizing religious institutions. A Democratic state senator from Missouri describes the ESA as a deliberate effort to circumvent a constitutional prohibition:

> Well, the direct appropriation is really unconstitutional, because if it allows for public tax dollars to go to religious schools, which this bill would have ... It can't be money that comes out of general revenue, so this ESA program was really an end run around our constitution, in my view, and that's how I characterized it on the floor when I talked about it. (Schupp 2018)

Supporters of ESAs also acknowledge the need to avoid constitutional challenges. Since ESAs are relatively new legislation, prospective bill sponsors look to other states to find the legislation with the greatest chances of success. Sponsors of recent ESA legislation acknowledge the importance of learning about successful legal strategies elsewhere:

> So we have learned what other states have done successfully in this area, learned that ESA is the newer up-and-coming way, especially because ESAs are immune to the Blaine Amendment problem, and Missouri has a very strongly written Blaine Amendment. So that's one of the reasons why ... I focus on ESAs. (Bahr 2018)

For modern voucher and ESA advocates, the *distanced-direct* rhetorical attenuation approach is common. Of the twelve pieces of model legislation, the American Legislative Exchange Council (ALEC) publishes for private school choice, just three employ a complex tax credit policy design. Nine are regular vouchers or ESAs. But the language that the bills use makes no mention of "vouchers," using instead the term "scholarship."

As yet there has been no wholesale switch to ESAs. Tax credit and regular voucher programs continue to pass state legislatures. *Doubly distanced* programs retain advantages over their more visible voucher cousins. But the broadening of voucher advocates' approach to include *distanced-direct* programs such as ESAs might signify greater confidence in the capacity of rhetorical attenuation alone to insulate such programs from attack.

When Losers Become Winners in Foundational Identity Struggles

This book advances the argument that the strategic imperative for policymakers to attenuate arises when an order opposed to its fundamental commitments holds sway within the judiciary or other organs of the state. Anticipating hot-button political controversy and likely losses, whether in court or on the ballot, policymakers seek to distance the state from the legally contentious policy purpose.

It follows that when members of the order mobilize to take control of the judiciary, its need to attenuate lessens and that of its opponent increases. The story of voucher advancement and retrenchment in this book tracks the rise of transformative egalitarian, secularist, and communitarian orders in courts and statehouses around the country, encouraging members of opposing white supremacist, accommodationist, and individualist orders to utilize attenuated governance to achieve their ends indirectly, despite political controversy.

However, since the 1990s, and accelerating in the first half of the twenty-first century, conservative, accommodationist, and individualist orders have gained control of the nation's high court, and courts and statehouses across America. Teles documents the rising power of the conservative legal movement (Teles 2008). The result is a radically changed strategic landscape for individual policymakers and advocacy organizations.

Accommodationism is resurgent. For example, the Supreme Court's *Trinity Lutheran Church of Columbia* v. *Comer* decision[8] (2017) found in favor of a church that wanted to take advantage of a government playground resurfacing grant, prompting commentators to prophesy the demise of the state no-aid provisions (NAPs), under which the church's action was challenged (Roberts 2017; Bailey 2017; Hess and Addison 2017).

In a nod to the formerly dominant secularist order, Trinity Lutheran Church had relied in part on an attenuation argument to bolster its claim to participate in the Missouri grant program. In front of a hostile district court, the church rooted its defense in the Missouri Supreme Court case *Americans United* v. *Rogers*[9] (1976), in which the court upheld a college tuition grant that paid for student attendance at private or public

[8] *Trinity Lutheran Church of Columbia* v. *Comer*, 582 US _ (2017).

[9] *Americans United* v. *Rogers*, 538 S.W. 2d 711 (Mo. 1976).

colleges, including religious ones. "The grant program did not directly pay the funds to private institutions; rather, the students received an individual check and would then endorse it over to the institution of their choice, so long as that institution had an independent board and a policy of academic freedom" (J. P. Morgan 1976).

Ultimately, however, Trinity Lutheran need not have introduced this attenuation defense because the Supreme Court majority favored accommodationism and found it in its favor. It was the secularist order's turn to distance the government from a newly contentious purpose. Religious subsidy was no longer in the hot seat, but interfering with religious Free Exercise was. The Supreme Court was alive to possible infringement of Free Exercise by the state: "As even the Department acknowledges, the Free Exercise Clause protects against 'indirect coercion or penalties on the free exercise of religion, not just outright prohibitions'" (Roberts 2017).

One way for secularists to pursue the strict interpretation of the Establishment Clause while avoiding litigation on Free Exercise grounds is to attenuate the connection between the government and the alleged religious burden. In *Trinity Lutheran*, the lower district court cited approvingly from a 1974 Supreme Court case, *Johnson* v. *Robison*,[10] in which the state had successfully defended itself from a Free Exercise claim brought by a conscientious objector for denial of veteran education benefits. The *Johnson* court had found any burden to be attenuated enough to avoid constitutional challenges. "The withholding of educational benefits involves only an incidental burden upon appellee's free exercise of religion – if, indeed, any burden exists at all" (W. J. Brennan 1974).

The district court in *Trinity Lutheran* found that the state could not be accused of animus toward religion because of the attenuated manner of policy delivery. "Nothing in the Complaint suggests that the decision to deny Trinity's grant application was motivated by hostility toward religion as opposed to a legitimate interest in avoiding government entanglement with religion" (Laughrey 2013). The Supreme Court was less receptive, ultimately finding in favor of the accommodationists, but secularists had learned their lesson: attenuation might help save their policies from hostile courts.

[10] *Johnson* v. *Robison*, 415 US 361 (1974).

The Supreme Court has also turned away from race-conscious and toward color-blind decision-making. Justice Anthony Kennedy – the swing justice who had authored the closely fought 2016 affirmative action case *Fisher* v. *University of Texas*[11] – resigned in June 2018, ushering in the prospect of a rollback of race-based college admissions practices. But even Kennedy had helped strike back against affirmative action programs on multiple occasions for a more conservative court, in cases such as *City of Richmond* v. *J.A. Croson Co.* (1989), *Adarand* v. *Pena* (1995), and *Gratz* v. *Bollinger* (2003)[12] (O'Connor 1989, 1995; Rehnquist 2003). Increasingly, the judiciary opposes quota-based affirmative action and other explicitly race-conscious measures.

Attenuated policies, in which the role of the state in promoting African American advancement is obscured, have a better chance of avoiding elimination by a court hostile to direct race-conscious measures. In her opinion in *Croson*, Justice Sandra Day O'Connor indicated a variety of measures that would be more acceptable than the quota-based minority-owned construction company set-aside plan that the court struck down:

> The city has at its disposal an array of race-neutral devices to increase the accessibility of city contracting opportunities to small entrepreneurs of all races who have suffered the effects of past societal discrimination, including simplification of bidding procedures, relaxation of bonding requirements, training, financial aid, elimination or modification of formal barriers caused by bureaucratic inertia, and the prohibition of discrimination in the provision of credit or bonding by local suppliers and banks. (O'Connor 1989)

Most of O'Connor's suggested alternatives – simplifying bidding, relaxing state requirements, and eliminating "barriers caused by bureaucratic inertia" – are quintessentially attenuated in their elevation of the marketplace over state action. Indirectly greasing the wheels of commerce, rather than imposing direct quotas, is a more acceptable way to promote race-conscious ends.

Accordingly, with the rise of the color-blind order, members of the race-conscious order tend to deemphasize direct action on behalf of underrepresented minorities. In the Michigan Law School case *Grutter*

[11] *Fisher* v. *University of Texas*, 579 US _ (2016).

[12] *City of Richmond* v. *J.A. Croson Co.*, 488 US 469 (1989); *Adarand* v. *Pena*, 515 US 200 (1995); *Gratz* v. *Bollinger*, 539 US 244 (2003).

v. *Bollinger* (2003),[13] "Dennis Shields, Director of Admissions when petitioner applied to the Law School, testified that he did not direct his staff to admit a particular percentage or number of minority students, but rather to consider an applicant's race along with all other factors" (O'Connor 2003). Rhetorically emphasizing "targeted goals" and "race awareness" rather than direct "quotas," affirmative action's proponents can sometimes save it even in the face of a hostile court. The Law School won in *Grutter*. That same year, the wider university's direct quotas were struck down in *Gratz*.

Increasingly popular "top-percentage" plans guarantee admission to top universities to the highest-achieving students from every high school. By avoiding direct entrance quotas, proponents hope to achieve racial diversity without attracting the ire of an ever-more powerful color-blind order. Both sides in America's foundational identity struggles can find use for attenuation.

Judges and the Future of Vouchers

The courts are central to the fate of school choice and of many other hot-button culture war issues. Former Goldwater Institute litigator Clint Bolick expresses their value: "At school choice conferences when asked what people could do to aid the effort, I would quip, 'Pray for the health of five members of the U.S. Supreme Court'" (Bolick 2003, 128). Statistical analysis of the universe of judicial decisions, during 1955–2016, demonstrates that – even controlling for program attenuation, partisanship, and a variety of other factors – judges have generally become more sympathetic to vouchers over time (Figure 7.3). Full logistic regression results with statistical controls are available in Table A11 in the Appendix.

As judges become more sympathetic to vouchers, thereby establishing a supportive body of case law (Figure 7.3), it may no longer be necessary for accommodationists and individualists to employ complex hidden mechanisms of tax credits in every instance. Communications are key. Both segregationists and later voucher supporters found – to their cost – that the way policymakers speak about their role in providing benefits has political and legal significance.

[13] *Grutter* v. *Bollinger*, 539 US 306 (2003).

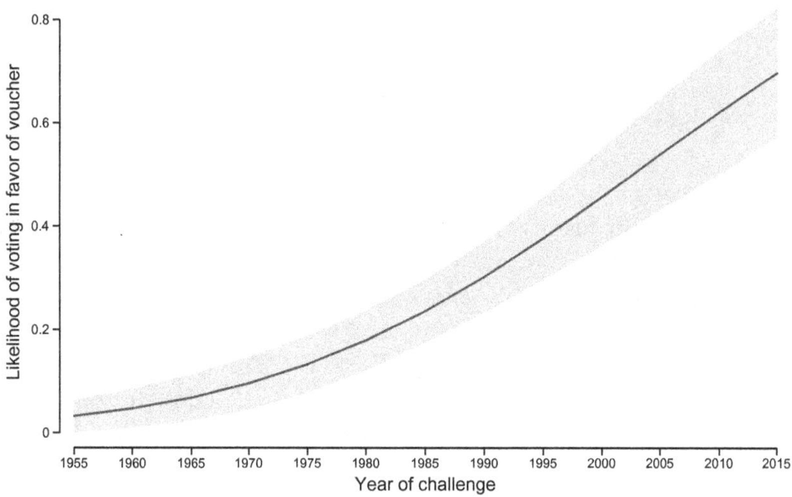

FIGURE 7.3. Likelihood of judicial vote in favor of voucher constitutionality over time.

CONCLUSION

Modern voucher programs represent the culmination of a decades-long period of policy learning by conservative color-blind, individualist, and accommodationist forces. Elites learn that certain communications strategies and policy designs are more likely to pass, and to avoid or survive legal challenge, than others. Where rival liberal, secularist, race-conscious, and communitarian forces enjoyed the power to mobilize organized interests and sway judges' votes, conservatives found it politically expedient to attenuate the connection between the state and the controversial policy output, the subsidy of private schools.

Attenuation involves the distancing of the state from a controversial policy output by drawing a sharp distinction between direct and indirect policy delivery and emphasizing the role of the marketplace or other nongovernment actors in the provision of certain benefits. Over the course of fifty years, these rationales for program constitutionality became more acceptable to judges, because Republican executives won power to appoint more sympathetic Republican judges, who could rely on growing precedent in making new determinations about voucher constitutionality, and because increasingly professionalized groups such as ALEC, IJ, and the Friedman Foundation financed advocacy and research into the most successful delivery mechanisms.

By 2018, sixty voucher programs existed across the nation, and a growing body of case law gave legal weight to color-blind, individualist, and accommodationist arguments. Judges had become more likely to vote in favor of the constitutionality of voucher programs than at any previous time in history (Figure 7.3). Hence, the pressures to attenuate diminished for conservative policymakers: they could pursue their policy aims openly instead, experimenting with policies such as ESAs that are only partially attenuated. And as individualism, accommodationism, and color blindness surged into the Trump presidency, communitarians, secularists, and racial egalitarians found their policy aims newly threatened, turning in some cases to an attenuation defense to insulate their programs from attack. Bitter contestation between rival orders in America's *foundational identity struggles* continued to play out in statehouses and courts across the nation.

Conclusion

Attenuated Governance and the State

"ANCILLARY INDIRECT BENEFITS TO SUCH INSTITUTIONS DO NOT RENDER IMPROPER THOSE GOVERNMENT EXPENDITURES THAT ARE OTHERWISE PERMISSIBLE"

On February 3, 1964, barely a week after little Bryan Poindexter and his mother were turned away from Ninth Ward Elementary in New Orleans, teenage brothers Anthony and Henry Lee prepared to reenter Tuskegee High School, a rural Alabama public school that Governor George C. Wallace had ordered closed in defiance of desegregation orders. That night, flaming crosses adorned the lawns of school board members. In April the boys' father, Detroit Lee, would be hanged in effigy in Tuskegee's downtown square. A dozen black children, including Anthony and Henry, entered Tuskegee High for the first time in fall 1963, but within a week, all 275 of their white classmates left, mostly for Macon Academy, a new segregated private school, their flight enabled by state-funded tuition grants. The Lee brothers' case against the white supremacist regime came to a head on July 13 when the US District Court for the Middle District of Alabama found against the segregationists in *Lee* v. *Macon County Board of Education.*[1]

The *Lee* court enjoined the payment of state tuition grants to segregated private schools, citing their creators' public racial animosity as evidence of unconstitutional discrimination. But the court did not argue that the tuition grants were unconstitutional on their face. "It is conceivable that the State of Alabama may choose to employ 'private' schools as

[1] *Lee* v. *Macon County Board of Education*, 231 F Supp 743 (M.D. Ala. 1964).

its instrument of discharging its obligation to provide education in lieu of its public school system" (Rives, Grooms, and Johnson 1964). The *Lee* judges thought that means mattered little and ends were what counted. Whether by public means or "private" ones, policymakers should be judged by their purposes. The white supremacists' inability to conceal their racist purposes through attenuating rhetoric had doomed their policies in court.

Fifty years later and 500 miles north, on March 26, 2013, single mom Heather Coffy prepared her three children, Delano, Alanna, and Darius, for another day at St. Monica Catholic School in Indianapolis, Indiana. But this would be no ordinary day for the Coffys. March 26 was the date set for the Indiana Supreme Court to decide *Meredith* v. *Pence*,[2] the voucher case to which Heather Coffy was appended as defendant-intervenor. Heather and her fellow scholarship parents were aided by the individualist public interest law firm, Institute for Justice (IJ), in their quest to place Indiana's vouchers on a firm constitutional footing. Both the families represented by the IJ sent their children to parochial schools. They were opposed in court by a phalanx of communitarian advocates led by kindergarten teacher Teresa Meredith and consisting of teacher union representatives, educationalists, and school board members plus Reverend Kevin Armstrong, a Methodist minister.

The communitarian opponents of Indiana's vouchers contended that the state had violated its obligation to provide a general, public, and uniform education for all children. Vouchers, Teresa Meredith argued, breached the separation of church and state and drained the public system of needed funds. In defense of the program, Heather Coffy and her legal team argued that the vouchers were simply designed to give parents options and that the attenuated nature of voucher programs rendered them constitutional by elevating the role of individual parents. The *Meredith* court found for the program, reasoning that "the voucher program does not directly fund religious activities because no funds may be dispersed to any program-eligible school without the private, independent selection by the parents of a program-eligible student" (Dickson 2013).

If they had lived to see it, the *Lee* judges might have recognized the *Meredith* court's declaration that the state's constitutional duty to provide for "intellectual improvement... by all suitable means" could be discharged by private, as well as public, methods. "The method and means of fulfilling this duty is thus delegated to the sound legislative discretion

[2] *Meredith* v. *Pence*, 984 N.E. 2d 1213 (Ind. 2013).

of the General Assembly" (Dickson 2013). As in *Lee*, *Meredith* turned upon the extent to which the state could distance itself from a legally contentious purpose, the subsidy of segregated, or religious, institutions, respectively. But unlike the white supremacists of Alabama, Indiana's voucher supporters did not trumpet the benefits to religious schools that flow from state-funded vouchers. Accordingly, they could characterize any benefit to religious schools as ancillary to the legislation's main purpose. "Ancillary indirect benefits to such institutions do not render improper those government expenditures that are otherwise permissible" (Dickson 2013). Attenuation matters.

Two court cases. Fifty years apart. Jim Crow's long death rattle incites white supremacists to create private school tuition grants, but blatantly racist rhetoric exposes their purposes. Conservatives watch and learn. They see that direct funding and communications are vulnerable because of the rise of racial egalitarian, secularist, and communitarian orders. The tenacity of teacher unions and a lingering commitment to public education make private school vouchers necessary but perilous for the individualist cause. Eventually, individualists and accommodationists hit upon the right formula: doubly distanced programs that obscure the role of the state and elevate that of the marketplace.

Attenuation helps distance the state from legally controversial policy goals through the intervention of private third parties and the tax system. Extensive use of distancing policy designs and communications strategies confirms the truth of Theodore Lowi's observation: "The typical American politician displaces and defers and delegates conflict where possible; he squarely faces conflict only when he must" (Lowi 1969, 76). Policymakers try to avoid conflict, particularly conflicts they expect to lose, by attenuating the connections between government and its contested, legally vulnerable policy goals.

Three Fundamental Struggles (and Six Institutional Orders): How the Hidden State Grows

Understanding the growth in the hidden state requires us to consider the forms attenuation takes. Voucher programs have been directed toward a variety of purposes over the past seventy years. I have argued that the hidden state grows because elites find it useful, strategically, to attenuate their policy designs and communications when their side in America's fundamental identity struggles is temporarily dethroned by rival ideas and institutions.

Chapter 3 shows how the crumbling of the white supremacist order in the mid-twentieth century, in favor of the transformative egalitarian order, gave rise to the strategic imperative to attenuate the connection between the government and the segregated institutions. After decades in which the white supremacist order was ascendant in the South – asserted by highly visible Jim Crow laws – the white supremacist order sought to sustain its policy commitments through hidden, attenuated means: contested-attenuated tuition grant legislation. The legislation was struck down as unconstitutional because its creators failed to rhetorically attenuate the connection between the state and its now illegal and discredited purposes: supporting segregated education.

As the accommodationist order gave way to secularist forces during the period of church–state activism by the Warren and Burger Courts (1953–86) on issues such as school prayer, evolution, and religious exemptions, accommodationists sought refuge in weakly attenuated policy delivery: voucher programs directed via parents instead of grants for religious school equipment, transportation, and other services. Chapter 4 shows how accommodationists came to rely on a defense in court that emphasized the benefits to the child rather than to the school. Like the white supremacist order of the 1950s facing racially egalitarian judicial action, accommodationists saw the rise of judicial secularism as a threat to their interests. Indirect benefits channeled through parents seemed to help insulate the state from secularist opposition. But most of these quasi-direct voucher programs of the latter half of the twentieth century were struck down as unconstitutional because they entangled the state with religious purposes.

Chapter 5 explains how teacher unions and school administrator associations rose to prominence in the middle of the twentieth century, empowering a communitarian order that supported public schools as civic institutions and bastions of community values. Although the 1925 Supreme Court case *Pierce* v. *Society of Sisters*[3] had struck down a law requiring public school attendance, the rival individualist order saw few victories during this period of collective bargaining expansion. Intellectually, the groundwork for the individualist order's overthrow of these socialized institutions was laid by Milton Friedman, Barry Goldwater, James Buchanan, and the public choice school. The conservative groups they founded became more adept at countering teacher union opposition during the latter half of the twentieth century,

[3] *Pierce* v. *Society of Sisters*, 268 US 510 (1925).

although they still faced the politically dangerous charge that they were intent upon undermining the public school system. Hence, as the individualist order grew in strength, it utilized attenuated policy forms to disguise the diversion of public dollars from public institutions.

The full fruits of attenuated governance matured with Republican victories during Barack Obama's presidency. Chapter 6 shows that the doubly distanced tax credit form enabled individualist and accommodationist forces to divert public funds to private religious institutions without appearing to do so. Due to the lingering importance of communitarian public schooling and secularist approaches to church–state relations among the nation's many judges, doubly distanced policies were safest. They were, and are, least likely to be challenged in court or struck down as unconstitutional.

Now, decades into the twenty-first century, the secularist, communitarian, and race-conscious orders' hold upon America's judicial institutions appears increasingly shaky. Growing partisan alignment within America's fundamental struggles binds the fate of these orders closer to the fortunes of the Democratic Party. Republican Party obstruction at the federal level – its ideological coherence, institutional strength, state-level victories, and strategic focus on judicial appointments – lends strength to individualist, accommodationist, and color-blind forces. Republican forces have *reconfigured* political dynamics in their favor (Patashnik 2008). Policy goals that were once likely to receive an unsympathetic hearing – whether white nativism, religious accommodation, or program privatization – are elevated by the Trump presidency. Hence, there is less need for individualists, accommodationists, and color-blind orders to attenuate the connection between the government and these policy goals. They can pursue them openly. The distanced-direct education savings accounts (ESAs) of Chapter 7 embody these characteristics.

It would be simplistic to argue that all aspects of the secularist, communitarian, and race-conscious orders have lost their hold upon American political development in the twenty-first century. America's fundamental identity struggles do not cease to be contested because of the temporary rise of one of the rival orders. As the tide turns against an order's political commitments, it becomes strategically valuable to attenuate. For secularist forces in the ongoing contestation about the limits of religious freedom under Religious Freedom Restoration Acts (RFRAs), for example, the ability to attenuate the connection between state mandates and contraceptive coverage is a valuable line of defense.

How Courts Construct the State

Existing literature on the growth of the hidden, submerged, or delegated state provides rich data on the experiences of ordinary citizens but largely ignores the role of the courts in incentivizing and sustaining these complex policy mechanisms. We know that special interests easily mobilize to defend submerged policies because of informational asymmetries between well-heeled, well-informed beneficiaries and a puzzled public (Mettler 2009; Campbell 2010).[4] These informational asymmetries disappear in court. Instead, legal rationales – spread by judges and advocates – help distinguish indirect from direct spending and publicly distance the government from legally contentious policy goals.

Powerful groups seek to resolve contested questions in constitutional law in ways that accord with their vital interests and fundamental values (Graber 2006). Litigation is "a site of civil rights strategy production" (Francis 2014, 10). The Supreme Court's rights revolution decisions in the 1960s and 1970s were powerfully influenced by well-organized advocacy groups, drawing upon a legal support structure (Epp 1998; Francis 2014). In the past few decades, the opposition to these advocacy groups has strengthened as the power of the secularist, race-conscious, and communitarian orders diminishes and that of accommodationist, color-blind, and individualist orders grows. Today, conservative litigation groups such as the IJ, Cato Institute, and Goldwater Institute play a crucial role in mobilization, awareness raising, and fundraising in support of vouchers.

As sites of contestation between rival institutional orders, courts also become sources of hidden state growth. Through reason giving and reason taking, they legitimate the use of attenuated policy delivery mechanisms. Judicial ideas and rationalizations are vital. Policymakers and advocates choose policy design and communications strategies strategically in order to insulate their policies from legal challenges. They do this by persuading, enabling, or pressuring judges to rule in their favor, drawing upon legal standards, reasoning, and categories. The state defines what counts as a legitimate legal grievance, offering "yet another channel for governing private outcomes while disguising public authority" (Thurston 2018, 6).

Courts have a preeminent position in the United States (Justice and Macleod 2016). Often, in America's voucher politics, there is no sharp

[4] Thurston uncovers important exceptions to this rule, when "boundary groups" mobilize low-income and marginalized populations by educating them about the distribution of hidden state benefits (Thurston 2018).

distinction between legal and political arguments, norms, and language. Policymakers care about law, and judges care about politics. Elites' efforts to avoid successful legal challenge involve not only making persuasive arguments in court but also attempting to avoid litigation in the first place. Arguments such as benefits to the child, freedom of association, entanglement between church and state, and providing children a decent, public education are deployed in statehouses as well as courts. When policymakers and advocates pay attention to what is legal in order to sustain their vulnerable policy commitments and survive challenges from rival orders, they utilize rhetoric that is both legal and intensely political.

Opposition to Doubly Distanced Policies: The Normative Case

Opponents of *doubly distanced* tax credit vouchers – and even some supporters – argue that these attenuated forms of governance are a smoke screen designed to conceal illicit and illegal governmental interference with private schools. This book has demonstrated that doubly distanced policies are adopted because they avoid – or at least *seem* to avoid – entangling the government with legally contentious purposes and hence are more likely to pass and survive a court challenge. But it is a further, value judgment to argue that it is *wrong* to conceal the government's purposes in this way.

For Mettler and other scholars of the submerged state, the growth of the hidden state is a worrying trend. Hiding the extent of the government's involvement in the creation and sustenance of consumer marketplaces and provision of services tends to weaken citizen understanding of the role of government. It augments the informational advantages enjoyed by special interests who benefit from such policies. The result is citizen apathy and anger, political sclerosis, and the impoverishment of democracy. Some scholars decry the regressive nature of tax expenditures. "Not only do wealthier citizens benefit from social tax expenditures but so too do the *private providers* of social welfare goods (such as large banks, private HMOs, and private drug companies, to name a few)" (Faricy 2015, 26) [italics in the original].

Unlike ordinary citizens, elites – policymakers, advocates, bureaucrats, and the judiciary – do not lack information about the size, scope, and significance of the hidden state. Elites are aware of doubly distanced indirect mechanisms for the delivery of public money, so they are in the position to criticize such mechanisms. The doubly distanced tax credit policy design is described by Republican and Democratic opponents as "a scam," "a gimmick," "an end run around the constitution," "a backdoor way of subsidizing private education" (Reick 2018; Flynn Currie 2018; Durkin and Reick 2018; Schupp 2018). "To me it's all a fig leaf, I mean, the reality is we are using public money to support private education" (Flynn Currie 2018). A Republican state representative from Illinois describes his opposition to doubly distanced policies in the following terms:

> We need to be fundamentally and philosophically honest with ourselves. If we're going to provide for this type of education and encourage this type of education, we need to do it out of money that we have appropriated. We're not being fair to the taxpayers by saying that we're gonna allow this backdoor method of paying for the something that we should be paying for. (Reick 2018)

For this representative, it is not the ends to which he objects (encouraging private education) but the means (a tax credit mechanism). Here the doubly distanced policy design – the means by which government distances itself from contentious issues of race and religion – *itself* becomes controversial.

Some liberals condemn attenuated governance as purposefully confusing. For example, King and Smith document Justice David Souter's concern about the race-conscious order's efforts to cloak affirmative action programs in attenuating rhetoric. Instead of instigating affirmative action programs directly as a remedy for racial injustice, courts encourage legislators to achieve the same results obliquely by focusing on "student diversity" and "guaranteeing admission to a fixed percentage of the top students from each high school." For Souter, these plans have "the disadvantage of deliberate obfuscation. The 'percentage plans' are just as race-conscious as the point scheme (and fairly so) but they get their racially diverse results without saying directly what they are doing or why they are doing it" (Souter 2003, 539:297–98).

On the conservative side, law professor Peter Schuck criticizes such policies on the grounds that they "may simply preserve the same objectionable use of ethno-racial preferences by disguising them and effectuating them indirectly" (Schuck 2002, 74). For opponents, there is a disingenuousness to *distanced-direct* policies. Even those who support the aim – college access for African Americans – criticize the means as complex, gimmicky, and obscure.

Yet unpalatable as the means might be to many liberals, attenuated governance may seem to be the only way for race-conscious forces to advance their aims, given that the modern Supreme Court, with its majority of Republican-appointed justices, favors color-blind forces and would be likely to resist any legislators attempting to advance race-conscious policies (D. King and Smith 2011). Appalling racial inequalities in access to quality education (Brittain and Kozlak 2007), health care (Braveman et al. 2010), housing (Krivo and Kaufman 2004), justice (S. Walker, Spohn, and Delone 2012), and full citizenship (Bonilla-Silva 2018) confer moral urgency upon the racial egalitarian cause. Racial egalitarians might conclude that they have a duty to pursue their aims howsoever they can be achieved, that the ends justify the means.

Secularists fearful of Free Exercise litigation under an increasingly conservative Supreme Court might feel the same way as racial egalitarians about attenuation, in spite of the fact that – as Chapters 4 and 6 demonstrate – the rival accommodationist order uses attenuation to defend vouchers against secularist challenge. With fresh conservative appointees (Neil Gorsuch and Brett Kavanaugh), octogenarian liberals (Ruth Bader Ginsburg and Stephen Breyer), and many Trump-appointed judges confirmed to appellate and district courts by a Republican Senate, secularists may conclude that means matter little in comparison to the urgency of their cause and their fear of the enemy.

Attenuation can help secularists defend themselves against the charge that they unconstitutionally burden Free Exercise, because merely private conduct, "no matter how discriminatory or wrongful," is not subject to civil action for the deprivation of rights,[5] and *indirect* burdens that do not explicitly discriminate between religions can be constitutional (Warren 1961). First Amendment rights are less easily invoked in support of proselytizing, for example, when restrictions on the distribution of religious literature are imposed by private organizations whose connections to the state are attenuated (Kaplan 2009).

Attenuation may also shore up organizations, such as Planned Parenthood, under assault from religious conservatives. Reproductive rights supporters repudiate their opponents' line of attack: that government subsidy of health-care services at organizations that use their own funds to provide abortions is really indirect taxpayer support for abortion (Dreweke 2016). *Direct* federal funding for abortion is outlawed, but *indirect* support – through tax advantages or subsidy of preventive services – is more easily defended in court. For example, the Supreme Court has proved receptive to an attenuation defense of organizations'

[5] Under 42 USC §1983, *state* action is subject to constitutional restriction, whereas *private* action is not.

abortion counseling and promotion of the legalization of prostitution (Rehnquist 1991; Roberts 2013). Since the Department of Health and Human Services' (HHS) regulations do not bar speech "outside the scope of the federally funded program," separating such advocacy from other programs can be sufficient to save it. By distancing the state from hot-button issues such as abortion counseling, liberals hope to protect their programs from legal challenges. Now it is conservatives' turn to seek *de*-attenuation: exposing the role of the state in supporting controversial policy outputs.

Attenuation strategies are naturally a better fit for conservative forces because of the nature of their policy desiderata, particularly support for privatization. For many communitarians, secularists, and racial egalitarians, there will always be something gimmicky or underhand about seeking to hide the role of the state and circumvent the power of their opponents. As legal challenges mount, however, some elites may choose to swallow their distaste for attenuation and pursue it in the hope of preserving their preferred policy aims against resurgent, rival orders.

Do Ideas Really Matter?

If attenuated governance is simply a sneaky means of achieving controversial policy objectives, then it follows that the rationales advanced to support it in court – child benefit theory (CBT), state action, and the distinction between indirect and direct expenditure – are mere window dressing. This book remains agnostic on that point, but the question to which it gives rise is central to ideational theories of political action: Do ideas really matter? Chapter 1's *fundamental struggles* framework suggests that they matter a great deal. Yet statistical analysis detailed in Chapter 6 (Figure 6.1) demonstrates that one of the strongest predictors of a legislative or judicial vote in favor of vouchers is partisanship. Ideas such as CBT clearly have instrumental power in helping to justify political and judicial action in favor of attenuated policies. But do these ideas have intrinsic validity, or are they mere instruments, helping to rationalize decisions and provide cover for elites already predisposed in their favor?

I do not propose a definitive answer here but suggest instead that the question poses a false dichotomy. Legal rationales can have both independent and instrumental power, not only in different cases or periods but also for individual judges and justices. There is no need to ascribe entirely cynical motives to elites relying on CBT or rejecting tax expenditure analysis. It would be equally foolish to ascribe wide-eyed naiveté. Ideas can be both convenient and convincing.

Elites form part of an order for many reasons (D. King and Smith 2011). Some are true believers in the cause of white supremacy or racial egalitarianism, communitarianism or individualism, and accommodationism or secularism. The importance of ideas waxes and wanes. For instance, ideas mattered greatly to the maturing conservative legal movement, which set out explicitly to foreground idealism as a strategy. By the 1980s, its activists' primary commitment was to a set of individualist *ideas* rather than to a particular set of interests or constituencies (Teles 2008).

Ideas "matter" in the sense that they provide impetus for, and structure, political action, as opposed to merely providing a convenient post hoc rationalization for that action. But ideas motivate in several ways. They can be intrinsically powerful (motivating action in themselves) or extrinsically powerful (motivating only in relation to their capacity to help people achieve other valued goals). Segregationists' cynical use of the "freedom of association" trope, detailed in Chapter 3, is an example of an extrinsically valuable idea, because it (temporarily) helped white supremacists uphold a racial hierarchy under attack. By contrast, the foundational ideas in America's foundational identity struggles – white supremacy or racial equality, secularism or accommodationism, and communitarianism or individualism – could be said to have intrinsic power because such ideas motivate action by themselves.

Nobody would argue that ideas are sufficient causes of policy change, but they might argue that an idea is necessary for policy change (if not a *specific* idea, then an idea of a particular sort). For example, as discussed in Chapters 3–7, there are many ways to couch legal arguments about the entanglement of government with legally contentious purposes. Ideas such as the distinction between purpose and effect, or the concept of "excessive entanglement," are available for use, but CBT – the idea that money distributed in the form of vouchers aids the child and not the religious institution – is deployed most frequently in amicus briefs and judgments. Therefore, CBT "matters" more than other ideas, in that it is most widely used to persuade judges to rule in favor of vouchers. This form of "mattering" is extrinsic. It is harder to find real-world evidence for (or against) the intrinsic power of an idea.

The question of whether ideas matter dramatizes the limits of interview-based social science: we live in a world of rationalizations. We can observe how elites justify their choices publicly and ask why they chose particular policy designs and communication strategies. We cannot –

and I suspect even *they* cannot – disentangle the underlying motives. In Teles's account of the development of the conservative legal movement, the intrinsic and instrumental values of ideas are intertwined. This book shows that ideas *as if* matter, because elites say they do, and mostly act as if they do.

I assert – supported in Chapters 3–7 by extensive interview evidence – that elites use attenuating rhetoric and policy design *deliberately* in order to insulate their programs from legal attack. Ultimately their intentions may be pure or cynical. Individual elites adhere to institutional orders and select political strategies for many reasons. They might not intend to benefit private segregated or religious schools by providing scholarships or may foresee but not intend the results. But as in Morgan and Campbell's work, where the language of delegation is used explicitly to denote "the deliberateness of this act" (K. J. Morgan and Campbell 2011), voucher supporters evidentially *intend* to create programs for private schools and their students that are insulated from legal challenges – and attenuation is the means to do it.

Attenuated Governance: Key Contributions

Attenuation is a process by which policymakers and organized interests distance local, state, or federal government from legally controversial policy outputs. This oblique form of policy delivery is a new addition to the modes of institutional change outlined by the historical institutionalism literature (Hacker 2005; Thelen 2004; Schickler 2001). Like "drift," attenuation enables policymakers to achieve their aims less visibly, but it involves actively redirecting funds through the tax system or individual consumer-citizens rather than merely failing to update existing legislation. New institutions (such as scholarship tuition organizations [STOs]) may be created to help attenuate the connection between the government and a particular policy output. In that sense, attenuation involves "layering" of new rules and institutions on top of old ones. Unlike layering, however, attenuation does not typically proceed by means of marginal amendments but often involves major institutional changes that "displace" existing rules.

"Conversion" is the strategic redeployment of existing rules; attenuation is the strategic redeployment of funds for existing ends. While a policy change by conversion involves a bottom-up renegotiation of institutional rules by participants within an institution, attenuation is an elite-driven process driven by leaders and advocates in response to strategic imperatives, specifically, the desire to avoid legal challenges. In this book I have shown that attenuation can help describe and explain decision-making by policymakers, advocates, and judges in the United States, but the concept has broader applicability as part of the theoretical apparatus of historical institutionalism.

This book identifies, measures, and deploys dimensions of attenuation to provide comprehensive treatment of the politics of vouchers. Alexander Hamilton asserts in Federalist No. 27, "A government continually at a distance and out of sight can hardly be expected to interest the sensations of the people" (Hamilton, Madison, and Jay 2008). I disentangle these two clauses: the quality of being *at a distance* in policy design is analytically separable from the quality of being *out of sight* to members of the public. Identifying two dimensions of attenuated governance offers greater analytical clarity in a field where these attributes are typically elided.

The submerged state consists of policies that utilize private mechanisms for the delivery of social policy, attenuating the connection between government and ultimate beneficiary compared to directly funded public provision: for example, subsidies to private lenders for student loans (as opposed to direct federal loans or grants), housing vouchers that provide a sum of public money to be spent in the private rental market (as opposed to public housing), tax expenditures for childcare, medical expenses, savings plans, home mortgage interest, or earned income tax credits (as opposed to in-kind benefits funded by direct governmental spending or lower headline tax rates).

In the rich field of scholarship connected with Mettler's submerged state, scholars identify the submerged state's associated characteristics: it is hidden from view, and the general public knows comparatively little about it (Haselswerdt and Bartels 2015); it enables politicians to claim credit for "shrinking government" and avoid blame for policy failures; and it is regressive, but its lack of visibility tends to dampen political mobilization on the part of the general public while increasing the informational advantages enjoyed by organized interests (Starr and Esping-Andersen 1979).

All of these characteristics are associated with the submerged state, but they do not always stand and fall as one, because what the public *feels* and *thinks it knows* about the *effects* of attenuated policies is not the same thing as objective institutional characteristics of policy design or political communications. The salience of such policies among different portions of the population rises and falls much more rapidly than any amendments to the design of the policy itself (Hackett 2017). Race, gender, and perceptions of socioeconomic status, as well as program design, can make policies more or less visible to recipients and affect their political beliefs, behaviors, and democratic engagement more generally (Michener 2018).

The case of vouchers underlines the fact that there is both a linguistic and policy design dimension to the submerged or hidden state, a dimensionality obscured in the literature. For many scholars, submerged policies are not intrinsically remote. Rather, "policymakers could reveal how they operate to the public by providing clear, simple, and straightforward information" (Mettler 2009, 67). The two dimensions of attenuated governance imply that this statement is conditionally true. Deeply attenuated policies have advantages over their weakly attenuated counterparts, but the rhetoric that seeks to attenuate the state–service connection also plays a part in the defense and expansion of the hidden state.

The conceptual apparatus of attenuated governance is capacious enough to accommodate different degrees of attenuation and to avoid dichotomies that can obscure the understanding of its operation and effects. Scholars working in the field of attenuated governance and the "hidden" or "submerged" state acknowledge the fuzziness of the concept's boundaries. For example, Mettler (2010) argues that "[i]t is appropriate…to think of all social programs as existing on a *continuum* from those that are most visible to those that are most submerged" (pp. 819–20).

Similarly, scholars refer to "more" or "less" visible social policies (Hacker 2002, 8–9; Howard 2007, 89–90). Yet by treating the submerged state dichotomously in empirical work, scholars might have missed important distinctions *within* the submerged state that reveal how different types of attenuated policy design raise or lower the risk of successful political or legal challenges. Understanding the origins, operation, and effects of attenuated governance arrangements helps illuminate the contours of state development and the strategies policymakers adopt to deal with its tensions and contradictions.

Attenuated Governance: The Strategic Landscape

Thirty years after the advent of New Public Management, amid the expansion of privatization and consumer-choice reforms to public services, attenuated governance thrives around the world. Much recent expansion of government has occurred through indirect means – grants, contracts, loans and loan guarantees, tax expenditures, and vouchers (Benjamin and Posner 2018). Vouchers are popular because they provide funds to individuals, taking advantage of the private sector and avoiding direct governmental management (Tighe, Hatch, and Mead 2017).

It is not only governments that have incentives to engage in attenuation. Corporations keen to avoid criticism for excessive executive pay during the financial crisis utilized "camouflage": attenuated mechanisms that hid the role of the company in providing benefits. "Out, for the most part, were seven- and eight-figure bonuses. In were complicated 'stock options' and 'deferred compensation' that promised equally big returns down the road" (Hacker and Pierson 2010, 2). Providing an attenuated benefit rather than a direct one was safer, by controlling reputational risk.

Attenuated programs are further bolstered by the fact that they offer substantial advantages to wealthy individuals and organizations. From 2011, the Internal Revenue Service allowed taxpayers to deduct the tax credit scholarship contributions from their federally taxable income as well. In combination with generous state-level credits and tax deductions, contributors in nine states – Alabama, Arizona, Georgia, Montana, Oklahoma, Pennsylvania, Rhode Island, South Carolina, and Virginia – could make a profit from their donation to tax credit scholarships (Greenmay 2017), otherwise known as "double-dipping."

Ironically, contributors in these mostly red states were prevented from double-dipping by the Trump administration's fight against high-tax blue states. The Tax Cuts and Jobs Act of 2017 capped the deductibility of state and local taxes. In 2018 the Treasury Department proposed a new rule on the federal income tax treatment of payments and property tax transfers under state and local tax credit programs, to prevent states from circumventing tax deduction limits (US Department of the Treasury 2018). By June 2019, after an outcry by private school advocates, the Treasury had published new rules intended to protect at least some donors to state tax credit scholarship programs (US Department of the Treasury 2019).

Policymakers face strategic decisions about the combination of policy design and presentation most conducive to passing and sustaining their policy reforms, decisions with consequences for the shape and scope of the state. By choosing attenuated governance – publicly distancing government from legally contentious purposes – those elites commodify public services and complicate lines of democratic accountability.

Attenuating policy design seems to present problems of *control*: principal-agent problems arise as the distance between funder and funded becomes more attenuated. Attenuating rhetoric seems to present problems of *credit-claiming*: it is more challenging to claim credit for policy successes where the role of the state in the provision of a benefit is verbally obscured. Yet attenuating policy design and rhetoric can be strategically rewarding for policymakers because they insulate such programs from challenges and enable policymakers to achieve the same ends through oblique, coded means.

Attenuated governance does not require government actually to disentangle itself from legally contentious purposes but merely seem to do so. Similarly, although proponents of New Public Management often claim it will clarify lines of responsibility, such reforms are embedded in political systems that can delegate authority on one dimension but increase oversight and control on another (Mortensen 2013, 232). Vouchers involve less active interference in private markets than other forms of public subsidy (Hays 1985, 140), but this "less active" interference enables the state to steer the direction of funds under the radar. The government may choose vouchers over cash because it has an interest in guiding consumption in a particular direction (Hevenstone 2015). Vouchers are tied to particular expenditures, often targeted at certain constituencies, and typically hedged by state regulations about usage.

In housing policy, for example, vouchers attenuate the connection between state and landlords by paying public funds to the consumer-citizen (typically) to spend on their choice of accommodation. But housing authorities who issue vouchers also conduct housing inspections to enforce minimum housing standards (Freeman 2011). Healthcare vouchers such as Medicare Part D also involve significant state involvement under the radar, as Morgan and Campbell explain, "At first, Medicare beneficiaries were given the option to have all benefits provided by managed care companies, but *when an insufficient number took up this option, advocates pushed to make this possibility more attractive*" (K. J. Morgan and Campbell 2011, 13) [italics added].

In addition to insulating the state from racial, religious, and civic controversy, attenuated governance helps government avoid pushback for growing inequality and financial mismanagement, regardless of underlying state support structures. This "winner-take-all" politics, in which the wealthiest gain the most, can be attributed to the "impersonal beneficence of

Adam Smith's 'invisible hand,' the natural outcome of free-market forces" (Hacker and Pierson 2010, 70–71). The government seems to have little to do with it. By privatizing policy administration, funding programs through tax expenditures, and complicating lines of accountability, elites protect themselves from blame. Many scholars of the submerged state argue that the solution is to make policy visible: providing citizens more and better information to help them make informed decisions (Mettler 2009).

However, it is not only through *de-attenuating* policy mechanisms and purposes that ordinary citizens can become aware of the significance of doubly distanced policies. One puzzle in Chapter 1 was that attenuated policies seem politically unattractive, despite documented uptake and growth, because they apparently prevent policymakers from claiming credit for policy successes. In fact, the credit-claiming problem is exaggerated. Politicians actually do take credit for attenuated policy delivery when communicating the policy benefits to its particular constituency, that is, to their issue public. When they do this successfully – unlike the visibly racist appeals of southern white supremacists – they utilize coded language and terms that appeal to relevant voters. Voucher proponents typically pitch their policies to conservatives in terms of empowerment, choice, and quality education. "We need to empower [parents] to make the best choices possible" (Wichmann 2018); "It's about evening the playing field" (Cupich 2018); "We're going to take those kids and give them school choice" (Koenig 2018).

Their opponents acknowledge the power of these appeals. "I think publicly their primary argument was probably around the kids, right, because that's everyone's first argument" (Guzzardi 2018). Telling conservatives that a policy "expands choice" or "empowers parents" would not alarm a court but enable policymakers to take credit for the policy in microtargeted ways. Coded, attenuating rhetoric has a dual function: strengthening the program legally even while allowing policymakers to take credit from relevant constituencies. An Illinoisan Republican representative describes the heightened awareness of the state tax credit scholarship for his Catholic constituents:

> Oh, I guarantee you they were aware of it. So every constituent, I guarantee you, every constituent that has a child in the parochial schools in my district were aware of this; one, because the schools themselves when they went to ... when the parishioners – and I happen to have a district that's heavily Catholic when the parishioners went to Mass they heard about it, that there were notices sent out that as of such-and-such a date you can begin applying. They knew exactly ... so they were very aware of it. (Harris 2018)

The director of government relations at the Illinois Catholic Conference confirms the representative's impression: "Our target audiences know about it I think" (Wichmann 2018). Policymakers can reach relevant issue publics despite attenuated tax credit policy designs.

Some policies may be more suited to attenuation than others, presenting a hierarchy of strategic possibilities to policymakers. Certain forms of threat – such as the threat of legal action – may be particularly susceptible to attenuation because of the significance of the direct–indirect funding distinction. It may be easier to engage in attenuating rhetoric in more technical policy areas, not experienced directly by the public. But this book demonstrates that even in education – a high-salience policy arena – policymakers find it politically rewarding to attenuate. The strategic advantages of attenuated governance sustain the hidden state.

Legacies of Losing

The strategic responses of policymakers to the prospect of legal challenge matter because America's fundamental struggles are *continually* contested. Uncertainty and contestation do not cease just because a particular set of policy commitments have been enacted into law (Patashnik 2008). The foundational rivalries continue to recur because institutional and ideational legacies of former regimes project themselves forward. "The entire historical record bears down with remarkable immediacy on present-day controversies" (Skowronek and Orren 2016, 27). None of the rival orders win out permanently even if they may temporarily gain ascendance in statehouses and courtrooms, because policymaking is a dynamic process in which opposing forces seek to bolster or undermine reforms. Hence, policymakers must always contend with the possibility that their policy goals will be challenged and even overturned in future.

We should rethink the prevailing understanding of political "winners" and "losers" in view of the fact that "losers" can prevail at other times and in other venues (Tulis and Mellow 2018). The lesson of attenuated governance is that directing benefits through indirect channels and rhetorically distancing government from controversial policy goals have an insulating effect on commitments that would otherwise be struck down.

Accommodationists can win in court, despite the lingering strength of the secularist order, by attenuating the connection between government and religious school. Individualists can outfox communitarian forces by channeling public funds through tax credits and private delivery mechanisms. Anticipating downstream political effects, policymakers strategically insulate their programs from challenge by means of attenuated delivery and attenuating rhetoric. Hence, members of "losing" orders can ultimately become winners. Through attenuated governance, these orders avoid painful defeats, gain a secure legal footing, and entrench their policy commitments in spite of the surging power of rivals.

Appendix

EMPIRICAL STRATEGY

This book combines quantitative and qualitative data collection for nine case study states (listed in Table A1 and shown in Figure A1) and the nation as a whole. I employ original datasets recording the creation and litigation of voucher programs, 1953–2018, and covering the entire nation. Two datasets, in particular, are crucial. First, I utilize state legislature websites to extract information about legislative votes on the forty-seven voucher bills passed across America between 2005 and 2017. The dataset contains the universe of state legislators who voted on those bills in 6,693 votes. I record individual and district-level characteristics (partisan affiliation, race, and sex; district ideology; private school enrollment; racial district characteristics; and government employees) and state or program-level characteristics (policy design, sponsor characteristics, program targets, state educational expenditure, and unionization rates).

In order to address the possibility of selection bias, I also use the legislative scanning programs, LegiScan and BillTrack50, to identify and incorporate twelve voucher bills that were brought to a vote before July 2017 but failed to become law because they were voted down on the floor, died in committee, or were vetoed by the state governor. The votes collected on failed vouchers came from all regions of the country and from states both with and without existing voucher programs. These 1,158 votes on bills that almost became law are added to those that did pass, yielding a total of 7,851 state legislator votes. Table A9 provides the full multilevel logistic regression results. Additional checks, detailed in Table A10, address potential selection concerns by examining 116 voucher bills that died without votes during the same period.

Second, drawing upon the universe of judicial votes in forty-six voucher cases (1955–2017), and 236 individual votes, I examine the vulnerability of these programs by recording each judge's decision about the constitutionality of the voucher program at issue. I note each judge or justice's sex, race, partisan affiliation, and vote in favor of or in opposition to the constitutionality of a voucher program, the year and region of challenge, and relevant state constitutional provisions.

In addition to these core datasets, I utilize archival sources pertaining to constitutional history, legislative bill jackets, and ballot initiative results. Most importantly, this book draws upon 101 interviews I conducted personally with policymakers, bureaucrats, and advocates, on the record, in nine states and in Washington, DC. Names, titles, and interview dates are listed in this Appendix. Interviews were conducted in the respondents' professional capacities and were professionally transcribed so that interviewees can be cited with precision. In several cases, interviewees are cited at length so that the reader can appreciate the complexity and the context of their statements.

Interviewing elites provides the best opportunity to capture strategic imperatives as policymakers themselves seek to explain or justify them. The attenuated governance thesis hypothesizes strategic action, and interviews reveal far more about policymaker motivations and intentions than a mere overview of actions taken. I cannot rule out the possibility that interviewees present only palatable motivations and conceal others (indeed, I expect this to be the case). But I do not think this danger too great, because – as Chapters 3–7 show in detail – in many cases both copartisan and politically opposing interviewees corroborate one other's accounts of policymaker actions.

INTERVIEWEES

Dr. Vicki Alger, Research Fellow for the Independent Institute, Oakland, California (March 23, 2012)

Anonymous staffer, Capitol Hill, Washington, DC (July 16, 2010)

Senator Conrad Appel, Chairman of the Education Committee, Louisiana State Senate (September 4, 2012)

Representative Kurt Bahr, Missouri House of Representatives (April 18, 2018)

Representative Gretchen Bangert, Member of the Education Committee, Missouri House of Representatives (April 18, 2018)
Erin Bendily, Deputy Superintendent of Policy and External Affairs at Louisiana Department of Education (September 27, 2012)
Holly Boffy, Member of the Louisiana Board of Elementary and Secondary Education (September 10, 2012)
Anna Borges, Transportation Supervisor for the California Department of Education (March 21, 2012)
Raymond Burnell, Education Specialist at the California Catholic Conference (March 13, 2012)
Representative Ingrid Burnett, Member of the Education Committee, Missouri House of Representatives (April 18, 2018)
Melissa Chapman, Executive Director of the Jewish Federation of the Sacramento Region, California (March 12, 2012)
Jordan Clark, Chief of Staff to Representative Glenn Thompson (July 13, 2010)
Dr. Raymond Colucciello, Superintendent of Schools for Albany City School District (March 8, 2012)
Dr. Andrew Coulson, Director of the Center for Educational Freedom at the Cato Institute (July 22, 2010)
Cardinal Blase J. Cupich, Archbishop of the Archdiocese of Chicago (April 25, 2018)
Representative Barbara Flynn Currie, Majority Leader of the Illinois House of Representatives (April 10, 2018)
Representative William Davis, Chairperson of the Appropriations – Elementary and Secondary Education Committee, Illinois House of Representatives (April 13, 2018)
Ned Dolejsi, Executive Director of the California Catholic Conference (March 13, 2012)
Representative Jim Durkin, Minority Leader of the Illinois House of Representatives (April 12, 2018)
Roger Eddy, Former Representative and Schools Superintendent, now Executive Director of the Illinois Association of School Boards (March 28, 2012)
Senator Edgar Emery, Member of the Committee on Education, Missouri State Senate (April 17, 2018)
Dr. Melanie Ezell, President of the Louisiana Association of Independent Schools and Former Headmistress of Parkview Baptist School (September 11, 2012)
Senator Teresa Fedor, Ohio State Senate (August 12, 2010)

Professor Chester E. Finn, Thomas B. Fordham Institute (July 14, 2010)

Carol Geddis, Executive Director of the Catholic School Administrators Association of New York State (March 5, 2012)

Representative Will Guzzardi, Member of the Elementary and Secondary Education: School Curriculum and Policies Committee, Illinois House of Representatives (April 13, 2018)

Patrick Haggarty, Superintendent of Catholic Schools for Montana (April 26, 2012)

Representative David Harris, Member of the Scholarship Tax Credit Oversight Subcommittee, Illinois House of Representatives (April 13, 2018)

James Herzog, Associate Director for Education for the Florida Catholic Conference (April 11, 2012)

Susan B. Hilton, Director of Governmental Relations for the Illinois Association of School Boards (April 19, 2012)

Representative Cliff Hite, Ohio House of Representatives (July 21, 2010)

Representative Jeanne Ives, Member of the Appropriations – Elementary and Secondary Education Committee, Illinois House of Representatives (April 13, 2018)

Lynn Jondahl, Former Chair of the Tax Committee, Michigan House of Representatives (July 28, 2010)

Todd Jones, President of the Association of Independent Colleges and Universities of Ohio (July 20, 2010)

Carolyn Jurkowitz, Director of the Ohio Catholic Conference (July 28, 2010)

Sister Catherine Kamphaus, Superintendent of Catholic Schools for Salt Lake City, Utah (April 2, 2012)

Cory Kanth, Statewide Online Education Program Specialist for the Utah State Office of Education (April 4, 2012)

Jan Kennedy, School Funding Advisory Council, Ohio (July 22, 2010)

Larry Keough, Associate Director of the Department on Education, Ohio Catholic Conference (July 29, 2010)

Senator David Koehler, Member of the Education Committee, Illinois State Senate (April 11, 2018)

Senator Andrew Koenig, Member of the Committee on Education, Missouri State Senate (April 18, 2018)

Dr. Jan Lancaster, Superintendent of Catholic Schools for the Archdiocese of New Orleans (September 6, 2012)

Patricia Levesque, Executive Director of Foundation for Florida's Future and Member of the Taxation and Budgetary Reform Commission (July 23, 2010, and May 4, 2012)

Senator Doug Libla, Member of the Committee on Education, Missouri State Senate (April 17, 2018)

David Little, Director of Government Relations for the New York State School Boards Association (March 5, 2012)

Senator Carol Liu, California State Senate Education Committee (March 21, 2012)

Danny Loar, Executive Director of the Louisiana Conference of Catholic Bishops (September 12, 2012)

Representative Rebecca Lockhart, Speaker of the Utah House of Representatives (April 5, 2012)

Jennifer Louie, Education Staffer to California State Senator Sharon Runner (March 13, 2012)

Bill Lucia, President and CEO of EdVoice (March 30, 2012)

Katherine Ludwig, Chief Housing Choice Voucher Officer, Chicago Housing Authority (April 9, 2018)

Assemblyman William B. Magnarelli, New York State Assembly Education Committee (February 29, 2012)

Joseph Mais, Staffer to Representative Raul Grijalva (D-AZ), US House of Representatives (July 15, 2010)

Assemblyman Alan Maisel, Member of the Education Committee, New York State Assembly (March 19, 2012)

Senator Andy Manar, Member of the Education Committee, Illinois State Senate (April 13, 2018)

Representative Mark Matthiesen, Missouri House of Representatives (April 18, 2018)

Dr. Mike McCarron, President of the Florida Catholic Conference (April 11, 2012)

Senator Dan McConchie, Member of the Education Committee, Illinois State Senate (April 12, 2018)

Sister Dale McDonald, Director of Public Policy and Education Research for the National Catholic Education Association (March 14, 2012)

Ruth Melton, Director of Legislative Affairs for the Florida School Boards Association (April 11, 2012)

Ronald Meyer, Attorney and Founding Partner of Meyer, Brooks, Demma and Blohm P.A., Tallahassee, Florida (April 13, 2012)

Assemblyman Joel M. Miller, New York State Assembly Education Committee (March 7, 2012)

Representative Jerry Mitchell, Republican Spokesperson for the Elementary and Secondary Education Committee of the Illinois General Assembly (March 27, 2012)

Senator Bill Montford, Chief Executive of the Florida Association of District School Superintendents and Minority Whip in the Florida Senate (April 12, 2012)

Dan Montgomery, President of the Illinois Federation of Teachers (April 5, 2018)

Representative Judy Morgan, Member of the Committee on Education, Missouri House of Representatives (April 17, 2018)

Representative Seth Morgan, Member of the Education Committee, Ohio House of Representatives (July 21, 2010)

Senator J. P. Morrell, Member of the Education Committee, Louisiana State Senate (September 6, 2012)

Representative Tom Morrison, Member of the Education Committee, Illinois General Assembly (March 29, 2012)

Mark Murphy, Legislative Aide to Assemblyman Mike Eng, California State Assembly (March 23, 2012)

Larry Newton, School Finance Director, Utah State Office of Education (April 4, 2012)

Don Noble, Lobbyist, Michigan Education Association (July 26, 2010)

Mary Obi, Church Volunteer and Leader, Our Lady of Guadalupe Parochial School, Sacramento, California (March 20, 2012)

Assemblyman Daniel O'Donnell, Member of the Education Committee, New York State Assembly (March 6, 2012)

State Senator Aaron Osmond, Member of the Education Committee, Utah State Senate (April 3, 2012)

Emmy Partin, Director of Ohio Policy and Research, Thomas B. Fordham Institute (July 22, 2010)

Representative Robert W. Pritchard, Republican Spokesperson for the Appropriations – Elementary and Secondary Education Committee, Illinois General Assembly (March 30, 2012)

James Quinn, Chief of Staff to Representative Bill Cassidy, US House of Representatives (July 16, 2010)

Representative Steve Reick, Member of the Appropriations – Elementary and Secondary Education Committee, Illinois House of Representatives (April 12, 2018)

Representative Rebecca Roeber, Vice Chair of the House Education Committee, Missouri House of Representatives (April 17, 2018)

Amy Rutschow, Staffer for the California State Republican Fiscal Office (March 15, 2012)
Assemblyman Joseph Saladino, Member of the Education Committee, New York State Assembly (March 7, 2012)
Professor Adam Schaeffer, Center for Educational Freedom and Adjunct Scholar at the Cato Institute, Washington, DC (July 13, 2010)
Senator Jill Schupp, Member of the Committee on Education, Missouri State Senate (April 17, 2018)
Michael Schwartz, Former Director of the Catholic League and Chief of Staff to Senator Tom Coburn, US Senate (July 15, 2010)
Jesse Sharkey, Vice President of the Chicago Teachers Union (April 5, 2018)
Sarah Spence, Legislative Aide to Senator Gary Cates, Ohio State Senate (July 20, 2010)
Representative Dan Stacy, Missouri House of Representatives (April 18, 2018)
David Stafford, Lobbyist, Michigan Education Association (July 26, 2010)
John Stanford, Governor's Policy Advisor on Education, Ohio (September 15, 2010)
Representative Kenneth Sumsion, Education Committee Member and Gubernatorial Candidate, Utah House of Representatives (April 3, 2012)
Representative Kathryn Swan, Member of the Education Committee, Missouri House of Representatives (April 18, 2018)
Lee Swift, President of the Florida School Boards Association (April 12, 2012)
Representative Glenn Thompson (R-PA), US House of Representatives (July 15, 2010)
Paul Upton, Senior Legislative Aide to Assemblyman Carl Heastie, New York State Assembly (March 7, 2012)
Senator Gerald Van Woerkom, Vice Chair of the Education Committee, Michigan State Senate (July 28, 2010)
Diana Vasquez, Legislative Aide to Assemblyman Mike Eng, California State Assembly (March 23, 2012)
Senator Chuck Weaver, Member of the Education Committee, Illinois State Senate (April 12, 2018)
Dr. John White, State Superintendent for Education in Louisiana (September 10, 2012)

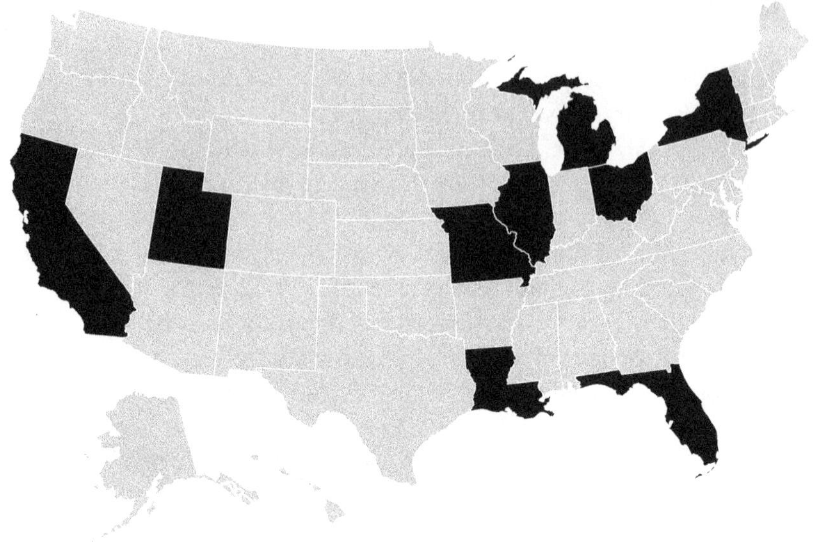

FIGURE A1. Location of case study states.

Professor Grover Whitehurst, Brookings Institute, Washington, DC (July 12, 2010)
Zachary Wichmann, Director of Government Relations for the Illinois Catholic Conference (March 27, 2012, and April 10, 2018)

VOUCHER VIGNETTES: VOUCHER PASSAGE IN THE STATES

American states vary widely in their experience with voucher programs. This geographical and temporal variation can be illustrated by a survey of voucher bill passage and failure across many states and regions. This book draws material from across America but incorporates additional archival and interview material from nine states – California, Florida, Illinois, Louisiana, Michigan, Missouri, New York, Ohio, and Utah – selected to represent the widest possible range of regions, cultures, and voucher program successes and failures, over seventy years (Figure A1).

Three case study states are red states, three blue, and three swing states, ranging from the Pacific West to the Northeast and the Deep South. Four are geographical neighbors (Illinois and Missouri, and Ohio and Michigan), and five are isolates. Table A1 summarizes characteristics

TABLE A1. *Case study states: relevant characteristics*

State	Population (m)	Region	Black population (%)[1]	Youth dependency ratio[2]	Religiosity (%)[3]	Party[4]	Unionization%[5]
CA	40	Pacific West	7.2 (low)	40.3 (high)	49 (moderately low)	Blue	15.5 (high)
FL	21	Atlantic South	17.0 (high)	36.0 (low)	54 (moderate)	Swing	5.6 (low)
IL	13	Midwest	15.4 (high)	39.0 (average)	51 (moderately low)	Blue	15.0 (high)
LA	5	Deep South	32.8 (very high)	39.9 (high)	71 (very high)	Red	4.4 (very low)
MI	10	Midwest	15.2 (high)	37.4 (low)	53 (moderate)	Swing	15.6 (high)
MO	6	Midwest	12.5 (average)	38.3 (average)	60 (high)	Red	8.7 (average)
NY	20	Northeast	17.2 (high)	35.4 (very low)	46 (low)	Blue	23.8 (very high)
OH	12	Midwest	13.4 (average)	37.6 (low)	58 (moderately high)	Swing	12.5 (average)
UT	3	Mountain West	1.6 (very low)	52.3 (very high)	64 (high)	Red	3.9 (very low)

1 "Black population" is the percentage of the state population who identify as black or African American alone or in combination, in their response to the 2010 US Census (Rastogi et al. 2010).

2 "Youth dependency ratio" is a measure of the relationship between under-18s and the working-age population. It is calculated by the following formula: (population under 18/population aged 18–64) × 100 (US Census Bureau 2009).

3 "Religiosity" here is a combined index composed by the 2014 US Religious Landscape Survey. The index is a combination of four indicators of religiosity, which are closely correlated: the "importance of religion" in one's life, frequency of prayer, worship attendance, and belief in God (Lipka and Wormald 2016).

4 "Party" is an overall determination of the partisan affiliation of the state, combining Gallup's measure of the party affiliation of state voters with recent state and federal election results (J. M. Jones 2016).

5 "Union membership" is the percentage of employed workers who are members of unions (and not simply represented by unions) (Bureau of Labor Statistics 2017).

of these case study states relevant to the racial, religious, and civic contests from which disputes about voucher constitutionality arise: the school-age population, racial and ethnic makeup, religiosity, unionization, and party affiliation.

Table A1 displays wide variation. Utah is the "youngest" state, in that it has the largest youth dependency ratio in the nation; Florida is the "oldest" with the highest old-age dependency ratio. A third of Louisianans, but fewer than one in twenty Utahns, identify as black. Almost a quarter of New Yorker workers belong to a union, but fewer than one in twenty Louisianans or Utahns do so. More than seven in ten Louisianans say that religion is "very important" in their lives while fewer than half of New Yorkers or Californians say the same. In between these extremes, neighboring Midwestern states Illinois, Michigan, Missouri, and Ohio match national averages and one another on many of these measures, though they vary in partisan affiliation.

The states from which I draw my interviewees also vary widely in the status of the voucher cause within their borders. The following vignettes encompass the full range of state experiences with voucher bills: school choice centers embracing both vouchers and tax credits, segregation tuition grants established during the Jim Crow era, vouchers overturned by referendum or struck down by court action, rare bipartisan votes for tax credit voucher bills, and states in which such bills fail repeatedly.

NEW YORK: NO VOUCHERS IN A DEMOCRATIC STATE

The Common School Fund and the Public School Society were founded in New York State in 1805. In 1812, the General School Act provided schools with an entitlement to a share of the Common School Fund, and several religious bodies established schools and participated in the fund. By 1824, the Free School Society, as the Public School Society became known, had begun to petition the New York state government to enjoin religious schools from participating in the Common School Fund. In 1825, an ordinance was passed that recognized the peculiar claims of orphan asylums as the only justifiable exemption to the general principle of providing public school moneys only for secular instruction.

The battles of the first half of the nineteenth century against the funding of Catholic schools reached their apogee in 1840, when Governor William Seward argued that the system of Catholic schools in New York State should be given public aid on the same basis as the public schools.

In response, the New York legislature passed Chapter 150 of 1842, which provided that "[n]o school ... in which any religious sectarian doctrine or tenet shall be taught, inculcated or practiced, shall receive any portion of the school moneys to be distributed by this act."

In 1867, a debate on compulsory education at the state constitutional convention generated evidence that Catholics would not send their children to public schools because of their Protestant character. The evidence had no effect on the convention's position on public and parochial schools. In 1873, another law was passed that provided money to be distributed from the education fund, "but no money shall be paid to any school under the control of any religious or denominational sect or society." In the early years of the twentieth century, however, the laws governing parochial schools shifted again.

In 1935, Democratic governor Herbert Lehman had vetoed a measure providing publicly funded transportation to children at private religious schools, but a year later he committed a volte-face by approving and signing a similar transportation measure known as the Kelly School Bus Transportation Bill, following lobbying from religious school interests. The New York Supreme Court ruled against the Kelly bill, but since the 1938 Constitutional Convention was then in session, the convention delegates quickly passed an exemption to the constitutional provision for transportation aid (Rippey 1938). The convention also established real estate tax exemptions for "real or personal property used exclusively for religious, educational or charitable purposes." Both provisions remain in force.

The development of New York aid continued in this lively vein during the 1940s. When Eleanor Roosevelt made the case against the public funding of religious schools in her *New York World-Telegram* column, Cardinal Spellman publicly excoriated her, and a vigorous public argument about church–state separation continued for several months. By the late 1960s, New York had established itself as a relatively generous state in terms of the provision of textbooks, transportation, and nursing services for children at private religious schools, but the state has never passed a voucher bill.

LOUISIANA: SEGREGATION GRANTS AND POSTHURRICANE VOUCHERS

Louisiana deployed segregation tuition grants in the immediate aftermath of the *Brown* v. *Board of Education* desegregation decision, to enable white families to escape the public schooling system for private segregated academies (1958).[6] The segregation tuition grants were struck down by a US district court in 1961, revived by the legislature, and struck down again in 1967 and 1968 with Bryan Poindexter's case. It took forty years for the voucher cause to be revived. The Louisiana state legislature passed vouchers in 2008 and tax credits in 2009.

Any account of the development of Louisiana's vouchers must include a major exogenous shock: Hurricane Katrina in 2005. The hurricane disaster destroyed a large portion of the educational infrastructure of New Orleans. In the immediate aftermath of the disaster, religious organizations were among the swiftest to return to the area and take in additional students who had lost their school. The importance of the hurricane was not merely providing the demand and physical space for the expansion of private religious schools and public charter schools but also providing a change of mind-set. "Alright," said the executive director of the Louisiana Conference of Catholic Bishops, describing the changes wrought by the hurricane, "half the city gone. Let's just start from a clean sheet of paper and let's try everything" (Loar 2012).

He suggests that the Louisianan voucher and tax credit programs stemmed from this period of disruption: "I don't think it would have happened without Katrina, I really don't" (Loar 2012). Although the number of Catholic schools in New Orleans dropped slightly since Katrina and charter schools have expanded most, the hurricane encouraged policymakers to consider radical solutions to the city's educational problems, including scholarship programs for private religious schools.

After his inauguration in 2008, Governor Bobby Jindal pushed for the introduction of tax credit and voucher programs. The 2008 Student Scholarships for Educational Excellence (vouchers) were limited in scope to New Orleans, but the 2008 Elementary and Secondary Tuition Deduction (tax credit) was statewide. In 2009, three more tax credit bills were passed, providing individual and corporate tax deductions for contributions to school tuition organizations that offer scholarships for nonpublic schools. Legislative activity on tax credits and vouchers in Louisiana has been swift and substantial. A further expansion occurred in June 2012, when the Louisianan voucher program was extended statewide.

In November 2012, a state judge ruled that the use of the Louisiana Minimum Foundation Program funding for statewide voucher scholarships was unconstitutional because it diverted funds from public

[6] Grants were not distributed until 1962.

education, a point I consider in Chapter 5. The judge did not issue an injunction to stop the scholarship program, however. By 2018, Louisiana had two tax credits and two vouchers in operation. Over 100,000 students utilize one or more of these voucher programs – more than 12 percent of all K–12 students and more than 60 percent of all private school enrollees (National Center for Education Statistics 2017a, 2017b).

CALIFORNIA: NO VOUCHERS AND A REFERENDUM DEFEAT

Under Governor Earl Warren's tenure during World War II, the Republican Senate and Democratic House of the California state legislature enacted transportation aid for private school students and exempted private school expenses from taxation, but the state has never come close to passing a voucher or tax credit private school tuition bill. California has never created a voucher or tax credit program, and it is highly unlikely to do so.

In 1993 Californians inflicted a "humiliating defeat" on a voucher ballot initiative, Proposition 174, which would have given parents a sum of public money equal to half the amount the state spent on each public school student (Menendez 1999, 77). By 69.5 to 30.4 percent overall, and with all fifty-eight counties in the state rejecting the proposal, the voucher cause was sunk. The voucher proposal did slightly better in heavily Republican areas but did not win more than 40 percent support in any county.

Seven years later Californian voters faced another voucher ballot initiative. Proposition 38, drafted by Silicon Valley entrepreneur Tim Draper, proposed to provide a sum to parents for private school enrollment: the greater of $4,000, half the national average of public school spending per pupil, or half California's public school spending per pupil (Brunner and Sonstelie 2003; Associated Press 2000b). Opposed by the state school board, the proposal would have allowed students to use any voucher amount in excess of private school tuition to pay for future educational expenses (Bolick 2003, 153–54; Associated Press 2000a). The initiative was defeated by 70.9 to 29.4 percent, and the voucher cause has not been revived since.

FLORIDA: SCHOOL CHOICE THROUGH VOUCHERS AND TAX CREDITS

By contrast with California, Florida is a school choice center with four tax credit and voucher programs in operation by 2018. The state never created segregation grants. Instead, it followed the Midwestern voucher pioneers of the 1990s closely. In 1999, Florida enacted major tax credit and voucher programs: the Florida Opportunity Scholarship Program and the

John McKay Scholarships for Students with Disabilities Program, under the Florida A+ Education Plan. The Opportunity Scholarship was open to students in public schools rated in the two lowest performance categories under the state's school standards, D or F, while the John McKay Scholarship was provided for students with an individual education plan (IEP), a statement of special educational needs.

These two programs were passed by a Republican state legislature under Republican governor Jeb Bush, a vocal proponent of school choice measures. They were followed in 2001 by the enactment of a tax credit program, again by Governor Bush through a Republican legislature, to "provide an income tax credit for corporations that contribute money to nonprofit Scholarship-Funding Organizations (SFOs) that award scholarships to students from families with limited financial resources" (Florida School Choice 2013).

One of these pieces of legislation, the Opportunity Scholarship Program, was found unconstitutional by the First District Court of Appeals in 2004 and by the Florida Supreme Court in 2006 on the grounds of the church–state separation and educational adequacy, respectively (Pariente 2006). But these court cases, *Bush* v. *Holmes*,[7] proved to be merely a brief hiatus in the rise of Floridian school choice programs.

Until 2009, tax credits under the scholarship program were only available against the state's corporate income tax. In that year the legislature expanded the revenue sources against which tax credits may be claimed to include the insurance premium tax and renamed the Corporate Income Tax Credit Scholarship Program the Florida Tax Credit Scholarship Program. In 2011, the legislature amended the Florida Tax Credits Scholarship Program to increase the value of contributions allowed. The program is large: in FY2010–11 the cap on the total tax credits was $140 million.

ILLINOIS: TAX CREDITS BUT NO VOUCHERS

In 1999, the Illinois legislature authorized a modest tax credit voucher, the Illinois Educational Expenses Tax Credit under the Illinois Income Tax Act, by amending the state revenue code. It provides a tax deduction of up to $500 per family for school-related expenses, including sports and computing equipment – and both public and private school children

[7] *Bush* v. *Holmes*, 29 Fla. L. Weekly D1877 (Fla. 1st DCA August 16, 2004); *Bush* v. *Holmes*, 886 So. 2d 340, 366 (Fla. 1st DCA 2004); *Bush* v. *Holmes*, 919 So. 2d 392 (2006).

are eligible to receive it. In 2008 an estimated $72 million was spent on the educational tax credit.

In 2011, Senator James Meeks – a Democratic state senator and pastor of a megachurch that operates a private Christian Academy – proposed a voucher bill for Chicago's low-income students. The bill passed in the state senate with the unanimous support of the chamber's thirty-three Republicans but failed in the House. It was followed by a second 2011 voucher proposal sponsored by Republican senator Matt Murphy, but this bill also split the Democratic Party representatives and failed to pass.

The voucher cause seemed dead until an unusual concatenation of circumstances arose in 2017. A new Republican governor, Bruce Rauner, was elected in 2014 opposite a Democratic-controlled legislature. An educational funding crisis connected to the inequitable distribution of resources between the state's 852 school districts and the funding of pensions for the city of Chicago had been growing for several years. It became acute under divided government, as Republicans and Democrats sought to achieve elusive consensus over the size and shape of the budget. After two years of discussions, the budget deal was finally passed and signed. It contained a tax credit scholarship for private school tuition: the $75 million Invest in Kids Act of 2017. Many Democrats, as well as Republicans, voted for the bill.[8]

MICHIGAN: REPEATED REFERENDUM FAILURES

Michigan has no voucher program and has limited the growth of charter schools. The state offers no financial aid in its budget for private schools' auxiliary services. Except for transportation, Michigan provides private schools with no public aid in any form. Three Michigan state ballot initiatives in 1970, 1978, and 2000, respectively, to prohibit public aid to religious schools (accepted), to establish a voucher program (rejected), and to permit the state indirectly to support nonpublic school students (rejected), demonstrated by a wide margin that Michigan would not support private schools, however indirectly.

The failed effort to enact the 2000 initiative, Proposal 1, was spearheaded by Dick and Betsy DeVos alongside the Mackinac Center, a Michigan-based free-market think tank, among others (Kronholz 2000). Clint Bolick, the Institute for Justice lawyer who litigated multiple voucher cases during the

[8] The Invest in Kids Act (SB1947) passed the Illinois House (which was controlled by Democrats 67–51) by a vote of 73–34 and the Senate (controlled by Democrats 37–22) by a vote of 38–13.

1990s and 2000s, attributes the failure of the Michigan voucher efforts to the fact that "the Michigan constitution contains the most stringent anti-school choice language in the nation, crafted precisely by the teachers unions in the 1960s to achieve that distinction" (Bolick 2003, 153).

MISSOURI: NO VOUCHERS DESPITE REPUBLICAN CONTROL

Unlike Illinois, neighboring Missouri had Republican control of at least one legislative chamber since 2001 and unified Republican government for six of those years. Yet despite many legislative efforts during successive legislative sessions, no voucher bill passed. At least twenty voucher bills were introduced since 2010, but none except a 2016 tax credit scholarship bill, HB1589, even received a vote in committee. A Republican state senator reflected upon the limited progress that the voucher cause had made in the state:

> How far in the legislature doesn't always mean a whole lot, because there may be a barrier that you may be closer to every time, but you never really get to the point where you can overcome that barrier. I think that's kind of where we are. We continue to move choice elements forward, maybe a little bit further each year, but the stopping point has never really changed, so even though we're getting closer to it, that doesn't mean we're getting closer to overcoming it. (Emery 2018)

Like Texas and Michigan, Missouri is unusual among Republican-controlled states in its repeated failure to pass voucher legislation of any kind. Chapter 5 considers the circumstances of these red states and explains their continued failure to enact a core Republican policy commitment.

OHIO: EARLY SUCCESS AND CONTINUED VOUCHER PASSAGE

Ohio operates what is arguably the most famous voucher program in America: the Ohio Cleveland Scholarship Program, which survived Supreme Court challenge in the *Zelman* v. *Simmons-Harris* decision of 2002.[9] Launched in 1995 through the efforts of Ohio governor George Voinovich and his business allies, the Cleveland program was the first in the nation to include religious schools from its inception. Emboldened by the 5–4 Supreme Court decision in *Zelman*, the Ohio state legislature passed further four voucher programs.

In 2003, the legislature wrote the Autism Scholarship Program, the nation's only private school choice program designed exclusively for autistic children, into law. In 2005, the legislature passed the Educational

[9] *Zelman* v. *Simmons-Harris*, 536 US 639 (2002).

Choice Scholarship Program for children in low-performing schools. The Jon Peterson Special Needs Scholarship and the Income-Based Scholarship Program were enacted in 2011 and 2013, respectively. All five Ohioan voucher programs operate today.

Ohio also experienced one of the largest expansions of charter schools in the United States during the past few decades. In the 2000–01 school year, there were seventy-one charter schools in Ohio (Bodwell 2018). By March 2017, 362 charter schools were operating in the state, enrolling a larger proportion of public school students (7.7 percent) than the national average (4.6 percent) (Ohio Department of Education 2017). The state operates two line items in its state budget for auxiliary services to private religious schools, offering state funding for school equipment, textbooks, transportation, and maintenance.

UTAH: VOUCHERS FALL BY REFERENDUM

Unlike Florida, Ohio, and Louisiana, Utah has only one small voucher program in existence. In 1896, when Utah finally became a state after several failed attempts, it was required to pass a no-aid provision (NAP) or Blaine Amendment in the first state constitution as one of the conditions for its entrance to the Union. A NAP is a constitutional provision prohibiting the granting of public aid to denominational institutions, including religious schools. No legislation was ever passed in Utah to provide aid for children at private religious schools, perhaps because the state was mindful of the strict conditions laid down by a federal Congress openly suspicious of the Church of Jesus Christ of Latter-Day Saints (LDS).

In 1986, the Utah Constitutional Revision Commission inserted the word "direct" into its NAP, but this move was surprisingly inconsequential. No record exists of the debate that occurred before this insertion, and the changing of the wording was not widely noted. Nor was the change consequential for children at private religious schools because the state provided no aid to such students until the passage of the Carson Smith Special Needs Voucher in 2005. The Carson Smith Program covers only a small section of the student population: those with disabilities. The state offers no other voucher or tax credit programs.

In 2007, the legislature passed HB 148 and HB 174, "Education vouchers" and "Education Voucher Amendments," respectively, to establish a generous statewide educational voucher program (Mero 2007). The former bill was passed by a single vote in the Utah House of Representatives, but both passed the state senate by wide margins and were signed into law by Governor Jon Huntsman. However, a 2007 referendum on the issue – initiated by the teachers' union, the Utah Education Association, and its parent National Education Association – found voters overwhelmingly opposed, and the program was revoked before it could take effect. Although Utah has embraced charter schools with enthusiasm, the 2007 referendum eliminated the voucher option for the foreseeable future.

VOUCHER TARGETING

Vouchers vary by target and take-up. Some are restricted to children with disabilities, low-income families, veteran-headed households, or children in foster care. Scholarships for children with disabilities run at a higher average cost because many recipients require expensive specialist equipment (EdChoice 2018). By contrast, scholarships aimed at low-income urban children are typically used at urban parochial schools that charge lower fees than their nonsectarian and rural counterparts. In 2007–08, the average private school fee was $8,549, but for Catholic schools, it was just $6,018 (National Center for Education Statistics, Schools and Staffing Survey (SASS) 2009). Catholic schools form almost half the total number of urban private schools, twice as numerous as nonsectarian urban private schools and more than four times as numerous as urban private schools of any other faith (Private School Universe Survey 2010). Their abundance is rooted in the period of combat between accommodationist and secularist forces during the nineteenth century, in which Catholic children were required to submit to Protestant practices in public schools (Hackett 2016). Many joined parochial schools as a result.

Table A2 gives examples of selected voucher schemes to illustrate the range of voucher policy designs and targets. This table is by no means exhaustive and is intended for illustrative purposes only.

THE MODERN VOUCHER LANDSCAPE

In this modern period, voucher programs stretch from Montana to Maryland and from New Hampshire to Nevada. Enrollments have grown to more than half a million children nationwide, across thirty states. In 2015, by my estimate, 665,759 students used some form of voucher. Southern legislatures have recently begun to embrace vouchers enthusiastically. Mississippi and Virginia passed their first modern voucher programs in 2012; Alabama and both Carolinas in 2013. By 2016, all seven of the original segregation tuition grant states had passed new voucher bills. Indeed, Alabama, Georgia, Louisiana, Mississippi, and

TABLE A2. *Vouchers, tax credit vouchers, and education savings account schemes by state, value, and participation (selected examples)*

State	Name	Average value per family ($)	Participating students
	Targeted at disabled students		
FL	John McKay Scholarship	7,193 (2017–18)	30,425 (2018–19)
OH	Jon Peterson Special Needs Scholarship	9,818 (2016–17)	4,930 (2016–17)
OK	Lindsey Nicole Henry Scholarships for Students with Disabilities	6,161 (2017–18)	669 (2018–19)
SC	Educational Credit for Exceptional Needs Children	5,136 (2016–17)	1,972 (2016–17)
TN	Individualized Education Account Program	5,092 (2017–18)	87 (2018–19)
UT	Carson Smith Special Needs Scholarship	5,905 (2016–17)	882 (2018–19)
	Targeted at low-income students		
AZ	Low-Income Corporate Income Tax Credit Scholarship Program	1,892 (2014–15)	16,573 (2014–15)
IA	School Tuition Organization Tax Credit	1,683 (2016–17)	10,771 (2016–17)
LA	Louisiana Scholarship Program	5,869 (2016–17)	6,995 (2016–17)
MD	Broadening Options and Opportunities for Students Today (BOOST)	2,294 (2017–18)	2,659 (2018–19)
WA	Opportunity Scholarship Program	9,570 (2016–17)	1,154 (2016–17)
WI	Milwaukee Parental Choice Program	7,503 (2017–18)	28,702 (2018–19)

(continued)

TABLE A2 *(continued)*

State	Name	Average value per family ($) (2017–18)	Participating students (2018)
Targeted at students in low-performing schools			
AL	Accountability Act of 2013 Parent-Taxpayer Refundable Tax Credits	2,425 (2016)	122 (2016)
OH	Educational Choice Scholarship Program	4,257 (2014–15)	22,892 (2016–17)
Multiple targets (foster care, children of military, etc.)			
AR	Succeed Scholarship Program	6,713	151
IN	Choice Scholarship	4,342	35,458
Universal (available to all students)			
AZ	Individual Income Tax Credit Scholarship	1,724 (2015–16)	31,578 (2015–16)
IA	Tuition and Textbook Tax Credit	116 (2015)	133,122 (2015)
MT	Tax Credits for Contributions to Scholarship Organizations	500 (2016–17)	25 (2016–17)
OH	Cleveland Scholarship Program	4,620 (2016–17)	8,594 (2016–17)

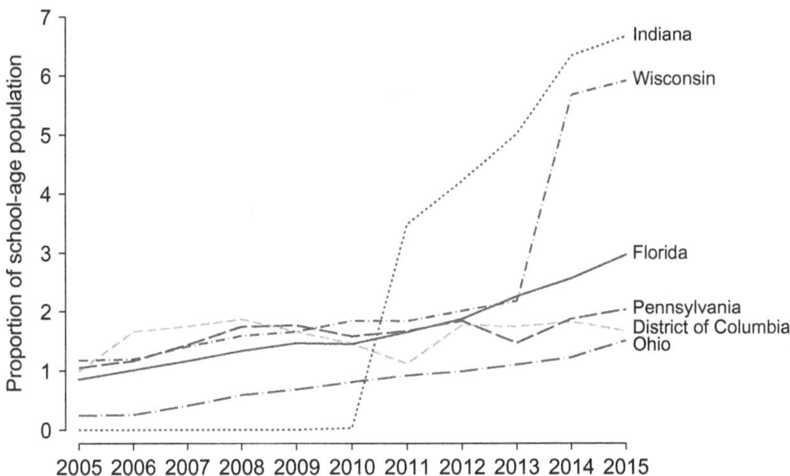

FIGURE A2. Growth of enrollments in voucher programs as a proportion of the school-age population in selected states, 2005–2015. *Sources*: Edchoice.org; US Census 1990, 2000, and 2010.

South Carolina each had more than one such program. Figure A2 displays the growth of enrollments in voucher programs as a proportion of the school-age population in selected states.

As Figure A2 shows, vouchers serve around 6–7 percent of the school-age population in school choice hot spots, Indiana and Wisconsin. That is three times as many, proportionately, as were served by tuition grants in the Deep South after *Brown*. Some states conspicuously failed to pass such programs, however. None of the three most populous states (California, Texas, and New York) had passed vouchers by 2019. New York and California were bastions of the liberal, increasingly Democratic, race-conscious alliance, so their absence is unremarkable. In Texas at least six legislative efforts to enact vouchers failed in committee or on the floor, defeated by Democrats and rural legislators fearing the loss of public school provision and associated jobs (Garrett 2017). I unpack the puzzle of the nonoccurrence of vouchers in Republican states in Chapter 5.[10]

Figure A3 displays the number of voucher programs in operation by state in June 2019. More than half of the states have some form of voucher, tax credit, or education savings account (ESA) program;

[10] Opposition to vouchers in Texas comes from an alliance of Democrats and Republican lawmakers with rural and suburban constituencies. For example, in the 2017 votes on SB1, a failed voucher bill, 62 percent of Republican lawmakers from less urbanized districts (those with an urbanized population of less than 80 percent according to the US Census Bureau) voted against vouchers, while 67 percent of Republican lawmakers

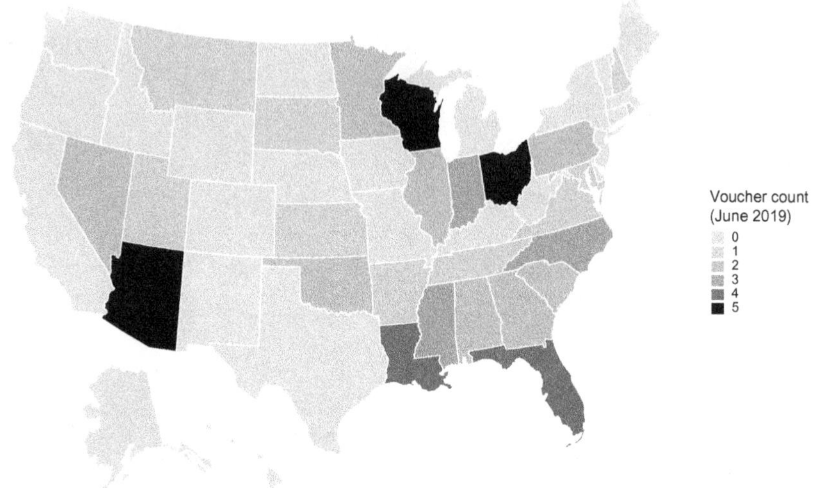

FIGURE A3. Number of voucher programs in operation by state in June 2019.

TABLE A3. *Southern states' years of first modern voucher program*

AL	2013	LA	2008	OK	2010
AR	2015	MD	2016	SC	2013
FL	1999	MS	2012	TN	2015
GA	2007	NC	2013	VA	2012

Source: Friedman Foundation for Educational Choice; National Conference of State Legislatures.

twenty-three states do not. Of the states that operate voucher programs, the five key centers of school choice are Arizona, Florida, Louisiana, Ohio, and Wisconsin, shown in dark gray in Figure A3.

There are also regional disparities on display in Figure A2. All but four southern states boast vouchers. These programs have expanded across the South relatively recently: those in Alabama, Arkansas, Maryland, North Carolina, South Carolina, and Tennessee were enacted in 2013 or later (Table A3).

from more urbanized districts (greater than 80 percent urbanization) voted in favor. In short, Texan Republicans from less urban districts helped scupper voucher bills alongside Democrats. This opposition may be related to practical questions about the viability of school choice in less-populated areas and concern about loss of public school jobs as much as fears of government regulation of private religious schools or perceptions of racial threat to white suburban school districts.

TABLE A4. *Attenuating and direct rhetoric cited in voucher cases*

Attenuating rhetoric: disclaiming government responsibility for policy outputs		
Speaker	**Attenuating rhetoric**	**Cited in**
Delegate, Colorado Constitutional Convention, 1876	The best way to avoid corruption is to distribute decision-making authority "to as small a degree as possible, and bring it home to each district. It should be left to the people at home."	*Owens* v. *Colorado Congress Of Parents Teachers* (2004)
James Lindsay Almond (Attorney General of Virginia), 1955	"Item 210 is not an appropriation *directly to* the institutions which the eligible children may attend, but is an appropriation to the parents or guardians of such children, is primarily for the benefit of such children, and only incidentally for the benefit of the selected private schools."	*Almond* v. *Day* (1955)
State Educational Finance Commission of Mississippi, 1969	The purpose of our bill is "to encourage the education of all of the children of Mississippi" and "to afford each individual freedom in choosing public or private schooling."	*Coffey* v. *State Educational Finance Commission* (1969)
Penny Kotterman (President of the Arizona Education Association), 1999	Credits are constitutionally different from deductions. A tax credit is the "functional equivalent of depleting the state treasury by a direct grant," while a tax deduction merely serves as "seed money" to encourage philanthropy.	*Kotterman* v. *Killian* (1999)
Daniel Boyd (Lowndes County, Alabama, Schools Superintendent), 2015	"[B]y appropriating public funds in this manner, the [program] effectively provides for an appropriation to educational institutions that are not under the absolute control of the State."	*Magee* v. *Boyd* (2015)

(continued)

TABLE A4 *(continued)*

Speaker	Attenuating rhetoric	Cited in
Julie Magee (Commissioner of Revenue) and Thomas L. White Jr. (Comptroller of the State of Alabama), 2015	"The tax-credit program … does not redirect or un-earmark the income-tax revenues that do enter the public coffers."	*Magee* v. *Boyd* (2015)
Julie Magee (Commissioner of Revenue) and Thomas L. White Jr. (Comptroller of the State of Alabama), 2015	"Because the [program] provides funds directly to parents and not to the nonpublic schools, the funds are not being improperly used to support religious schools."	*Magee* v. *Boyd* (2015)
Julie Magee (Commissioner of Revenue) and Thomas L. White Jr. (Comptroller of the State of Alabama), 2015	"Tax-credit programs are religiously neutral student-assistance programs under which parents are free to choose religious and nonreligious schools."	*Magee* v. *Boyd* (2015)
Julie Magee (Commissioner of Revenue) and Thomas L. White Jr. (Comptroller of the State of Alabama), 2015	"Although the payment of refundable tax credits does use public funds, those funds are paid to, and used for the support of, parents and students, not religious schools."	*Magee* v. *Boyd* (2015)
Julie Magee (Commissioner of Revenue) and Thomas L. White Jr. (Comptroller of the State of Alabama), 2015	"The [program] does not use any funds that have been raised for the support of public schools because the scholarships are funded by voluntary private donations, not by public funds."	*Magee* v. *Boyd* (2015)

Direct rhetoric: taking direct responsibility for policy outputs		
Speaker	Direct rhetoric	Cited in
Sidney C. Day (Comptroller of Virginia), 1955	"The provision for the payment of tuition, institutional fees and other designated expenses at a private school, to be attended by children eligible under the Act, is a direct and substantial aid to such institution."	*Almond* v. *Day* (1955)
Wade O. Martin (Secretary of State of Louisiana), 1960	Louisiana [will] go from public to private schools so that every child would have a check or money to go to the school of his choice; the white schools would accept white students, and the "black schools" would accept Negro students.	*Poindexter* v. *Louisiana Financial Assistance Commission* (1967)
Frank Voelker Jr. (Chairman of the Louisianan State Sovereignty Commission), 1961	"If the present grants in aid is carried to the federal courts it probably would be knocked out because it is really the state operating the schools."	*Poindexter* v. *Louisiana Financial Assistance Commission* (1967)
Louisianan Representative Risley Triche (Administration Floor Leader and Sponsor of Act 2), 1961	"[The bill] does not authorize any school system to operate integrated schools. We haven't changed our position one iota. This bill allows the voters to change to a private segregated school system. That's all that it's intended to do. I don't think we want to fall into the trap of authorizing integrated schools by the votes of the people. This bill doesn't allow that and we're not falling into that trap."	*Poindexter* v. *Louisiana Financial Assistance Commission* (1967)

(continued)

TABLE A4 *(continued)*

Speaker	Direct rhetoric	Cited in
President pro tempore of the Louisiana Senate, 1961	"As I see it, Louisiana is entering into a new phase in its battle to maintain its segregated school system. The keystone to this new phase is the local option plan we have under consideration."	*Poindexter* v. *Louisiana Financial Assistance Commission* (1967)
Louisianan Representative Wellborn Jack, 1961	"It gives the people an opportunity to help fight to keep the schools segregated. We are the ones who have been speaking for segregation. This is going to give the people in all 64 parishes the right to speak by going to the polls. This is just to recruit more people to keep our schools segregated, and we're going to do it in spite of the federal government, the brainwashers and the Communists."	*Poindexter* v. *Louisiana Financial Assistance Commission* (1967)
James D. Fountain (Assistant Director of the Louisiana Sovereignty Commission), 1962	"I think we can operate within our present revenues, unless there is a mass integration effort."	*Poindexter* v. *Louisiana Financial Assistance Commission* (1967)
Alabama Governor George C. Wallace, 1963	The threat of integration "is detrimental to the public interest" and the "integration of the public schools will totally disrupt and effectively destroy the educational process."	*Lee* v. *Macon County Board of Education* (1964)
Alabama State Superintendent of Education, 1963	"Teachers, administrators and parents have firmly held the line for our way-of-life and in opposition to misguided parents who have tried to force the entry of their children into schools for a different race."	*Lee* v. *Macon County Board of Education* (1964)

Alabama State Board of Education, 1964	"BE IT RESOLVED That the State Board of Education deplores the order of Judge Johnson and pledges every resource at our command to defend the people of our State against every order of the Federal courts in attempting to integrate the public schools of this State and will use every legal means at our command to defeat said integration orders and pledges our full support to the local boards of education in supporting the public school system as now constituted with the law, and will give every assistance possible to support every effort to maintain our way of life and high educational standards for all citizens of our State."	*Lee* v. *Macon County Board of Education* (1964)
Alabama State Board of Education, 1964	We will "defend the people of our State against every order of the Federal courts in attempting to integrate the public schools of this State and will use every legal means at our command to defeat said integration orders and pledges our full support to the local boards of education in supporting the public school systems as now constituted."	*Lee* v. *Macon County Board of Education* (1964)
E. W. Gravolet Jr. (Chairman of the Louisiana Financial Assistance Commission), 1964	[Letter distributed during the second gubernatorial primary election in January 1964] "I enclose a New Orleans clipping showing Morrison's statement that he is unalterably opposed to state grant-in-aid to help your children go to a private segregated school of your choice, instead of having to go to a racially integrated school. Your only hope to continue to get school checks to help your children go to private schools is by electing John McKeithen governor on Saturday, January 11. E. W. Gravolet, Jr. Chairman Louisiana Financial Assistance Commission."	*Poindexter* v. *Louisiana Financial Assistance Commission* (1967)

(continued)

TABLE A4 *(continued)*

Speaker	Direct rhetoric	Cited in
Charles LaCoste (Former Director of the Carrollton Elementary School), 1967	"The basic purpose for the organization of the school was to avoid public school desegregation and ... the existence of tuition grants allowed that purpose to be accomplished."	*Poindexter* v. *Louisiana Financial Assistance Commission* (1967)
Nebraskan Senator Terry Carpenter, 1972	"We have a large number, not a large, a number of privately owned schools of all denominations who I think, as I recall, have about anywhere from 12-1500 vacancies in their dormitories and area of education in which they cannot fill. Now if we don't do something for these private schools, they're going to have to close the doors to some of them.'"	*Rogers* v. *Swanson* (1974)
Nebraskan Senator Terry Carpenter, 1972	"I would like to find some legal way in order to have the state make a contribution, either in the bill or any other area, in order to use up the unused parts of these private schools."	*Rogers* v. *Swanson* (1974)
Nebraskan Senator E. Thome Johnson, 1972	"Mr. President, members of the legislature, it has been brought out that there are campuses over the state where fine facilities, fine instructors, but they lack students."	*Rogers* v. *Swanson* (1974)
Nebraskan Senator Harold Moylan, 1972	"Now it's not only a thing of keeping these colleges alive, it's the case of financial assessts [*sic*] to the state."	*Rogers* v. *Swanson* (1974)

TABLE A5. *No-aid provision strength: full scoring by criterion*

A: Direct and indirect aid forbidden?		
Doesn't mention (–1)	**Only direct (–2)**	**Direct and indirect (0)**
AL, AZ, AR 1868, CO, DE 1967, DE 1897, DC, ID, IL, IN, IA, KS, KY, LA 1879, MA 1855, MA 1917, MA 1974, MI 1835, MI 1850, MN, MS 1890, MS 1868, NE 1875, NE 1976, NV 1864, NV 1880, NH, NJ 1844, NM, ND, OH, OR, PA 1874, PA 1975, SD, TX, UT 1896, VA, WA, WI 1848, WI 1967, WI 1972, WY	AK, SC, UT 1986	CA, FL, GA, HI, MI 1970, MO, MT, NY 1894, NY 1938, OK
B: Tone of No-Aid Provision language		
Strident (0)	**Not Strident (–1)**	**Placatory (–2)**
CA, CO, DC, IL, KY, MA 1917, MA 1974, MI 1970, MS 1890, MT, NV 1880, NM, OK, OR, SD, WY	AL, AK, AZ, AR 1868, FL, GA, ID, IN, IA, KS, LA 1879, MI 1850, MN, MS 1868, NV 1864, NH, ND, PA 1874, PA 1975, SC, TX, UT 1896, UT 1986, VA, WI 1848, WI 1967, WI 1972, WA	DE 1897, DE 1967, HI, MA 1855, MI 1835, MO, NE 1875, NE 1976, NJ 1844, NY 1894, NY 1938, OH

(continued)

TABLE A5 *(continued)*

C: Extent of explicit no-aid provision bans		
Only public appropriations (–2)	**Money plus property/land (–1)**	**Long list of bans (0)**
AL, AK, AR 1868, DE 1897, DE 1967, FL, GA, IN, IA, KS, KY, LA 1879, MA 1855, MI 1835, MS 1890, MS 1868, NE 1976, NE 1875, NV 1864, NV 1880, NH, NJ 1844, ND, OH, OK, OR, PA 1874, PA 1975, SC, UT 1896, UT 1986, WI, 1848, WI 1967, WI 1972, WY	AZ, CO, DC, HI, ID, IL, MI 1850, MN, MO, MT, NM, NY 1938, NY 1894, TX, VA, WA	CA, MA 1917, MA 1974, MI 1970, SD

D: Qualifications and exceptions	
Qualifying statement supportive of religion (–1)	**Exceptions to no-aid provision bans (–2)**
CO, FL, HI, MO, NE 1875, UT 1896, UT 1986, WI 1848, WI 1967, WI 1972	CA, DE 1897, DE 1967, HI, ID, MA 1917, MA 1974, MI 1970, MO, NE, NY 1938, PA 1975, WI 1967, WI 1972

E: No no-aid provision (–10)
AR 1874, CT, LA 1975, ME, MD, NJ 1948, NC, RI, TN, VT, WV

TABLE A6. *No-aid provision scoring table*

State	A	B	C	D	E	Score
AL	−1	−1	−2	0		6
AK	−2	−1	−2	0		5
AZ	−1	−1	−1	0		7
AR (1868)	−1	−1	−2	0		6
AR (1874)					−10	0
CA	0	0	0	2		8
CO	−1	0	−1	−1		7
CT					−10	0
DE (1897)	−1	−2	−2	−2		3
DE (1967)	−1	−2	−2	−3		2
DC	−1	0	−1	0		8
FL	0	−1	−2	−1		6
GA	0	−1	−2	0		7
HI	0	−2	−1	−3		4
ID	−1	−1	−1	−2		5
IL	−1	0	−1	0		8
IN	−1	−1	−2	0		6
IA	−1	−1	−2	0		6
KS	−1	−1	−2	0		6
KY	−1	0	−2	0		7
LA (1879)	−1	−1	−2	0		6
LA (1975)					−10	0
ME					−10	0
MD					−10	0
MA (1855)	−1	−2	−2	0		5
MA (1917)	−1	0	0	−2		7
MA (1974)	−1	0	0	−2		7
MI (1835)	−1	−2	−2	0		5
MI (1850)	−1	−1	−1	0		7
MI (1970)	0	0	0	−2		8
MN	−1	−1	−1	0		7
MS (1868)	−1	−1	−2	0		6
MS (1890)	−1	0	−2	0		7
MO	0	−2	−1	−3		4
MT	0	0	−1	0		9

(continued)

TABLE A6 *(continued)*

State	A	B	C	D	E	Score
NE (1875)	−1	−2	−2	−1		4
NE (1976)	−1	−2	−2	−3		2
NV (1864)	−1	−1	−2	0		6
NV (1880)	−1	0	−2	0		7
NH	−1	−1	−2	0		6
NJ (1844)	−1	−2	−2	0		5
NJ (1948)					−10	0
NM	−1	0	−1	0		8
NY (1894)	0	−2	−1	0		7
NY (1938)	0	−2	−1	−2		5
NC					−10	0
ND	−1	−1	−2	0		6
OH	−1	−2	−2	0		5
OK	0	0	−2	0		8
OR	−1	0	−2	0		7
PA	−1	−1	−2	−2		4
RI					−10	0
SC	−2	−1	−2	0		5
SD	−1	0	0	0		9
TN					−10	0
TX	−1	−1	−1	0		7
UT (1896)	−1	−1	−2	−1		5
UT (1986)	−2	−1	−2	−1		4
VT					−10	0
VA	−1	−1	−1	0		7
WA	−1	−1	−1	0		7
WV					−10	0
WI (1848)	−1	−1	−2	−1		5
WI (1967)	−1	−1	−2	−3		3
WI (1972)	−1	−1	−2	−3		3
WY	−1	0	−2	0		7

TABLE A7. *States listed with no-aid provision scores*

AL	6	ME	0	NY (1938)	5
AK	5	MD	0	NC	0
AZ	7	MA (1855)	5	ND	6
AR (1868)	6	MA (1917)	7	OH	5
AR (1874)	0	MA (1974)	7	OK	8
CA	8	MI (1835)	5	OR	7
CO	7	MI (1850)	7	PA	4
CT	0	MI (1970)	8	RI	0
DE (1897)	3	MN	7	SC	5
DE (1967)	2	MS (1868)	6	SD	9
DC	8	MS (1890)	7	TN	0
FL	6	MO	4	TX	7
GA	7	MT	9	UT (1896)	5
HI	4	NE (1875)	4	UT (1986)	4
ID	5	NE (1976)	2	VT	0
IL	8	NV (1864)	6	VA	7
IN	6	NV (1880)	7	WA	7
IA	6	NH	6	WV	0
KS	6	NJ (1844)	5	WI (1848)	5
KY	7	NJ (1948)	0	WI (1967)	3
LA (1879)	6	NM	8	WI (1972)	3
LA (1975)	0	NY (1894)	7	WY	7

TABLE A8. *Successful and selected unsuccessful voucher bills, 2005–17*

State	Bill number	Voucher type	Year	Relevant law
		Successful bills		
OH Educational Choice Scholarship Program	HB66 (Sec. 3310.03)	Voucher	2005	Ohio Rev. Code §§ 3310.01 through 17
UT Carson Smith Special Needs Scholarships	HB249	Voucher	2005	Utah Code 53A-1a-701 through 710
AZ Low-Income Corporate Income Tax Credit Scholarship	SB1499/HB2154	Tax credit	2006	Ariz. Rev. Stat. §§ 43-1183; 43-1501 through 1507; and 20-224.06
IA School Tuition Organization Tax Credit	SF2409	Tax credit	2006	Iowa Stat. § 422.11S
RI Tax Credits for Contributions to Scholarship organizations	H 7120Aam	Tax credit	2006	R.I.G.L. §§ 44-62-1 through 44-62-7
GA Special Needs Scholarship	SB10	Voucher	2007	O.C.G.A. §§ 20-2-2110 through 20-2-2118
GA Qualified Education Expense Tax Credit	HB1133	Tax credit	2008	O.C.G.A. §§ 20-2A-1 through 7 and 48-7-29.16
LA Elementary and Secondary School Tuition Deduction	SB5	Tax credit	2008	La. Rev. Stat. §§ 47:293(9)(a)(xiv) and 297.10
LA Scholarship Program	HB1347	Voucher	2008	La. Rev. Stat. §§ 17:4011 through 4025
AZ Lexie's Law for Disabled and Displaced Students Tax Credit Scholarships	HB2001	Tax credit	2009	Ariz. Rev. Stat. §§ 15-891; 43-1184; 43-1501 through 1507; and 20-224.07
IN School Scholarship Tax Credit	Budget (HB1001) and SB528	Tax credit	2009	Ind. Code §§ 6-3.1-30.5 and 20-51-1 through 3
LA School Choice Program for Certain Students with Exceptionalities	HB216	Voucher	2010	La. Rev. Stat. § 17:4031
OK Lindsey Nicole Henry Scholarships for Students with Disabilities	HB3393	Voucher	2010	Okla. Stat. §§ 70-13-101.1 and 101.2

AZ Empowerment Scholarship Accounts	SB1553	ESA	2011	Ariz. Rev. Stat. §§ 15-2401 through 2404
IN Private School/Homeschool Deduction	HB1003	Tax credit	2011	Ind. Code § 6-3-2-22
IN Choice Scholarships	HB1003	Voucher	2011	Ind. Code §§ 20-51-1 through 4
OK Equal Opportunity Scholarships	SB969	Tax credit	2011	Okla. Rev. Stat. § 68-2357.206
OH Jon Peterson Special Needs Scholarship Program	HB153 (budget)	Voucher	2011	Ohio Rev. Code §§ 3310.51 through 64
WI Parental Private School Choice (Racine)	AB40	Voucher	2011	Wis. Stat. § 118.60
LA Tuition Donation Rebate Program	HB969	Tax credit	2012	La. Rev. Stat. § 47:6301
NH Education Tax Credit Program	SB372	Tax credit	2012	N.H. Rev. Stat. §§ 77-G:1 through 10
PA Opportunity Scholarship Tax Credit Program	HB761	Tax credit	2012	72 P.S. §§ 8701-G.1 through 8712-G.1
VA Education Improvement Scholarships Tax Credits Program	SB131	Tax credit	2012	Code of Va. §§ 58.1-439.25-28
MS Dyslexia Therapy Scholarship for Students with Dyslexia	HB1031	Voucher	2012	Miss. Code Ann. §§ 37-173-1 through 31
AZ "Switcher" Individual Income Tax Credit Scholarships	SB1047	Tax credit	2012	Ariz. Rev. Stat. § 43-1089.03
NC Special Education Scholarship Grants for Children with Disabilities	HB269	Voucher	2013	N.C. Rev. Stat. §§ 115C-112.5–9
AL Education Scholarship Program	HB84	Tax credit	2013	Ala. Code §§ 40-2A-7(a)(5) and 16-6D
AL Accountability Act of 2013 Parent-Taxpayer Refundable Tax Credits	HB84	Tax credit	2013	Ala. Code §§ 40-2A-7(a)(5) and 16-6D
SC Educational Credit for Exceptional Needs Children	Budget	Tax credit	2013	S.C. State Budget Proviso 109.15

(continued)

TABLE A8 *(continued)*

State	Bill number	Voucher type	Year	Relevant law
MS Nate Rogers Scholarship for Students with Disabilities	HB896	Voucher	2013	Miss. Code Ann. §§ 37-175-1 through 29
NC Opportunity Scholarships	SB402/HB944	Voucher	2013	N.C. Rev. Stat. §§ 115C-562.1 through 562.7
OH Income-Based Scholarship Program	HB59	Voucher	2013	Ohio Rev. Code § 3310.032
WI K–12 Private School Tuition Deduction	AB40	Tax credit	2013	Wis. Stat. § 71.05(6)(b)49
WI Parental Choice Program	AB40	Voucher	2013	Wis. Stat. § 118.60
FL Personal Learning Scholarship Account Program	SB850	ESA	2014	Fla. Stat. §§ 393.063 & 1002.385
KS Tax Credit for Low Income Students Scholarships	HB2506	Tax credit	2014	K.S.A. §§ 72-99a01(Supp) through 72-99a07 (Supp); 79-32,138 (Supp)
MS Equal Opportunity for Students with Special Needs Program	SB2695	ESA	2015	Miss. Code Ann. §§ 37-181-1 through 21
MT Tax Credits for Contributions to Student Scholarship Organizations	SB410	Tax credit	2015	Mont. Code Ann. §§ 15-30-3101 through 3114
NV Education Savings Accounts	SB302	ESA	2015	N.R.S. §§ 353B.850-880; 388D.100-140; 392.070(3)
NV Educational Choice Scholarships	AB165	Tax credit	2015	N.R.S. 388D.250 through 280
SC Refundable Educational Credit for Exceptional Needs Children	Budget	Tax credit	2015	S.C. State Budget Proviso 109.15
TN Individualized Education Account Program	SB0027	ESA	2015	Tenn. Code Ann. §§ 49-10-1401 through 1406

AR Succeed Scholarship Program for Students with Disabilities	HB1552 (Act 1178)	Voucher	2015	Ark. Code Ann. §§ 6-41-801 through 807
WI Special Needs Scholarship Program	SB615 (Act 289)	Voucher	2015	Wis. Stat. §115.7915
MD Broadening Options and Opportunities for Students Today (BOOST) Program	SB190	Voucher	2016	Fiscal 2017 Budget Bill § R00A03.05
SD Partners in Education Tax Credit Program	SB159	Tax credit	2016	S.D. Codified Laws §§ 13-65-1 through 12
Failed bills				
IL	SB2494	Voucher	2010	
TN	SB196	Voucher	2014	
ID	HB507	Tax credit	2014	
TX	SB1	ESA	2017	
AK	SB746	Tax credit	2017	
CO	SB39	Tax credit	2017	
VA	HB1605	ESA	2017	
AR	HB1222	ESA	2017	
WY	HB228	Tax credit	2017	
TN	SB161	Voucher	2017	
TN	SB380	Voucher	2017	
NH	HB647	ESA	2017	

Despite the South's recent expansion of vouchers, two of the most prolific voucher-creating states, as shown in Figure A2, are in the Midwest: Wisconsin and Ohio. Other prolific voucher states include Arizona, Florida, and Louisiana (Tables A4–A9).

MULTILEVEL LOGISTIC REGRESSION RESULTS

TABLE A9. *Individual legislator votes on successful and unsuccessful voucher bills, 2005–17*

Individual-level variables		
Partisan affiliation (Republican)		5.080*** (0.258)
Sex (male)		0.311** (0.137)
Race (black)		−0.392* (0.231)
Government workers in district (%)		−3.500*** (1.323)
African Americans in district (%)		0.021*** (0.006)
Ideological conservatism of district (MRP)		0.747*** (0.292)
Private school enrolment in district (%)		0.015*** (0.004)
State-level variables		
Right to Work state at time of passage		−3.643*** (0.732)
State unionization rate (%)		−0.682*** (0.128)
State expenditure on education (%)		−0.204** (0.090)
Program-level variables		
Partisanship of sponsor (Republican)		−0.085 (0.188)
Gender of sponsor (male)		0.402** (0.200)
Target population (reference category: universal programs for all students)	Disabled children	0.881*** (0.228)
	Low-income children	1.076*** (0.217)
	Students in failing schools	2.338*** (0.571)
	Mixture of targets	0.209 (0.258)
Submergence of policy (Deeply submerged)		*0.372** (0.164)*
Constant		13.211*** (3.846)

N: 6,026; $p < 0.01$***; $p < 0.05$**; $p < 0.1$*.

ADDRESSING SELECTION CONCERNS

To address selection concerns, I gathered and amalgamated data on bills that (a) died without votes ($N = 116$), (b) died after a failed vote ($N = 12$), and (c) passed ($N = 47$) during the period 2005–17.

Due to the very large number of failed bills, I used a random number generator in Excel to select states for data gathering. The sample of failed

TABLE A10. *Modeling the likelihood of a voucher vote being held: logistic regression with standard errors clustered by state*

Partisanship of bill sponsor (Republican)		−0.127 (0.601)
Gender of bill sponsor (male)		−0.794* (0.447)
Target population (reference category: universal program; all students)	Disabled students	−0.827* (0.430)
	Low-income students	−0.745 (0.541)
	Students in failing schools	−1.64* (0.873)
	Multiple target categories	−0.953* (0.563)
Program design (reference category: voucher)	Tax credit scholarship	−0.220 (0.466)
	ESA	−0.623 (0.443)
Region (reference category: Northeast)	Midwest	1.779 (1.346)
	South	1.586 (1.169)
	West	1.046 (1.208)
Constant		−0.416 (1.120)

N: 170; Pseudo R^2: 0.0836.
$p < 0.01$***; $p < 0.05$**; $p < 0.1$*

TABLE A11. *Logistic regression with clustered standard errors: individual judicial opinions, dissents, and concurrences in voucher cases, 1955–2017*

Partisan affiliation (Republican)	0.870**(0.423)
Sex (male)	0.416 (0.440)
Race (white)	0.822* (0.456)
Year of challenge	0.068*** (0.015)
No-aid provision strength	0.032 (0.104)
Submergence of policy (deeply submerged)	0.947** (0.419)
Region	
Northeast	−0.288 (0.694)
Midwest	0.388 (0.548)
West	−1.429*** (0.480)
Constant	−138.051*** (30.190)

N: 236; Pseudo R^2: 0.249; $p < 0.01$***; $p < 0.05$**; $p < 0.1$*.

bills used in this analysis represents the universe of failed bills in the selected states for this time period. Random generation produced a sample of states that varies widely by region and existing voucher programs.

I modeled the likelihood of a vote being held (dichotomous DV: vote held/not held) by bill and state-level characteristics: the partisanship and gender of the bill sponsor, the type of program proposed (tax credit,

TABLE A12. *Program age at time of legal challenge by decision*

	Decision			
Program age at time of legal challenge (years)	Constitutional	Unconstitutional	% Constitutional	% Unconstitutional
<1	12	16	43	57
2	18	10	64	36
3	8	5	62	38
4	4	5	44	56
5–9	12	10	55	45
10–15	3	5	38	63
16–20	1	2	33	67
21–30	1	3	25	75
31–40	3	0	100	0
>41	1	4	20	80
TOTAL	63	60		

voucher, or ESA), the target population (disabled students, low-income students, students in failing schools, students living within target areas, or all students), and the region in which the bill was proposed. The unit of analysis is the bill.

The weak and insignificant relationships in Table A10 help counter concerns that there are important bill-level differences between bills that do and do not receive a vote. There is a marginal effect for some target categories and for the gender of the sponsor (bills aimed at all students, and those sponsored by women or a mix of sponsors, are slightly more likely to come to a vote than those targeting certain students or sponsored by men). But these differences are only just significant. As expected, the key proposed IV – the program design – is not statistically significant here (Tables A.11 and A.12).

References

Adler, Donna D. 1993. "The Internal Revenue Code, the Constitution, and the Courts: The Use of Tax Expenditure Analysis in Judicial Decision Making." *Wake Forest Law Review* 28 (4): 855–917.

Albertson, Bethany L. 2015. "Dog-Whistle Politics: Multivocal Communication and Religious Appeals." *Political Behavior* 37 (1): 3–26. https://doi.org/10.1007/s11109-013-9265-x.

Alito, Samuel. 2014. *Burwell* v. *Hobby Lobby Stores, Inc.*, 573 US, Supreme Court of the United States, p. 682.

Almond v. Day. (1955). Supreme Court of Virginia. 89 S.E.2d 851 (Va. 1955).

Alpert, Bruce. 2012. "Jindal Calls Teacher Unions Shameful for Opposing Private School Vouchers." *Times-Picayune,* December 11. www.nola.com/news/politics/article_137ae59c-9bd4-5035-883e-0ef1175eaace.html.

American Federation for Children. 2012. "What Public Opinion Says about School Choice: An Analysis of Attitudes toward Educational Options in America." *American Federation for Children: The Nation's Voice for School Choice.* s3.amazonaws.com/assets.clients/Afc/legacy_assets/uploads/213/original/Polling_Report.pdf?1347295528.

Appel, Conrad. 2012. Author interview with Conrad Appel, Louisianan State Senator and Chairman, Education Committee.

Arend, Harry Oscar. 1961. *Matthews* v. *Quinton*, 362 P 2d 932, Supreme Court of Alaska.

Associated Press. 1958. "Little Rock's White School Opens Monday." *Chicago Tribune*, October 18. http://archives.chicagotribune.com/1958/10/18/page/17/article/little-rocks-white-school-opens-monday.

1965a. "Tuition Grants Voted by Alabama Senate." *Washington-Times Herald*, August 8 p. A7.

1965b. "White School Faces Challenge in Selma." *New York Times*, July 28, p. 40.

1969. "NAACP Won't Appeal Tuition-Grant Ruling." *Washington-Times Herald*, February 22, p. A20.

2000a. "State School Board Votes to Oppose Vouchers." *Los Angeles Times*, July 14. http://articles.latimes.com/2000/jul/14/news/mn-53031.

2000b. "Voucher Initiative Lagging, Survey Finds." *Los Angeles Times*, October 14. http://articles.latimes.com/2000/oct/14/news/mn-36593.

2011. "State Republicans Push for Education Tax Credit Plan: Bill Would Divert Business Taxes." *News section*, December 5, p. 15. https://issuu.com/tnhstaff/docs/issue24_2011.

Bahr, Kurt. 2018. Author interview with Representative Kurt Bahr, Missouri House of Representatives.

Bailey, Sarah Pulliam. 2017. "The Supreme Court Sided with Trinity Lutheran Church. Here's Why That Matters." *Washington Post*, June 26, Sec. Acts of Faith. www.washingtonpost.com/news/acts-of-faith/wp/2017/06/26/the-supreme-court-sided-with-trinity-lutheran-church-heres-why-that-matters/.

Baldwin, Raymond E. 1960. *Snyder* v. *Newtown*, 147 Conn. 374, Supreme Court of Connecticut.

Balogh, Brian. 2009. *A Government Out of Sight: The Mystery of National Authority in Nineteenth-Century America*. Cambridge: Cambridge University Press.

Bangert, Gretchen. 2018. Author interview with Representative Gretchen Bangert, Missouri House of Representatives.

Barham, Mack. 1970. *Seegers* v. *Parker*, 241 So. 2d 213, Supreme Court of Louisiana.

Barrow, Bill. 2008. "Jindal May Back Tuition Tax Breaks." *Times-Picayune*, March 3.

2011. "American Legislative Exchange Conference Critics Say Group Too Cozy with Business." *Times-Picayune*, August 4.

Baumgartner, Frank R., and Bryan D. Jones. 1993. *Agendas and Instability in American Politics*. Chicago: University of Chicago Press.

Bedrick, Jason, Jonathan Butcher, and Clint Bolick. 2016. "Taking Credit for Education: How to Fund Education Savings Accounts through Tax Credits." Washington, DC: Cato Institute, January 20. www.cato.org/publications/policy-analysis/taking-credit-education-how-fund-education-savings-accounts-through-tax.

Bendily, Erin. 2012. Author interview with Erin Bendily, Deputy Superintendent of Policy and External Affairs at the Louisiana Department of Education.

Benjamin, Lehn M., and Paul L. Posner. 2018. "Tax Expenditures and Accountability: The Case of the Ambivalent Principals." *Journal of Public Administration Research and Theory* 28 (4): 569–582.

Berg, Thomas C. 2003. "Vouchers and Religious Schools: The New Constitutional Questions." *University of Cincinnati Law Review* 72 (1): 151–222.

Berner, Ashley, and Mai Miksic. 2014. "What Are Education Tax Credits, and Why Should We Care?" CUNY Institute for Education Policy, Roosevelt House. http://ciep.hunter.cuny.edu/education-tax-credits-care/.

Bernhard, Michael, and Daniel I. O'Neill. 2018. "The New (Ab)Normal in American Politics." *Perspectives on Politics* 16 (2): 307–10. https://doi.org/10.1017/S1537592718000713.

Bice, Daniel. 2013. "School Voucher Battle Erupts with Charges of Racism and Religious Bigotry." *Wisconsin Journal Sentinel*, May 29. http://archive.jsonline.com/newswatch/209290011.html.

Black, Justice. 1964. *Griffin* v. *County School Board of Prince Edward County (Va.)*, 377 US 218, Supreme Court of the United States.

Blanshard, Paul. 1949. *American Freedom and Catholic Power*. Boston: Beacon Press.

Bodwell, Gregory B. 2018. "Charter Schools." Case Western Reserve University. https://case.edu/ech/articles/c/charter-schools.

Boffy, Holly. 2012. Author interview with Holly Boffy, Member, Louisiana Board of Elementary and Secondary Education (BESE).

Bohannon, John. 2016. "Mechanical Turk Upends Social Sciences." *Science* 352 (6291): 1263–64. https://doi.org/10.1126/science.352.6291.1263.

Bolick, Clint. 2003. *Voucher Wars: Waging the Legal Battle over School Choice*. Washington, DC: Cato Institute.

2008. "Voting Down Vouchers: Lessons Learned from Utah." *Education Next* 8 (2): 46–51.

Bolin, Michael F. 2015. *Magee* v. *Boyd*, 175 So. 3d 79, Supreme Court of Alabama.

Bolton, Charles C. 2005. *The Hardest Deal of All: The Battle over School Integration in Mississippi, 1870–1980*. Jackson: University Press of Mississippi.

Bonastia, Christopher. 2012. *Southern Stalemate: Five Years without Public Education in Prince Edward County, Virginia*. Chicago: University of Chicago Press.

Bonilla-Silva, Eduardo. 2018. *Racism without Racists: Color-Blind Racism and the Persistence of Racial Inequality in America*. 5th ed. Lanham, MD: Rowman & Littlefield.

Bonner, Lynn. 2013. "Proposal of Vouchers for Special Needs Students Moves Forward." *News & Observer*, April 16.

Boudreau, Cheryl, and Scott A. MacKenzie. 2014. "Informing the Electorate? How Party Cues and Policy Information Affect Public Opinion about Initiatives." *American Journal of Political Science* 58 (1): 48–62. https://doi.org/10.1111/ajps.12054.

Bownes, Hugh. 1980. *Rhode Island Federation of Teachers* v. *Norberg*, 630 F. 2d 850, United States Court of Appeals, First Circuit.

Boyer, Jonathan D. 2009. "Education Tax Credits: School Choice Initiatives Capable of Surmounting Blaine Amendments." *Columbia Journal of Law and Social Problems* 43 (1): 117–50.

Braveman, Paula A., Catherine Cubbin, Susan Egerter, David R. Williams, and Elsie Pamuk. 2010. "Socioeconomic Disparities in Health in the United States: What the Patterns Tell Us." *American Journal of Public Health* 100 (S1): S186–96. https://doi.org/10.2105/AJPH.2009.166082.

Brennan, William J. 1974. *Johnson* v. *Robison*, 415 US 361, Supreme Court of the United States.

Brittain, John, and Callie Kozlak. 2007. "Racial Disparities in Educational Opportunities in the United States." *Seattle Journal for Social Justice* 6 (2): 58.

Brown, Emma. 2015. "Two Teachers Explain Why They Want to Take Down Their Union." *Washington Post*, August 11, Sec. Education. www.washingtonpost.com/news/education/wp/2015/08/11/two-teachers-explain-why-they-want-to-take-down-their-union/?utm_term=.058e0362fc54.

Brunner, Eric, and Jon Sonstelie. 2003. "Homeowners, Property Values, and the Political Economy of the School Voucher." *Journal of Urban Economics* 54 (2): 239–57. https://doi.org/10.1016/S0094-1190(03)00063-9.

Buhrmester, Michael, Tracy Kwang, and Samuel D. Gosling. 2011. "Amazon's Mechanical Turk: A New Source of Inexpensive, Yet High-Quality, Data?" *Perspectives on Psychological Science* 6 (1): 3–5. https://doi.org/10.1177/1745691610393980.

Bunch, Will. 2011. "Pennsylvania: Voucher Ground Zero." *Philadelphia Daily News*, May 23. www.inquirer.com/philly/education/20110523_Pennsylvania__Voucher_Ground_Zero.html

Bureau of Labor Statistics. 2017. "Table 5. Union Affiliation of Employed Wage and Salary Workers by State." US Department of Labor. www.bls.gov/news.release/union2.t05.htm.

Burke, Cathy. 2016. "Trump Unveils Plan to Destroy 'Education Monopoly.'" *NewsMax*, September 8. www.newsmax.com/Newsfront/donald-trump-policies-education-reform/2016/09/08/id/747380/.

Burnell, Raymond. 2012. Author interview with Raymond Burnell, Education Specialist at the California Catholic Conference.

Burnett, Ingrid. 2018. Author interview with Representative Ingrid Burnett, Missouri House of Representatives.

Butzner, John D. 1964. *Pettaway* v. *County School Board of Surry County*, 230 E.D. Va. 480, US District Court for the Eastern District of Virginia.

Callow, William G. 1992. *Davis* v. *Grover*, 166 Wis. 2d 501, Supreme Court of Wisconsin. Campbell, Andrea L. 2010. "The Public's Role in Winner-Take-All Politics." *Politics & Society* 38 (2): 227–32. https://doi.org/10.1177/0032329210365046.

2011. "Policy Feedbacks and the Impact of Policy Designs on Public Opinion." *Journal of Health Politics, Policy and Law* 36 (6): 961–73.

Carl, Jim. 2011. *Freedom of Choice: Vouchers in American Education*. Santa Barbara, CA: ABC-CLIO.

Carper, Elsie. 1960. "Tuition Grants Seen Hurting Va. Schools." *Washington-Times Herald*, November 20, p. D20.

Carr, Sarah. 2009. "School Vouchers' Future Is Uncertain in Louisiana." *Times-Picayune,* September 5. www.nola.com/news/education/article_0c75de68-3ce2-5b51-86c4-adb27d88636b.html

2012. "In Southern Towns, 'Segregation Academies' Are Still Going Strong." *Atlantic,* December 13. www.theatlantic.com/national/archive/2012/12/in-southern-towns-segregation-academies-are-still-going-strong/266207/.

Carr, Sarah, and Bill Barrow. 2008. "Jindal Avoids Calling It Voucher Program." *Times-Picayune*, April 2, p. 1.

Cartwright-Smith, Lara, and Sara Rosenbaum. 2012. "Controversy, Contraception, and Conscience: Insurance Coverage Standards under the Patient Protection and Affordable Care Act." *Public Health Reports* 127 (5): 541–45.

Catholic Conference of Ohio. 1995. "Catholic Conference of Ohio." Box, Needles Files, Misc. – Education, Box 1KK. Folder, Non-Public – Catholic Conference. Voinovich Archives.

Cato Institute. 2016. "The Way Forward: Scholarship Tax Credits or Vouchers?" www.cato.org/education-wiki/scholarship-tax-credits-vouchers.

Catsam, Derek C. 2009. *Freedom's Main Line: The Journey of Reconciliation and the Freedom Rides*. Civil Rights and the Struggle for Black Equality in the Twentieth Century. Lexington: University Press of Kentucky.

Cauthen, James. 2012. "State Constitutions and Challenges to Nonpublic School Transportation Programs." *Journal of Church and State* 55 (3): 498–526.

Chapman, William. 1964. "Virginia Tuition Help Held Unconstitutional by U.S. Appeals Court." *Washington-Times Herald*, December 3. ProQuest Historical Newspapers: The Washington Post, p. A1.

Charities Aid Foundation. 2016. "Gross Domestic Philanthropy: An International Analysis of GDP, Tax and Giving." www.cafonline.org/docs/default-source/about-us-policy-and-campaigns/gross-domestic-philanthropy-feb-2016.pdf.

Chin, Gabriel J., Roger Hartley, Kevin Bates, and Rona Nichols. 2006. "Still on the Books: Jim Crow and Segregation Laws Fifty Years after Brown v. Board of Education." *Michigan State Law Review* 2006 (2): 457–76.

Christie, Bob. 2018. "Judge Rejects Effort to Block Vote on School Voucher Law." *AP News*, January 31. https://apnews.com/dfb50de010cb4a74a9eb4ecf9aba9c66.

Chubb, John E., and Terry M. Moe. 1990. *Politics, Markets, and America's Schools*. Washington, DC: Brookings Institution Press.

Church of St. Gregory the Great. 1995. "Church of St. Gregory the Great." Box, Needles Files, Misc. – Education, Box 1KK. Folder, Non-Public – Catholic Conference. Voinovich Archives.

Cibulka, James G. 2000. "The NEA and School Choice." In *Conflicting Missions? Teachers Unions and Educational Reform*, edited by Tom Loveless, 150–73. Washington, DC: Brookings Institution Press.

Clark, Jordan. 2010. Author interview with Jordan Clark, Chief of Staff to Representative Glenn Thompson (R-PA).

Clark, Tom C. 1961. *Burton* v. *Wilmington Parking Authority*, 365 US 715, Supreme Court of the United States.

Clotfelter, Charles T. 2004. *After Brown: The Rise and Retreat of School Desegregation*. Princeton, NJ: Princeton University Press.

Coles, Adrienne D. 1997. "Poll Finds Growing Support for School Choice." *Education Week*, September 3. www.edweek.org/ew/articles/1997/09/03/01pdk.h17.html?qs=african+american+support+vouchers+daterange:1981-07-01..2000-01-01.

Collins, Paul M. 2004. "Friends of the Court: Examining the Influence of Amicus Curiae Participation in U.S. Supreme Court Litigation." *Law & Society Review* 38 (4): 807–32. https://doi.org/10.1111/j.0023-9216.2004.00067.x.

2007. "Lobbyists before the U.S. Supreme Court: Investigating the Influence of Amicus Curiae Briefs." *Political Research Quarterly* 60 (1): 55–70. https://doi.org/10.1177/1065912906298535.

Compitello, Michael J., Gregory S. Baylor, and Heather G.Hacker. 2013. "In the Superior Court for Strafford County, New Hampshire, Amicus Curiae Brief of Alliance Defending Freedom, Cornerstone Policy Research, and Liberty Institute for Duncan vs State of New Hampshire." Alliance Defending Freedom, Cornerstone Policy Research, and Liberty Institute. www.adfmedia.org/files/NHamicus.pdf.

Congressional Budget Office. 2017. "Federal Subsidies for Health Insurance Coverage for People under Age 65: 2017 to 2027." Congress of the United States. www.cbo.gov/system/files/115th-congress-2017-2018/reports/53091-fshic.pdf.

Connell, Christopher. 2000. *Parochial Schools and Public Aid: Today's Catholic Schools*. Washington, DC: Thomas B. Fordham Institute.

Cookson, Peter W. 1994. *School Choice: The Struggle for the Soul of American Education*. New Haven, CT: Yale University Press.

Corella, Hipolito. 2013. "Court Backs Arizona on Use of Taxpayer-Funded 'Scholarships' to Send Kids to Private Schools." *Arizona Daily Star*, October 1. http://azstarnet.com/news/state-and-regional/court-backs-arizona-on-use-of-taxpayer-funded-scholarships-to/article_d7fc270e-2ac3-11e3-bf51-0019bb2963f4.html.

Coulson, Andrew. 2010a. Author interview with Dr. Andrew Coulson, Cato Institute, Washington, DC.

2010b. "The Effects of Teachers Unions on American Education." *Cato Journal* 30 (1): 155–70.

Crespino, Joseph. 2007. *In Search of Another Country: Mississippi and the Conservative Counterrevolution*. Politics and Society in Twentieth-Century America. Princeton, NJ: Princeton University Press.

Cupich, Blase J. 2018. Author interview with Cardinal Blase J. Cupich, Archbishop of the Archdiocese of Chicago.

Curry, Patricia E. 1981. "James Madison and the Burger Court: Converging Views of Church-State Separation." *Indiana Law Journal* 56 (4): 615–36.

Dahl, Robert. 1957. "Decision-Making in a Democracy: The Supreme Court as National Policy-Maker." *Journal of Public Law* 6 (2): 279–95.

Dalianis, Linda Stewart. 2014. *Duncan* v. *State of New Hampshire*, 102 A. 3d 913, Supreme Court of New Hampshire.

Davis, William F. 1999. "The Reauthorization of the Elementary and Secondary Education Act in a Republican-Controlled Congress: A View from the Bishops' Conference." *Catholic Education: A Journal of Inquiry and Practice* 3 (1): 97–106.

De Tocqueville, Alexis. 1998. *Democracy in America*. Wordsworth Classics of World Literature. London: Wordsworth Editions.

Denniston, Lyle. 2016. "Opinion Analysis: Result but No Guidance on Public Unions' Fees." *SCOTUSblog*. www.scotusblog.com/2016/03/opinion-analysis-result-but-no-guidance-on-public-unions-fees/.

Denny, Dann. 2011. "Democrats Frustrated by GOP Attitude on Labor, Public Schools." *Herald Times*, April 3.

Department of Education, Office of Innovation and Improvement, Office of Non-Public Education. 2009. "State Regulation of Private Schools." www2.ed.gov/admins/comm/choice/regprivschl/index.html.

Dickson, Brent E. 2013. *Meredith* v. *Pence*, 984 N.E. 2d 1213, Supreme Court of Indiana.

Dinan, John. 2018. *State Constitutional Politics: Governing by Amendment in the American States*. Chicago: University of Chicago Press.

Dolejsi, Ned. 2012. Author interview with Ned Dolejsi, Executive Director of the California Catholic Conference.

Dooley, John. 1994. *Campbell* v. *Manchester Board of School District Directors*, 641 A. 2d 352, Supreme Court of Vermont.

Dorfman, Jeffrey. 2016. "Teachers Unions, Faulty Economics, and School Choice." *Forbes*, November 13. www.forbes.com/sites/jeffreydorfman/2016/11/13/teachers-unions-faulty-economics-and-school-choice/#f94e48d7c73f.

Douglas, Davison M. 2005. *Jim Crow Moves North: The Battle over Northern School Segregation, 1865–1954*. Cambridge Historical Studies in American Law and Society. Cambridge: Cambridge University Press.

Dreweke, Joerg. 2016. "'Fungibility': The Argument at the Center of a 40-Year Campaign to Undermine Reproductive Health and Rights." *Guttmacher Policy Review* 19 (October): 53–60.

Durkin, Jim, and Steve Reick. 2018. Author interview with Minority Leader Jim Durkin and Representative Steve Reick, Illinois House of Representatives.

Eckes, Suzanne E., Julie Mead, and Jessica Ulm. 2016. "Dollars to Discriminate: The (Un)Intended Consequences of School Vouchers." *Peabody Journal of Education* 91 (4): 537–58. https://doi.org/10.1080/0161956X.2016.1207446.

EdChoice. 2018. "School Choice in America Dashboard." www.edchoice.org/school-choice/school-choice-in-america/.

Eddy, Roger. 2012. Author interview with Roger Eddy, Executive Director of the Illinois Association of School Boards and former Representative and Schools Superintendent.

Elam, Stanley M. 1999. "Florida's Voucher Program: Legislating What Can't Be Done by Referendum." *Phi Delta Kappan* 81 (1): 81–82, 84–86, 88.

Elazar, Daniel J. 1970. *Cities of the Prairie: The Metropolitan Frontier and American Politics*. Lanham: University Press of America.

Ellis, Christopher, and Christopher Faricy. 2011. "Social Policy and Public Opinion: How the Ideological Direction of Spending Influences Public Mood." *Journal of Politics* 73 (4): 1095–110.

Emery, Edgar G. H. 2018. Author interview with Senator Edgar G. H. Emery, Missouri State Senate.

Epp, Charles R. 1998. *The Rights Revolution: Lawyers, Activists, and Supreme Courts in Comparative Perspective*. Chicago: University of Chicago Press.

Evans-Brown, Sam. 2013. "N.H. House Votes to Repeal School Choice Tax Credit." *Concord Monitor*, February 20. www.concordmonitor.com/Archive/2013/02/HouseRoundup-CM-022113.

Ezell, Melanie. 2012. Author interview with Melanie Ezell, President, Louisiana Association of Independent Schools and former Headmistress of Parkview Baptist School.

Faith and Reason Institute. 2000. "Are Vouchers Good for Catholic Education?" Catholic Education Resource Center. www.catholic-education.org/en/education/catholic-contributions/are-vouchers-good-for-catholic-education.html.

Faricy, Christopher. 2011. "The Politics of Social Policy in America: The Causes and Effects of Indirect versus Direct Social Spending." *Journal of Politics* 73 (1): 74–83. https://doi.org/10.1017/S0022381610000873.

2015. *Welfare for the Wealthy: Parties, Social Spending, and Inequality in the United States*. New York: Cambridge University Press.

2016. "The Distributive Politics of Tax Expenditures: How Parties Use Policy Tools to Distribute Federal Money to the Rich and the Poor." *Politics, Groups, and Identities* 4 (1): 110–25. https://doi.org/10.1080/21565503.2015.1066688.

Feldman, Noah. 2005. *Divided by God: America's Church-State Problem – and What We Should Do about It*. New York: Farrar, Straus & Giroux.

Finger, Leslie K. 2018. "Vested Interests and the Diffusion of Education Reform across the States." *Policy Studies Journal* 46 (2): 378–401. https://doi.org/10.1111/psj.12238.

Finn, Chester E. 2010. Author interview with Professor Chester E. Finn, Thomas B. Fordham Institute.

Fischer, Howard. 2013a. "Public Schools Challenge State Vouchers for Private and Parochial Schools." *Arizona Daily Star*, October 19. http://azstarnet.com/news/local/education/public-schools-challenge-state-vouchers-for-private-and-parochial-schools/article_7442748a-64da-5dca-a51c-242b52805cfd.html.

2013b. "Schools Chief Urges Court to Uphold School Voucherlike Program." *Arizona Daily Star*, December 8. http://azstarnet.com/news/local/education/schools-chief-urges-court-to-uphold-school-voucherlike-program/article_cf23e5dc-5cc4-5918-a2df-155e50508792.html.

2017. "Legislature Ends Session, Passes Tax Breaks, Reverses Cuts to Public Benefits." *Arizona Capitol Times*, May 10. https://azcapitoltimes.com/news/2017/05/10/legislature-ends-session-passes-tax-breaks-reverses-cuts-to-public-benefits/.

Florida. 1838. "Constitution of the State of Florida." State of Florida. www.leg.state.fl.us/statutes/index.cfm?submenu=3.

Florida School Choice. 2013. "Florida Tax Credit Scholarship Program: Definition and Eligibility." Florida Department of Education. www.fldoe.org/schools/school-choice/k-12-scholarship-programs/ftc/ftc-faqs.stml.

Florida Statutes. 2001. Florida Tax Credit Scholarship Program. Section 220.187.

Flynn Currie, Barbara. 2018. Author interview with Majority Leader Barbara Flynn Currie, Illinois House of Representatives.

Ford, Chris, Stephenie Johnson, and Lisette Partelow. 2017. "The Racist Origins of Private School Vouchers." Center for American Progress. www.americanprogress.org/issues/education/reports/2017/07/12/435629/racist-origins-private-school-vouchers/.

Forman, James. 2007. "The Rise and Fall of School Vouchers: A Story of Religion, Race, and Politics." *UCLA Law Review*, Yale Law School Faculty Scholarship Series, 54 (3): 547.

Francis, Megan M. 2014. *Civil Rights and the Making of the Modern American State*. New York: Cambridge University Press.

Freeman, Lance. 2011. "The Impact of Source of Income Laws on Voucher Utilization and Locational Outcomes." Washington, DC: US Department of Housing and Urban Development, Office of Policy Development and Research. http://prrac.org/pdf/FreemanSOIreport_2-11.pdf.

Friedman Foundation for Educational Choice. 2016. "School Choice – The Friedman Foundation for Educational Choice." www.edchoice.org/.

Friedman, Milton. 1955. "The Role of Government in Education." *In Economics and the Public Interest*, edited by Robert A. Solo. New Brunswick, NJ: Rutgers University Press, pp. 123–44.

1997. "Public Schools: Make Them Private." *Education Economics* 5 (3): 341–44. https://doi.org/10.1080/09645299700000026.

Frymer, Paul. 2008. *Black and Blue: African Americans, the Labor Movement, and the Decline of the Democratic Party*. Princeton Studies in American Politics: Historical, International, and Comparative Perspectives. Princeton, NJ: Princeton University Press.

Frymer, Paul, and John D. Skrentny. 1998. "Coalition-Building and the Politics of Electoral Capture during the Nixon Administration: African Americans, Labor, Latinos." *Studies in American Political Development* 12 (1): 131–61.

Fusarelli, Lance D. 2003. *The Political Dynamics of School Choice: Negotiating Contested Terrain*. New York: Palgrave Macmillan.

Galewitz, Phil. 2018. "Medicare Advantage Riding High as New Insurers Compete to Sell to Seniors." *USA Today*, October 15. www.usatoday.com/story/news/2018/10/15/medicare-advantage-enrollment-growing-affordable-care-act-obamacare-insurance-plans/1618652002/.

Gamble, Barbara S. 1997. "Putting Civil Rights to a Popular Vote." *American Journal of Political Science* 41 (1): 245–69. https://doi.org/10.2307/2111715.

Garman, Rita B. 2001. Toney v. Bower. 744 N.E. 2d 351, Ill. App. 4th Dist.

Garrett, Robert T. 2017. "Texas House Passes Budget with Provision Banning School-Voucher Funding." *Dallas News*, April 7. www.dallasnews.com/news/politics/2017/04/07/texas-house-passes-budget-with-provision-banning-school-voucher-funding/.

Gauri, Varun. 1999. *School Choice in Chile: Two Decades of Educational Reform*. Pittsburgh, PA: University of Pittsburgh Press.

Geddis, Carol. 2012. Author interview with Carol Geddis, Director of the Catholic School Administrators Association of New York State.

Georgia. 1868. "Constitution of the State of Georgia." State of Georgia. https://georgiainfo.galileo.usg.edu/topics/government/related_article/constitutions/georgia-constitution-of-1868.

1877. "Constitution of the State of Georgia." State of Georgia. https://georgiainfo.galileo.usg.edu/topics/government/related_article/constitutions/georgia-constitution-of-1877-as-ratified-without-subsequent-amendments.

1945. "Constitution of the State of Georgia." State of Georgia. https://georgiainfo.galileo.usg.edu/topics/government/related_article/constitutions/georgia-constitution-of-1945-as-ratified-without-subsequent-amendments#Article%20VIII.

Gingrich, Jane. 2011. *Making Markets in the Welfare State: The Politics of Varying Market Reforms*. Cambridge Studies in Comparative Politics. Cambridge: Cambridge University Press.

2014. "Visibility, Values, and Voters: The Informational Role of the Welfare State." *Journal of Politics* 76 (2): 565–80.

Glendon, Mary A. 1991. *Rights Talk: The Impoverishment of Political Discourse*. New York: Free Press.

Godbold, John C., William H. Cox, and Dan M. Russell. 1969. *Coffey* v. *State Educational Finance Commission*, 296 F Supp 1389, US District Court for the Southern District of Mississippi.

Gooden, Mark A., Huriya Jabbar, and Mario S. Torres. 2016. "Race and School Vouchers: Legal, Historical, and Political Contexts." *Peabody Journal of Education* 91 (4): 522–36. https://doi.org/10.1080/0161956X.2016.1207445.

Graber, Mark. 2006. *Dred Scott and the Problem of Constitutional Evil*. Cambridge Studies on the American Constitution. New York: Cambridge University Press.

Grado, Gary. 2011. "Advocates in Arizona to Seek Choices for Kids in Failing Schools." *Arizona Capitol Times*, December 4, Sec. News.

Grant, Ulysses S. 1875. "To the Society of the Army of the Tennessee." American Civic Forum. https://archive.org/stream/wordsofourherouloogran/wordsofourherouloogran_djvu.txt.

Green, Stephen K. 1992. "The Blaine Amendment Reconsidered." *American Journal of Legal History* 36 (1): 38–69.

2004. "'Blaming Blaine': Understanding the Blaine Amendment and the 'No Funding' Principle." *First Amendment Law Review* 2 (1): 107–52.

Greenmay, Erica L. 2017. "In Some States, Donating to Private Schools Can Earn You a Profit." *New York Times*, May 17. www.nytimes.com/2017/05/17/us/politics/in-some-states-donating-to-private-schools-can-earn-you-a-profit.html?_r=0.

Guzzardi, Will. 2018. Author interview with Representative Will Guzzardi, Illinois House of Representatives.

Hacker, Jacob S. 2002. *The Divided Welfare State: The Battle over Public and Private Social Benefits in the United States*. New York: Cambridge University Press, pp. 40–82.

2004. "Privatizing Risk without Privatizing the Welfare State: The Hidden Politics of Social Policy Retrenchment in the United States." *American Political Science Review* 98 (2): 243–60. https://doi.org/10.1017/S0003055404001121.

2005. "Policy Drift: The Hidden Politics of US Welfare State Retrenchment." In *Beyond Continuity: Institutional Change in Advanced Political Economies*, edited by Wolfgang Streeck and Kathleen Thelen. New York: Oxford University Press, pp. 40–82.

2016. "America's Welfare Parastate." *Perspectives on Politics* 14 (3): 777–83. https://doi.org/10.1017/S1537592716002760.

Hacker, Jacob S., and Paul Pierson. 2010. "Winner-Take-All Politics: Public Policy, Political Organization, and the Precipitous Rise of Top Incomes in the United States." *Politics & Society* 38 (2): 152–204. https://doi.org/10.1177/0032329210365042.

Hackett, Ursula. 2014. "Republicans, Catholics and the West: Explaining the Strength of Religious School Aid Prohibitions." *Politics and Religion* 7 (3): 499–520. https://doi.org/10.1017/S1755048313000242.

2016. "The Exit-Voice Choice: Religious Cleavages, Public Aid, and America's Private Schools." *Politics and Religion* 9 (2): 249–70. https://doi.org/10.1017/S1755048316000201.

2017. "Theorizing the Submerged State: The Politics of Private Schools in the United States." *Policy Studies Journal* 45 (3): 464–89. https://doi.org/10.1111/psj.12170.

2019. "Attenuated Governance: How Policymakers Insulate Private School Choice from Legal Challenge." *Policy Studies Journal* 47 (2): 237–73.

Hackett, Ursula, and Desmond King. 2019. "The Reinvention of Vouchers for a Color-Blind Era: A Racial Orders Account." *Studies in American Political Development* 33 (2): 234–57. https://doi.org/10.1017/S0898588X19000075.

Hamburger, Philip. 2002. "Separation and Interpretation." *Journal of Law & Politics* 18 (1): 7–64.

Hamilton, Alexander, James Madison, and John Jay. 2008. *The Federalist Papers*. Oxford: Oxford University Press.

Hammond, Phillip E. 2001. "American Church/State Jurisprudence from the Warren Court to the Rehnquist Court." *Journal for the Scientific Study of Religion* 40 (3): 455–64.

Hannah, John A., Eugene Patterson, Frankie M. Freeman, Erwin N. Griswold, Theodore M. Hesburgh, and Robert S. Rankin. 1964. "1964 Staff Report: Public Education." US Commission on Civil Rights. https://books.google.co.uk/books?id=PUhHAQAAIAAJ&pg=PR1&dq=%221964+Staff+Report:+Public+Education%22&hl=en&sa=X&ved=0ahUKEwi5x4Df8aPnAhV2UBUIHSKhCioQ6AEIKDAA#v=onepage&q=%221964%20Staff%20Report%3A%20Public%20Education%22&f=false.

Hardesty, James. 2016. *Schwartz* v. *Lopez*, 132 Nev. Adv. Opn. No. 73, Supreme Court of Nevada.

Harris, David. 2018. Author interview with Representative David Harris, Illinois House of Representatives.

Harter, Jerome C., and Peter M. Hoffman. 1973. "Segregation Academies and State Action." *Yale Law Journal* 82 (7): 1436–61.

Hartney, Michael, and Patrick Flavin. 2011. "From the Schoolhouse to the Statehouse: Teacher Union Political Activism and U.S. State Education Reform Policy." *State Politics & Policy Quarterly* 11 (3): 251–68. https://doi.org/10.1177/1532440011413079.

Haselswerdt, Jake. 2014. "The Lifespan of a Tax Break: Comparing the Durability of Tax Expenditures and Spending Programs." *American Politics Research* 42: 731–59.

Haselswerdt, Jake, and Brandon L. Bartels. 2015. "Public Opinion, Policy Tools, and the Status Quo Evidence from a Survey Experiment." *Political Research Quarterly* 68 (3): 607–21. https://doi.org/10.1177/1065912915591217.

Hays, R. Allen. 1985. *The Federal Government and Urban Housing: Ideology and Change in Public Policy*. Albany: State University of New York Press.

Hertel-Fernandez, Alexander. 2018. "Policy Feedback as Political Weapon: Conservative Advocacy and the Demobilization of the Public Sector Labor Movement." *Perspectives on Politics* 16 (2): 364–79. https://doi.org/10.1017/S1537592717004236.

Hess, Frederick M. 2004. *Revolution at the Margins: The Impact of Competition on Urban School Systems.* Washington, DC: Brookings Institution Press.

Hess, Frederick M., and Grant Addison. 2017. "The Supreme Court Can Deliver a Pivotal Win for School Choice." *National Review*, April 18, Sec. Education. www.nationalreview.com/2017/04/supreme-court-church-state-case-trinity-lutheran/.

Hevenstone, Debra. 2015. *The American Myth of Markets in Social Policy: Ideological Roots of Inequality.* New York: Palgrave Macmillan.

Hill, David. 1998. "Class Action." *Education Week Teacher*, April 1. www.edweek.org/tm/articles/1998/04/01/07denver.h09.html?qs=african+american+support+vouchers+daterange:1981-07-01..2000-01-01.

Hill, Paul T., Christopher T. Cross, and Sally Kilgore. 2000. "The Federal Role in Education." *Brookings Papers on Education Policy* 3 (3): 11–57.

Hollander, Robyn, and Haig Patapan. 2017. "Morality Policy and Federalism: Innovation, Diffusion and Limits." *Publius: The Journal of Federalism* 47 (1): 1–26. https://doi.org/10.1093/publius/pjw027.

Holmes, Oliver W. 1927. *Miller* v. *City of Milwaukee*, 272 US 713, Supreme Court of the United States.

Hood, Christopher. 2002. "The Risk Game and the Blame Game." *Government and Opposition* 37 (1): 15–37. https://doi.org/10.1111/1477-7053.00085.

2007. "What Happens When Transparency Meets Blame-Avoidance?" *Public Management Review* 9 (2): 191–210. https://doi.org/10.1080/14719030701340275.

Hood, Christopher, Will Jennings, Ruth Dixon, Brian Hogwood, and Craig Beeston. 2009. "Testing Times: Exploring Staged Responses and the Impact of Blame Management Strategies in Two Examination Fiasco Cases." *European Journal of Political Research* 48 (6): 695–722. https://doi.org/10.1111/j.1475-6765.2009.01830.x.

Howard, Christopher. 1997. *The Hidden Welfare State: Tax Expenditures and Social Policy in the United States.* Princeton, NJ: Princeton University Press.

2007. *The Welfare State Nobody Knows: Debunking Myths about U.S. Social Policy.* Princeton, NJ: Princeton University Press.

Hsu, Spencer S. 2006. "How Vouchers Came to D.C." In *Choice and Competition in American Education*, edited by Paul E. Peterson, 219–32. Lanham, MD: Rowman & Littlefield.

Hughes, Charles E. 1930. *Cochran* v. *Louisiana State Board of Education*, 281 US 370, Supreme Court of the United States.

Hunter, James D., and Alan Wolfe, eds. 2006. *Is There a Culture War? A Dialogue on Values and American Public Life.* The Pew Forum Dialogues on Religion and Public Life. Washington, DC: Pew Research Center, Brookings Institution Press.

Huntington, Samuel P. 2004. *Who Are We? The Challenges to America's National Identity.* New York: Simon and Schuster.

Illescas, Carlos. 2011. "Douglas County School District Pitches Voucher Program." *Denver Post*, February 23. www.denverpost.com/2011/02/22/douglas-county-school-district-pitches-voucher-program/.

2013. "Plaintiffs in Douglas County School Voucher Fight Turn to High Court." *Denver Post*, April 11 www.denverpost.com/2013/04/11/plaintiffs-in-douglas-county-school-voucher-fight-turn-to-high-court/.

Institute for Justice. 2016. "School Choice Issue Backgrounder." https://ij.org/issues/school-choice/backgrounder/.

The Institute for Justice, and the American Legislative Exchange Council. 2007. "School Choice and State Constitutions: A Guide to Designing School Choice Programs." files.eric.ed.gov/fulltext/ED514959.pdf.

Internal Revenue Service. 2017. "Exemption Requirements – 501(c)(3) Organizations." www.irs.gov/charities-non-profits/charitable-organizations/exemption-requirements-section-501c3-organizations.

Ives, Jeanne. 2018. Author interview with Representative Jeanne Ives, Illinois House of Representatives.

Jacobs, Lawrence R., and Suzanne Mettler. 2018. "When and How New Policy Creates New Politics: Examining the Feedback Effects of the Affordable Care Act on Public Opinion." *Perspectives on Politics* 16 (2): 345–63. https://doi.org/10.1017/S1537592717004182.

Jeynes, William H. 2014. *School Choice: A Balanced Approach*. Santa Barbara, CA: Praeger.

Joint Committee on Taxation. 2008. "Estimates of Federal Tax Expenditures for Fiscal Years 2008–2012." US Government Printing Office. www.jct.gov/publications.html?func=select&id=5.

2013. "Estimates of Federal Tax Expenditures for Fiscal Years 2012–2017." US Government Printing Office. www.jct.gov/publications.html?func=select&id=5.

Jones, Jeffrey M. 2016. "Red States Outnumber Blue for First Time in Gallup Tracking." Gallup. https://news.gallup.com/poll/188969/red-states-outnumber-blue-first-time-gallup-tracking.aspx?g_source=Politics&g_medium=lead&g_campaign=tiles.

Jones, Todd. 2010. Author interview with Todd Jones, President of the Association of Independent Colleges and Universities of Ohio.

Justice, Benjamin, and Colin Macleod. 2016. *Have a Little Faith: Religion, Democracy, and the American Public School*. The History and Philosophy of Education Series. Chicago: University of Chicago Press.

Kagan, Elena. 2011. *Arizona Christian School Tuition Organization* v. *Winn* (dissent), 563 US 125, Supreme Court of the United States.

Kagan, Robert A. 1991. "Adversarial Legalism and American Government." *Journal of Policy Analysis and Management* 10 (3): 369–406.

Kahlenberg, Richard D. 2007. *Tough Liberal: Albert Shanker and the Battles over Schools, Unions, Race, and Democracy*. Columbia Studies in Contemporary American History. New York: Columbia University Press.

Kamphaus, Catherine. 2012. Author interview with Catherine Kamphaus, Superintendent of Catholic Schools for Salt Lake City, Utah.

Kaplan, Jeff. 2009. *Rundus* v. *City of Dallas*, N.D. Tex. US District Court for the Northern District of Texas, Dallas Division. https://casetext.com/case/rundus-v-city-of-dallas-2.

Kay, Richard S. 1993. "The State Action Doctrine, the Public/Private Distinction, and the Independence of Constitutional Law." *Constitutional Commentary* 10 (2): 329.

Keller, Timothy D. 2013. "Response to Plaintiffs-Appellants' Petition for Review in the Case Niehaus v Huppenthal." Institute for Justice. https://ij.org/wp-content/uploads/2011/09/niehaus-response-to-petition-for-review.pdf.

Kennedy, Anthony. 2011. *Arizona Christian School Tuition Organization* v. *Winn*, 563 US 125, Supreme Court of the United States.

Key, Valdimer Orlando 1949. *Southern Politics in State and Nation*. New York: Vintage Books.

Kincaid, John. 2016. "The Rational Basis of Irrational Politics: Examining the Great Texas Political Shift to the Right." *Politics & Society* 44 (4): 525–50.

King, Desmond. 2017. "Forceful Federalism against American Racial Inequality." *Government and Opposition* 52 (2): 356–82. https://doi.org/10.1017/gov.2016.52.

King, Desmond, and Rogers M. Smith. 2005. "Racial Orders in American Political Development." *American Political Science Review* 99 (1): 75–92.

2011. *Still a House Divided*. Princeton Studies in American Politics: Historical, Institutional, and Comparative Perspectives. Princeton, NJ: Princeton University Press.

King, Erika. 1998. "Tax Exemptions and the Establishment Clause." *Syracuse Law Review* 49 (3): 971–1037.

Klein, Alyson. 2018a. "DeVos: State Bans on Public Money to Religious Schools Should Go to 'Ash Heap of History.'" *Education Week – Politics K-12*, May 16. http://blogs.edweek.org/edweek/campaign-k-12/2018/05/devos_religious_money_public_private_new_york.html?cmp=SOC-SHR-FB.

2018b. "GOP Bill Would Create ESAs for Military Families, Using Impact Aid." *Education Week – Politics K-12*, March 7. http://blogs.edweek.org/edweek/campaign-k-12/2018/03/Banks_impact_aid_ESA_choice_military.html?cmp=SOC-SHR-FB.

Koehler, David. 2018. Author interview with Senator David Koehler, Illinois State Senate.

Koenig, Andrew P. 2018. Author interview with Senator Andrew P. Koenig, Missouri State Senate.

Koppich, Julia E. 2005. "A Tale of Two Approaches – the AFT, the NEA, and NCLB." *Peabody Journal of Education* 80 (2): 137–55.

Kramer, John. 1999. "In Major First Amendment Ruling, Arizona Supreme Court Upholds School Choice Tax Credit." Institute for Justice. https://ij.org/press-release/arizona-tax-credits-release-1-27-1999/.

Krivo, Lauren J., and Robert L. Kaufman. 2004. "Housing and Wealth Inequality: Racial-Ethnic Differences in Home Equity in the United States." *Demography* 41 (3): 585–605. https://doi.org/10.1353/dem.2004.0023.

Kronholz, June. 2000. "In Michigan, Amway Chief and Wife Give School Vouchers a Higher Profile." *Wall Street Journal*, October 25. www.wsj.com/articles/SB972434493337200201.

Kruse, Kevin M. 2005. *White Flight: Atlanta and the Making of Modern Conservatism*. Princeton, NJ: Princeton University Press.

Lacorne, Denis. 2011. *Religion in America: A Political History*. Translated by George Holoch. New York: Columbia University Press.

Ladson-Billings, Gloria. 2004. "Landing on the Wrong Note: The Price We Paid for Brown." *Educational Researcher* 33 (7): 3–13.

Lancaster, Jan. 2012. Author interview with Jan Lancaster, Superintendent of Catholic Schools for the Archdiocese of New Orleans, Louisiana.

Landrigan, Kevin. 2012. "Lynch Vetoes Education Tax Credit Bill; House, Senate Could Override." *Concord Monitor*, June 19.

2014. "Gov. Hassan Urges High Court Affirm Strike Down Tax Credits for Religious Schools." *Concord Monitor*, January 14.

Laughrey, Nanette K. 2013. *Trinity Lutheran Church of Columbia* v. *Pauley*, 976 F Supp 2d 1137, US District Court for the Western District of Missouri, Central Division.

Lawton, Millicent. 1992. "Gallup Poll Finds Wide Support for Tuition Vouchers." *Education Week*, September 23. www.edweek.org/ew/articles/1992/09/23/03-3cho.h12.html?qs=african+american+support+vouchers.

Leach, Robert E. 1968. *Honohan* v. *Holt*, 17 Ohio 57, Common Pleas Court of Franklin County.

Leal, David L. 2004. "Latinos and School Vouchers: Testing the 'Minority Support' Hypothesis." *Social Science Quarterly* 85 (5): 1227–37.

Lerman, Amy E., Meredith L.Sadin, and Samuel Trachtman. 2017. "Policy Uptake as Political Behavior: Evidence from the Affordable Care Act." *American Political Science Review* 111 (4): 755–70. https://doi.org/10.1017/S0003055417000272.

Leubsdorf, Ben. 2013. "Judge Says N.H.'s New Education Tax Credit Violates State Constitution." *Concord Monitor*, June 18 www.concordmonitor.com/Archive/2013/06/EduTaxCredit-CM-061813.

Levesque, Patricia. 2012. Author interview with Patricia Levesque, Executive Director for the Foundation for Florida's Future and Member of the Taxation and Budgetary Reform Committee.

Lewis, Andrew R. 2017. *The Rights Turn in Conservative Christian Politics: How Abortion Transformed the Culture Wars*. Cambridge: Cambridge University Press.

Libla, Doug. 2018. Author interview with Senator Doug Libla, Missouri State Senate.

Lieberman, Myron. 1997. *The Teachers' Unions : How the NEA and AFT Sabotage Reform and Hold Students, Parents, Teachers, and Taxpayers Hostage to Bureaucracy*. 1st ed. New York: Free Press.

2000. *The Teacher Unions: How They Sabotage Educational Reform and Why*. San Francisco: Encounter Books.

Lieberman, Robert C. 2002. "Ideas, Institutions, and Political Order: Explaining Political Change." *American Political Science Review* 96 (4): 697–712. https://doi.org/10.1017/S0003055402000394.

Lipka, Michael, and Benjamin Wormald. 2016. "How Religious Is Your State?" Pew Research Center. www.pewresearch.org/fact-tank/2016/02/29/how-religious-is-your-state/.

Lips, Dan, and Jonathan Butcher. 2015. "The Next Frontier in Education." Goldwater Institute, August 31. http://goldwaterinstitute.org/en/work/topics/education/education-savings-accounts/the-next-frontier-in-education/.

Little, David. 2012. Author interview with David Little, Director of Government Relations for the New York State School Boards Association.

Loar, Danny. 2012. Author interview with Danny Loar, Executive Director of the Louisiana Conference of Catholic Bishops.

Lockhart, Rebecca. 2012. Author interview with Representative Rebecca Lockhart, Speaker of the Utah House of Representatives.

Lowi, Theodore J. 1969. *The End of Liberalism: Ideology, Policy and the Crisis of Public Authority*. New York: W. W. Norton & Co.

Luckhaupt, Timothy. 1994. Letter to Tom Needles. "Luckhaupt to Needles." June 2. Box, Needles Files, Misc. – Education, Box 1KK. Folder, Non-Public – Catholic Conference. Voinovich Archives.

MacLean, Nancy. 2017. *Democracy in Chains: The Deep History of the Radical Right's Stealth Plan for America*. Melbourne: Scribe Publications.

Magleby, David. 2001. *Direct Legislation: Voting on Ballot Propositions in the United States*. Baltimore: Johns Hopkins University Press.

Magnarelli, William B. 2012. Author interview with Representative William B. Magnarelli, Member, New York State Assembly Education Committee.

Maier, Harold G. 1982. "Extraterritorial Jurisdiction at a Crossroads: An Intersection between Public and Private International Law." *American Journal of International Law* 76 (2): 280–320. https://doi.org/10.2307/2201454.

Maisel, Alan. 2012. Author interview with Representative Alan Maisel, Member, New York State Assembly Education Committee.

Manar, Andy. 2018. Author interview with Senator Andy Manar, Illinois State Senate.

Marley, Patrick. 2013. "Past School Voucher Advocate Rips Gov. Walker's Plan." *Wisconsin Journal Sentinel*, May 16. http://archive.jsonline.com/newswatch/207753841.html.

Marley, Patrick, and Jason Stein. 2011. "Walker: Budget Could Expand School Choice to Other Cities." *Wisconsin Journal Sentinel*, May 10. http://archive.jsonline.com/news/statepolitics/121581839.html/.

Matheson, Scott. 2015. *Little Sisters of the Poor* v. *Burwell*, 10th Cir. 13-1540, US Court of Appeals for the Tenth Circuit.

Matthiesen, Mark. 2018. Author interview with Representative Mark Matthiesen, Missouri House of Representatives.

McBee, Susanna. 1963. "Report Shows South's Fight to Keep Schools Segregated Has Been Costly." *Washington-Times Herald*, July 14, p. A6.

McCann, Michael. 1986. *Taking Reform Seriously: Perspectives on Public Interest Liberalism*. Ithaca, NY: Cornell University Press.

McCarron, Mike, and James Herzog. 2012. Author interview with Mike McCarron and James Herzog, President and Associate Director for Education, respectively, at the Florida Catholic Conference.

McConchie, Dan. 2018. Author interview with Senator Dan McConchie, Illinois State Senate.

McDonald, Dale. 2012. Author interview with Sister Dale McDonald, Director of Public Policy and Education Research for the National Catholic Education Association.

McGuigan, Patrick B., and Stacey Martin. 2011. "Opportunity Scholarship Act Passes Oklahoma State Senate." CapitolBeatOK, March 16. www.capitolbeatok.com/reports/opportunity-scholarship-act-passes-oklahoma-state-senate.

McMurray, Coleen. 2003. "Voucher Issue Elicits No Clear Public Sentiment." Gallup. http://news.gallup.com/poll/9523/Voucher-Issue-Elicits-Clear-Public-Sentiment.aspx.

Mellor, William H. 2013. "Intervenor-Respondent Families' Opposition Brief to Petitions for Writ of Certiorari in the Case Taxpayers for Public Education et al. v. Douglas County School District." Institute for Justice. www.google.com/url?sa=t&rct=j&q=&esrc=s&source=web&cd=9&cad=rja&uact=8&ved=2ahUKEwiJ5uTn9qPnAhWTN8AKHQqnAy4QFjAIegQICRAB&url=https%3A%2F%2Fwww.au.org%2Fsites%2Fdefault%2Ffiles%2FColo%2520intervenors%2527%2520motion%2520to%2520dismiss.pdf&usg=AOvVawoYOJSb_ZS3fUVgxTZLeZx9.

Melton, Ruth. 2012. Author interview with Ruth Melton, Director of Legislative Affairs for the Florida School Boards Association.

Menendez, Albert J. 1999. "Voters versus Vouchers: An Analysis of Referendum Data." *Phi Delta Kappan* 81 (1): 76–78.

Meola, Olympia. 2011. "Senate Panel Votes Down Tax Credits for Private School Scholarships." *Richmond Times-Dispatch*, February 16.

Mero, Paul T. 2007. *Vouchers, Vows, and Vexations*. Salt Lake City, UT: The Sutherland Institute.

Mettler, Suzanne. 2009. *The Submerged State: How Invisible Government Policies Undermine American Democracy*. Chicago: University of Chicago Press.

2010. "Reconstituting the Submerged State: The Challenges of Social Policy Reform in the Obama Era." *Perspectives on Politics* 8 (3): 803–24.

Metzger, Gillian E. 2003. "Privatization as Delegation." *Columbia Law Review* 103 (6): 1367. https://doi.org/10.2307/3593390.

Meyer, Ronald G. 2012. Author interview with Ronald G. Meyer, Attorney at Meyer, Brooks, Demma and Blohm, P.A.

Michener, Jamila. 2018. *Fragmented Democracy: Medicaid, Federalism, and Unequal Politics*. New York: Cambridge University Press.

Miller, Joel M. 2012. Author interview with Representative Joel M. Miller, Member, New York State Assembly Education Committee.

Mills, Jon, and Timothy McLendon. 1998. "Strengthening the Duty to Provide Public Education." *The Florida Bar Journal*, LXXII (9): 28–39.

Mitchell, Jerry. 2012. Author interview with Representative Jerry Mitchell, Republican Spokesperson for the Elementary and Secondary Education Committee of the Illinois General Assembly.

Moe, Terry M. 2003. "Reform Blockers." *Education Next* 3 (2): 56–61.

2006. "A Union by Any Other Name." In *Choice and Competition in American Education*, edited by Paul E. Peterson, 123–35. Lanham, MD: Rowman & Littlefield.

2014. "Teachers Unions and American Education Reform: The Power of Vested Interests." In *The Politics of Major Policy Reform in Postwar America*, edited by Jeffery A. Jenkins and Sidney M. Milkis, 129–56. Cambridge: Cambridge University Press.

Molnar, Alex. 2001. "School Vouchers: The Law, the Research, and the Public Policy Implications." National Education Policy Studies Laboratory, Arizona State University, CERA-01-17 https://nepc.colorado.edu/publication/school-vouchers-the-law-research-and-public-policy-implications.

Montana. 1889. "Constitution of the State of Montana: As Adopted by the Constitutional Convention August 17, 1889." Indianapolis, IN: A. Smith; Helena, MT: Published by authority, F. Murray, Secretary of State. https://archive.org/details/constitutionofstoomontrich/page/n31.

Montford, Bill. 2012. Author interview with Bill Montford, Chief Executive of the Florida Association of District School Superintendents and Minority Whip in the Florida Senate.

Montgomery, Dan. 2018. Author interview with Dan Montgomery, President of the Illinois Federation of Teachers.

Moore, Colin D. 2011. "State Building through Partnership: Delegation, Public-Private Partnerships, and the Political Development of American Imperialism, 1898–1916." *Studies in American Political Development* 25 (1): 27–55. https://doi.org/10.1017/S0898588X11000034.

Morgan, Judy. 2018. Author interview with Representative Judy Morgan, Missouri House of Representatives.

Morgan, June P. 1976. *Americans United* v. *Rogers*, 538 S.W. 2d 711, Supreme Court of Missouri.

Morgan, Kimberly J., and Andrea L. Campbell. 2011. *The Delegated Welfare State: Medicare, Markets, and the Governance of Social Policy*. New York: Oxford University Press.

Morgan, Seth. 2010. Author interview with Representative Seth Morgan, Ohio House of Representatives.

Morrell, Jean-Paul. 2012. Author interview with J. P. Morrell, Louisianan State Senator and Member, Education Committee.

Morrison, Tom. 2012. Author interview with Tom Morrison, Member, Illinois General Assembly Education Committee.

Mortensen, Peter B. 2012. "'It's the Central Government's Fault': Elected Regional Officials' Use of Blame-Shifting Rhetoric." *Governance* 25 (3): 439–61. https://doi.org/10.1111/j.1468-0491.2012.01585.x.

2013. "Public Sector Reform and Blame Avoidance Effects." *Journal of Public Policy* 33 (2): 229–53. https://doi.org/10.1017/S0143814X13000032.

Murphy, Marjorie. 1990. *Blackboard Unions: The AFT and the NEA, 1900–1980*. Ithaca, NY: Cornell University Press.

Muse, Benjamin. 1961. *Virginia's Massive Resistance*. Bloomington: Indiana University Press.

National Center for Education Statistics. 2017a. "Enrollment in Public Elementary and Secondary Schools, by Region, State, and Jurisdiction: Selected Years, Fall 1990 through Fall 2027." Institute of Education Sciences. https://nces.ed.gov/programs/digest/d17/tables/dt17_203.20.asp.

2017b. "Private Elementary and Secondary Schools, Enrollment, Teachers, and High School Graduates, by State: Selected Years, 2005 through 2015." Institute of Education Sciences. https://nces.ed.gov/programs/digest/d17/tables/dt17_205.80.asp.

National Center for Education Statistics, Schools and Staffing Survey (SASS). 2009. "Private Elementary and Secondary Enrollment, Number of Schools, and Average Tuition, by School Level, Orientation, and Tuition: 1999–2000, 2003–04, and 2007–08." US Department of Education. http://nces.ed.gov/programs/digest/d10/tables/dt10_063.asp.

Needles, Tom. 1994. Letter to George Voinovich. "Needles to Voinovich." June 6. Box, GVV, 42, CAP-CH1. Folder, Catholic Conference. Voinovich Archives.

Newport, Frank, and Joseph Carroll. 2001. "No Public Consensus Yet on School Voucher Programs." Gallup News Service. http://news.gallup.com/poll/2122/Public-Consensus-Yet-School-Voucher-Programs.aspx.

Newton, Larry, and Cory Kanth. 2012. Author interview with Larry Newton and Cory Kanth, School Finance Director and Statewide Online Education Program Specialist, respectively, Utah State Office of Education.

Noll, Mark A. 2002. *America's God: From Jonathan Edwards to Abraham Lincoln*. New York: Oxford University Press.

Northeast Mississippi Daily Journal. 2012. "Voucher-like Path Not Right for State." McClatchy-Tribune Regional News, December 3.

Novak, William J. 1996. *The People's Welfare: Law and Regulation in Nineteenth-Century America*. Studies in Legal History. Chapel Hill: University of North Carolina Press.

O'Brien, Molly T. 1996. "Private School Tuition Vouchers and the Realities of Racial Politics." *Tennessee Law Review* 64 (2): 359–408.

O'Connor, Sandra D. 1989. *City of Richmond* v. *J. A. Croson Co.*, 488 US 469, Supreme Court of the United States.

1995. *Adarand Constructors* v. *Pena*, 515 US 200, Supreme Court of the United States.

1997. *Agostini* v. *Felton*, 521 US 203, Supreme Court of the United States.

2003. *Grutter* v. *Bollinger*, 539 US 306, Supreme Court of the United States.

Ohio Business Roundtable. 1994. "Ohio Business Roundtable." May 31. Box, GVV, 47, ED:AD-ED:GEM. Folder, Education Choice Committee. Voinovich Archives.

Ohio Department of Education. 2017. "Charter Schools Program Monitoring Report: Final Report Prepared for the U.S. Department of Education." WestEd. http://education.ohio.gov/getattachment/Topics/Community-Schools/Charter-Schools-Program-Grant-CSP/Ohio-CSP-Final-Monitoring-Report-2017.pdf.aspx?lang=en-US.

Ohio Federation of Teachers. 1992. Letter to George Voinovich. "Ohio Federation of Teachers to Voinovich." March 12. Box, Governor's, Box 46, DRO-ED ACH. Folder, Education – General. Voinovich Archives.

Ollstein, Alice M. 2015. "The Rise of Anti-Union Rhetoric in the 2016 Race." ThinkProgress, July 1. https://thinkprogress.org/the-rise-of-anti-union-rhetoric-in-the-2016-race-139fe15c1cec.

Open Secrets. 2018. "Top Organization Contributors." Center for Responsive Politics. www.opensecrets.org/orgs/list.php?cycle=2016.

Orren, Karen, and Stephen Skowronek. 2004. *The Search for American Political Development*. Cambridge: Cambridge University Press.

Owens v. Colorado Congress Of Parents Teachers. (2004). Supreme Court of Colorado. 92 P.3d 933 (Colo. 2004).

Pager, Devah. 2007. "The Use of Field Experiments for Studies of Employment Discrimination: Contributions, Critiques, and Directions for the Future." *ANNALS of the American Academy of Political and Social Science* 609 (1): 104–33. https://doi.org/10.1177/0002716206294796.

Pariente, Barbara R. 2006. *Bush* v. *Holmes*, 886 So. 2d 340, Supreme Court of Florida.

Patashnik, Eric M. 2008. *Reforms at Risk: What Happens after Major Policy Changes Are Enacted*. Princeton, NJ: Princeton University Press.

Pear, Robert. 2004. "Education Chief Calls Union 'Terrorist,' Then Recants." *New York Times*, February 24, Sec. U.S. www.nytimes.com/2004/02/24/us/education-chief-calls-union-terrorist-then-recants.html.

Peltason, Jack W. 1971. *Fifty-Eight Lonely Men: Southern Federal Judges and School Desegregation*. Urbana: University of Illinois Press.

Per Curiam. 1968. *Brown* v. *South Carolina State Board of Education*, 296 F Supp 199, US District Court for the District of South Carolina.

2016a. *Friedrichs* v. *California Teachers Association*, 578 US, Supreme Court of the United States.

2016b. *Zubik* v. *Burwell*, 578, US, Supreme Court of the United States.

Peterson, Paul E., Michael Henderson, and Martin R. West. 2014. *Teachers versus the Public*. Washington, DC: Brookings Institution Press.

Pilarczyk, Daniel E. 1991. Letter to George Voinovich. "Pilarczyk to Voinovich." July 3. Box, GVV, 47, ED:AD-ED:GEM. Folder, Education Choice Committee. Voinovich Archives.

1993a. Letter to George Voinovich. "Pilarczyk to Voinovich (August)." August 27. Box, GVV, 47, ED:AD-ED:GEM. Folder, Education Choice Committee. Voinovich Archives.

1993b. Letter to George Voinovich. "Pilarczyk to Voinovich (March)." March 17. Box, GVV, 42, CAP-CH1. Folder, Catholic Diocese – Pilarczyk, Dan Archbishop. Voinovich Archives.

1994. Letter to George Voinovich. "Pilarczyk to Voinovich." March 21. Box, Needles Files, Misc. – Education, Box 1KK. Folder, Non-Public – Catholic Conference. Voinovich Archives.

1995. Letter to George Voinovich. "Pilarczyk to Voinovich." February 2. Box, Needles Files, Misc. – Education, Box 1KK. Folder, Non-Public – Catholic Conference. Voinovich Archives.

Powell, Lewis. 1973a. *San Antonio Independent School District* v. *Rodriguez*, 411 US 1, Supreme Court of the United States.

1973b. *Sloan* v. *Lemon*, 413 US 825, Supreme Court of the United States.

Prasad, Monica. 2016. "American Exceptionalism and the Welfare State: The Revisionist Literature." *Annual Review of Political Science* 19 (1): 187–203. https://doi.org/10.1146/annurev-polisci-042214-044323.

Private School Universe Survey. 2010. "Table 5. Number and Percentage Distribution of Private School Students, by Urbanicity Type and Selected Characteristics: United States, 2009–10." National Center for Education Statistics. http://nces.ed.gov/surveys/pss/tables/table_2009_05.asp.

Prothero, Arianna. 2018. "Is 'Voucher' a Bad Word? What the Public Thinks about School Choice." *Education Week*, August 21. http://blogs.edweek.org/edweek/charterschoice/2018/08/is_voucher_a_bad_word_heres_what_the_public_thinks_about_school_choice.html?cmp=eml-enl-eu-news2&M=58585970&U=1473140.

Quaratiello, Arlene. 2013. "What's Really behind Scholarship Repeal Effort?" *Concord Monitor*, February 15, Sec. My Turn.

Quinn, James. 2010. Author interview with James Quinn, Chief of Staff to Representative Bill Cassidy (R-LA).

Rai, Arti K. 2001. "Health Care Fraud and Abuse: A Tale of Behavior Induced by Payment Structure." *Journal of Legal Studies* 30 (S2): 579–87.

Rarick, Philip J. 2001. *Griffith v. Bower*. 747 N.E. 2d 423, Ill. App. 5th Dist.

Rastogi, Sonya, Tallese D. Johnson, Elizabeth M. Hoeffel, and Malcolm P. Drewery, Jr. 2010. "The Black Population: 2010 Census Briefs." US Census Bureau. www.census.gov/prod/cen2010/briefs/c2010br-06.pdf.

Ravitch, Diane. 2001. "The Right Thing: Why Liberals Should Be Pro-Choice." Brookings Institution Press. www.brookings.edu/articles/the-right-thing-why-liberals-should-be-pro-choice/.

Ray, Julie. 2004. "Public Opinion Still 'Soft' on Voucher Issue." Gallup. www.gallup.com/poll/13210/public-opinion-still-soft-voucher-issue.aspx.

Rehnquist, William. 1983. *Mueller* v. *Allen*, 463 US 388, Supreme Court of the United States.

1991. *Rust* v. *Sullivan*, 500 US 173, Supreme Court of the United States.

2002. *Zelman* v. *Simmons-Harris*, 536 US 639, Supreme Court of the United States.

2003. *Gratz* v. *Bollinger*, 539 US 244, Supreme Court of the United States.

Reick, Steve. 2018. Author interview with Representative Steve Reick, Illinois House of Representatives.

Reid, Karla S. 2001. "Poll Finds Support for Vouchers Wanes If Public Schools Affected." *Education Week*, October 3. www.edweek.org/ew/articles/2001/10/03/05nsba.h21.html?qs=african+american+support+vouchers.

Resmovits, Joy. 2017. "Betsy DeVos Would Not Agree to Bar Discrimination by Private Schools That Get Federal Money." *Los Angeles Times*, May 24. www.postguam.com/the_globe/nation/devos-won-t-agree-to-bar-discrimination-by-private-schools/article_437d4dfc-4111-11e7-b29e-871b4333d447.html.

Rice, Nancy E. 2015. *Taxpayers for Public Education* v. *Douglas County School District*, C.O., Supreme Court of Colorado, 351 P.3d 461 (2015).

Richards, Erin, and Kevin Crowe. 2013. "Vouchers a Boon for Private Schools in Milwaukee, Racine Counties." *Wisconsin Journal Sentinel*, May 4. http://archive.jsonline.com/news/education/vouchers-a-boon-for-private-schools-in-milwaukee-racine-counties-rr9pa6l-206122011.html.

Ringle, Hayley. 2011. "Arizona Scholarship Program Faces Lawsuit: Funds Allow Tailored Options for Disabled Kids." *Arizona Republic*, October 2. www.azcentral.com/news/articles/2011/10/02/20111002arizona-empowerment-scholarship-lawsuit.html.

Rippey, Harlan W. 1938. *Judd et al.* v *Board of Education*, 15 N.E. 2d 576, Court of Appeals of the State of New York.

Rives, Richard T., Harlan H. Grooms, and Frank M. Johnson. 1964. *Lee* v. *Macon County Board of Education*, 231 F Supp 743, US District Court for the Middle District of Alabama.

Roberts, John. 2013. *Agency for International Development* v. *Alliance for Open Society International, Inc.*, 570 US 205, Supreme Court of the United States.

2017. *Trinity Lutheran Church of Columbia, Inc.* v. *Comer*, 582 US, Supreme Court of the United States.

Roeber, Rebecca. 2018. Author interview with Representative Rebecca Roeber, Missouri House of Representatives.

Rogers, Judith W. 2006. *Village of Bensenville* v. *Federal Aviation Administration*, 457 F 3d 52, US Court of Appeals, District of Columbia Circuit.

Rogers, Todd, and Joel A. Middleton. 2012. "Are Ballot Initiative Outcomes Influenced by the Campaigns of Independent Groups? A Precinct-Randomized Field Experiment." John F. Kennedy School of Government, Harvard University, HKS Faculty Research Working Paper Series RWP12-049. https://dash.harvard.edu/bitstream/handle/1/9830357/RWP12-049_Rogers.pdf?sequence=1.

Rogers, Wynne G. 1929. *Borden* v. *Louisiana*, 168 La. 1005, Supreme Court of Louisiana.

Ronayne, Kathleen. 2014. "Hassan Files Brief Encouraging Prohibition of Scholarships for Religious Schools." *Concord Monitor*, January 13.

Rowe, Lori S. 2016. *McCall* v. *Scott*, 199 So. 3d 359, District Court of Appeal of Florida, First District.

Ryan, Michael D. 2009. *Cain* v. *Horne*, 202 P 3d 1178, Supreme Court of Arizona.

Saladino, Joseph. 2012. Author interview with Joseph Saladino, Member, New York State Assembly Education Committee.

Sandefur, Rebecca L. 2008. "Access to Civil Justice and Race, Class, and Gender Inequality." *Annual Review of Sociology* 34 (1): 339–58. https://doi.org/10.1146/annurev.soc.34.040507.134534.

Sawchuk, Stephen. 2017. "NEA to DeVos: Address Our Concerns or Resign." *Education Week*, July 4. http://blogs.edweek.org/edweek/teacherbeat/2017/07/nea_devos_address_concerns_or_resign.html.

Scanlan, Michael. 1993. Letter to George Voinovich. "Scanlan to Voinovich." January 18. Box, GVV, 47, ED:AD-ED:GEM. Folder, Education Choice Committee. Voinovich Archives.

Schickler, Eric. 2001. *Disjointed Pluralism: Institutional Innovation and the Development of the U.S. Congress*. Princeton, NJ: Princeton University Press.

Schickler, Eric, and Ruth B. Rubin. 2016. "Congress and American Political Development." In *The Oxford Handbook of American Political Development*, edited by Richard Valelly, Suzanne Mettler, and Robert Lieberman. New York: Oxford University Press.

Schneider, Anne, and Helen Ingram. 2019. "Social Constructions, Anticipatory Feedback Strategies, and Deceptive Public Policy." *Policy Studies Journal* 47 (2): 206–236.

Schuck, Peter H. 2002. "Affirmative Action: Past, Present, and Future." *Yale Law & Policy Review* 20 (1): 1–96.

Schueler, Beth E., and Martin R. West. 2016. "Sticker Shock: How Information Affects Citizen Support for Public School Funding." *Public Opinion Quarterly* 80 (1): 90–113. https://doi.org/10.1093/poq/nfv047.

Schupp, Jill. 2018. Author interview with Senator Jill Schupp, Missouri State Senate.

Schwartz, Bernard. 1983. *Super Chief: Earl Warren and His Supreme Court – A Judicial Biography*. New York: New York University Press.

Schwartz, Michael. 2010. Author interview with Michael Schwartz, former Director of the Catholic League and Chief of Staff to Senator Tom Coburn (R-OK).

Semuels, Alana. 2016. "Why Are Unions So Worried about an Upcoming Supreme Court Case?" *Atlantic*, January 8. www.theatlantic.com/business/archive/2016/01/friedrichs-labor/423129/.

Sharkey, Jesse. 2018. Author interview with Jesse Sharkey, Vice President of the Chicago Teachers Union.

Skocpol, Theda, and Alexander Hertel-Fernandez. 2016. "The Koch Network and Republican Party Extremism." *Perspectives on Politics* 14 (3): 681–99. https://doi.org/10.1017/S1537592716001122.

Skowronek, Stephen, and Karen Orren. 2016. "Pathways to the Present: Political Development in America." In *The Oxford Handbook of American Political Development*, edited by Richard Valelly, Suzanne Mettler, and Robert Lieberman, 27–47. Oxford Handbooks. Oxford: Oxford University Press.

Smith, Bill. 2014. "Half of Scholarship Cash from Business Tax Credit Donations Returned." *New Hampshire Union Leader*, February 2.

Smith Richards, Jennifer. 2012. "Special-Needs Students Seeking New Vouchers." *Columbus Dispatch*, April 23. www.google.com/url?sa=t&rct=j&q=&esrc=s&source=web&cd=1&cad=rja&uact=8&ved=2ahUKEwihoZj6_KPnAhWXiVwKHQjoChoQFjAAegQIBRAB&url=https%3A%2F%2Fwww.dispatch.com%2Farticle%2F20120423%2FNEWS%2F304239694&usg=AOvVaw1PHMsSh8dZ4WzHlTXxUlbj.

Sobeloff, Simon. 1964. *Griffin* v. *Board of Supervisors of Prince Edward County*, and *Pettaway* v. *Board of Supervisors of Surry County*, 339 F 2d 486, US Court of Appeals for the Fourth Circuit.

Souter, David. 1995. *Rosenberger* v. *Rector and Visitors of University of Virginia*, 515 US 819, Supreme Court of the United States.

2003. *Gratz* v. *Bollinger* (dissent), 539 US 244, Supreme Court of the United States.

Special to the New York Times. 1959. "State Tuition Aid Urged by Faubus." *New York Times*, February 10, p. 30.

1961. "Faubus Proposes Integration Bar." *New York Times*, January 22, p. 40.

1964. "Mississippi Faces New School Step." *New York Times*, August 10, p. 17.

1967. "Maddox Is Rebutted on Private Pupils." *New York Times*, August 28, p. 26.

Spence, Sarah. 2010. Author interview with Sarah Spence, Legislative Aide to Ohioan Senator Gary Cates.

Spencer, Harry A. 1974. *Rogers* v. *Swanson*, 219 N.W. 2d 726, Supreme Court of Nebraska.

Spriggs, James F., and Paul J.Wahlbeck. 1997. "Amicus Curiae and the Role of Information at the Supreme Court." *Political Research Quarterly* 50 (2): 365–86. https://doi.org/10.1177/106591299705000206.

Stacy, Dan. 2018. Author interview with Representative Dan Stacy, Missouri House of Representatives.

Stanley, Bill. 2012. "New Tax Credits Empower Parents with School Choice." *Roanoke Times & World News*, June 17.

Starr, Paul, and Gosta Esping-Andersen. 1979. "Passive Intervention." *Working Papers for a New Society*. 7 (2): 15–25.

Steinmetz, Donald W. 1998. *Jackson* v. *Benson*, 578 N.W. 2d 602, Supreme Court of Wisconsin.

Stone Sweet, Alec. 2002. "Path Dependence, Precedent, and Judicial Power." In *On Law, Politics, and Judicialization*, edited by Martin Shapiro and Alec Stone Sweet, 112–35. Oxford: Oxford University Press.

Suitts, Steve, and Katherine Dunn. 2011. "A Failed Experiment: Georgia's Tax Credit Scholarships for Private Schools." Southern Education Foundation, Inc. https://www.southerneducation.org/publications/afailedexperiment/.

Sumsion, Ken. 2012. Author interview with Ken Sumsion, Representative, Gubernatorial Candidate and Member, Utah House of Representatives Education Committee.

Super, David A. 2003. "Offering an Invisible Hand: The Rise of the Personal Choice Model for Rationing Public Benefits." *Yale Law Journal* 113 (4): 815–94.

Surrey, Stanley S. 1970. "Federal Income Tax Reform: The Varied Approaches Necessary to Replace Tax Expenditures with Direct Governmental Assistance." *Harvard Law Review* 84 (2): 352–408.

Swaby, Aliyya. 2017. "School Choice Bill Pitches Savings Accounts, Tax Credit Scholarships." *Texas Tribune*, January 30 www.kut.org/post/school-choice-bill-pitches-savings-accounts-tax-credit-scholarships.

Swan, Kathryn. 2018. Author interview with Representative Kathryn Swan, Member of the Education Committee, Missouri House of Representatives.

Tabachnik, Rachel. 2011. "The DeVos Family: Meet the Super-Wealthy Right-Wingers Working with the Religious Right to Kill Public Education." AlterNet: The Independent Media Institute, May 6. www.rawstory.com/2016/11/meet-the-devos-family-super-wealthy-right-wingers-working-with-the-religious-right-to-destroy-public-education/.

Tausanovitch, Chris, and Christopher Warshaw. 2013. "Measuring Constituent Policy Preferences in Congress, State Legislatures, and Cities." *Journal of Politics* 75 (2): 330–42.

Teles, Steven M. 2008. *The Rise of the Conservative Legal Movement: The Battle for Control of the Law.* Princeton Studies in American Politics: Historical, Institutional, and Comparative Perspectives. Princeton, NJ: Princeton University Press.

2013. "Kludgeocracy in America." *National Affairs.* Fall 2013 issue: 97–114.

Thelen, Kathleen. 2004. *How Institutions Evolve: The Political Economy of Skills in Germany, Britain, the United States, and Japan.* New York: Cambridge University Press.

Thomas, Clarence. 2000. *Mitchell* v. *Helms*, 530 US 793, Supreme Court of the United States.

Thomas, George. 2015. "Rethinking the Dartmouth College Case in American Political Development: Constituting Public and Private Educational Institutions." *Studies in American Political Development* 29 (1): 23–39. https://doi.org/10.1017/S0898588X14000121.

Thompson, Jon W. 2013. *Niehaus* v. *Huppenthal*, 310 P 3d 983, Court of Appeals of Arizona.

Thurston, Chloe N. 2015. "Policy Feedback in the Public–Private Welfare State: Advocacy Groups and Access to Government Homeownership Programs, 1934–1954." *Studies in American Political Development* 29 (2): 250–67. https://doi.org/10.1017/S0898588X15000097.

2018. *At the Boundaries of Homeownership: Credit, Discrimination, and the American State.* Cambridge: Cambridge University Press.

Tighe, J. Rosie, Megan E. Hatch, and Joseph Mead. 2017. "Source of Income Discrimination and Fair Housing Policy." *Journal of Planning Literature* 32 (1): 3–15.

Timmins, Annemarie. 2012. "Voter ID, Tax Credit Bills to Become Law." *Concord Monitor*, June 28. www.concordmonitor.com/Archive/2012/06/999661249-999661250-1206-CM.

Tomlins, Christopher L. 1985. *The State and the Unions: Labor Relations, Law, and the Organized Labor Movement in America, 1880–1960.* Cambridge: Cambridge University Press.

Toppo, Greg. 2012. "USA's Top Teachers Union Losing Members." *USA Today*, July 3. https://usatoday30.usatoday.com/news/education/story/2012-06-28/Teacher-unions-education/55993750/1.

2017. "Union Leader: School Vouchers 'Polite Cousins of Segregation.'" *USA Today*, July 20, US Edition. www.pressreader.com/usa/usa-today-us-edition/20170720/281565175817281.

Torruella, Juan R. 2005. *Wirzburger* v. *Galvin*, 412 F 3d 271, First Circuit Court of Appeals.

Tulis, Jeffrey, and Nicole Mellow. 2018. *Legacies of Losing in American Politics.* Chicago Studies in American Politics. Chicago: University of Chicago Press.

Tuohy, Carolyn J. 1992. *Policy and Politics in Canada: Institutionalized Ambivalence.* Policy and Politics in Industrialized States. Philadelphia, PA: Temple University Press.

Tyack, David. 1974. *The One Best System: A History of American Urban Education*. Cambridge, MA: Harvard University Press.

Uetricht, Micah. 2014. *Strike for America: Chicago Teachers against Austerity*. The Jacobin Series. London: Verso.

Ujifusa, Andrew. 2017. "Ed. Dept. Has No Plans for a 'Federal Voucher Program.' Let's Break That Down." *Education Week – Politics K-12*, May 31. http://blogs.edweek.org/edweek/campaign-k-12/2017/05/federal_voucher_program_no_plans_education_department.html?cmp=SOC-SHR-FB.

2018. "House Vote Could Decide Fate of School Choice Plan for Key Group of Students." *Education Week – Politics K-12*, May 10. http://blogs.edweek.org/edweek/campaign-k-12/2018/05/house_vote_school_choice_plan_fate_key_students.html?cmp=eml-enl-eu-news3&M=58482764&U=1473140.

Umhoefer, Dave. 2016. "For Unions in Wisconsin, a Fast and Hard Fall since Act 10." *Milwaukee Journal Sentinel*, October 9. https://projects.jsonline.com/news/2016/11/27/for-unions-in-wisconsin-fast-and-hard-fall-since-act-10.html.

Underkuffler, Laura S. 2004. "The 'Blaine' Debate: Must States Fund Religious Schools?" *First Amendment Law Review* 179 (1): 179–198.

US Census Bureau. 2009. "Table 17. Age Dependency Ratios by State: 2000 and 2009." ftp://ftp.census.gov/library/publications/2010/compendia/statab/130ed/tables/11s0017.pdf.

US Department of the Treasury. 2018. "Treasury Issues Proposed Rule on Charitable Contributions and State and Local Tax Credits." US Government. https://home.treasury.gov/news/press-releases/sm467.

2019. "Treasury Issues Final Regulations on Charitable Contributions and State and Local Tax Credits." US Government. https://home.treasury.gov/news/press-releases/sm705.

Vale, Lawrence J., and Yonah Freemark. 2012. "From Public Housing to Public-Private Housing: 75 Years of American Social Experimentation." *Journal of the American Planning Association* 78 (4): 379–402. https://doi.org/10.1080/01944363.2012.737985.

Van Woerkom, Gerald. 2010. Author interview with Senator Gerald Van Woerkom, Vice Chair, Michigan Senate Education Committee.

Verney, Kevern, and Lee Sartain. 2009. *Long Is the Way and Hard: One Hundred Years of the NAACP*. Fayetteville, NC: University of Arkansas Press.

Viteritti, Joseph P. 1997. "Blaine's Wake: School Choice, The First Amendment, and State Constitutional Law." *Harvard Journal of Law and Public Policy* 21 (3): 657–718.

Voinovich, George. 1991a. Letter to Daniel Edward Pilarczyk. "Voinovich to Pilarczyk." June 14. Box, GVV, 42, CAP-CH1. Catholic Diocese – Pilarczyk, Dan Archbishop. Voinovich Archives.

1991b. Letter to Ken Unger. "Voinovich to Unger." October 21. Box, Governor's Box 46, DRO-ED ACH. Folder, Education-Choice Committee. Voinovich Archives.

1992. Letter to Jean Droste. "Voinovich to Droste." April 30. Box, GVV, 47, ED:AD-ED:GEM. Folder, Education-Choice Committee. Voinovich Archives.

1993. Letter to Ted Sanders. "Voinovich to Sanders." January 4. Box, Governor's, Box 46, DRO-ED ACH. Folder, Education – General. Voinovich Archives.

1994a. Letter to David Brennan. "Voinovich to Brennan; Includes Attachment from Ohio Business Roundtable on School Choice." May 31. Box, GVV, 47, ED:AD-ED:GEM. Folder, Education Choice Committee. Voinovich Archives.

1994b. Letter to Tom Needles. "Voinovich to Needles." February 25. Box, Needles Files, Misc. – Education, Box 1Y. GVV & Education. Voinovich Archives.

1995. Letter to Daniel Edward Pilarczyk. "Voinovich to Pilarczyk." March 24. Box, GVV, 42, CAP-CH1. Catholic Diocese – Pilarczyk, Dan Archbishop. Voinovich Archives.

Walker, Julian. 2012. "Tax Credits Don't Violate Constitution, Cuccinelli Says." *Virginian-Pilot*, May 30.

Walker, Samuel, Cassia Spohn, and Miriam Delone. 2012. *The Color of Justice: Race, Ethnicity, and Crime in America*. 5th ed. Belmont, CA: Wadsworth, Cengage Learning.

Wall, J. K. 2012a. "Charter, Voucher Backers Wary of Ritz." *Indianapolis Business Journal*, November 26. www.ibj.com/articles/38099-charter-voucher-backers-wary-of-schools-chief-ritz.

2012b. "Private Schools Raking in Cash Thanks to 2011 Reform Law." *Indianapolis Business Journal* 33 (6): 1.

2012c. "Round 2?" *Indianapolis Business Journal*, January 9. www.ibj.com/articles/31764-indiana-schools-chief-bennett-gears-up-for-re-election-bid.

Walsh, Kevin. 2014. "Symposium: Looking Forward from the Supreme Court's Important but Unsurprising *Hobby Lobby* Decision."*Supreme Court of the United States Blog*, July 1. www.scotusblog.com/2014/07/symposium-looking-forward-from-the-supreme-courts-important-but-unsurprising-hobby-lobby-decision/.Warren, Earl. 1961. *Braunfeld* v. *Brown*, 366 US 599, Supreme Court of the United States.

1968. *Flast* v. *Cohen*, 392 US 83, Supreme Court of the United States.

Wearne, Eric. 2013. "From 'Fear-Based' Choice to 'Freedom-Based' Choice: Georgia's Tuition Grants Act, 1960–1997." *Journal of School Choice* 7 (2): 196–224.

Weaver, Chuck. 2018. Author interview with State Senator Chuck Weaver, Illinois State Senate.

Weaver, Robert K. 1986. "The Politics of Blame Avoidance." *Journal of Public Policy* 6 (4): 371–98.

Weimer, John L. 2013. *Louisiana Federation of Teachers et al.* v. *State of Louisiana*, 118 So. 3d 1033, Supreme Court of Louisiana.

Weingarten, Randi. 2014. *2012–2014 State of the Union*. Washington, DC: American Federation of Teachers.

Weir, Margaret, and Jessica Schirmer. 2018. "America's Two Worlds of Welfare: Subnational Institutions and Social Assistance in Metropolitan America." *Perspectives on Politics* 16 (2): 380–99. https://doi.org/10.1017/S1537592717004248.

White, Tim. 2012. "A Brilliant Run around North Carolina's Constitution." *Fayetteville Observer*, May 27.

Wichmann, Zach. 2012. Author interview with Zach Wichmann, Director of Government Relations for the Illinois Catholic Conference.

2018. Author interview with Zach Wichmann, Director of Government Relations at the Illinois Catholic Conference.

Wilson, John F., and Donald Drakeman. 2003. *Church and State in American History: Key Documents, Decisions and Commentary from the Past Three Centuries*. Boulder, CO Westview Press.

Winkler, Amber M., Janie Scull, and Dara Zeehandelaar. 2012. "How Strong Are U.S. Teacher Unions? A State-By-State Comparison." Washington, DC: Thomas B. Fordham Institute.

Wisdom, John M. 1961. *Hall* v. *St. Helena Parish School Board*, 197 F Supp 649, US District Court for the Eastern District of Louisiana.

1967. *Poindexter* v. *Louisiana Financial Assistance Commission*, 275 F Supp 833, US District Court for the Eastern District of Louisiana.

1968. *Poindexter* v. *Louisiana Financial Assistance Commission*, 296 F Supp 686, US District Court for the Eastern District of Louisiana.

Wolters, Raymond. 1984. *The Burden of Brown: Thirty Years of School Desegregation*. Knoxville: University of Tennessee Press.

Worden, Amy, and Dan Hardy. 2011. "Corbett Appears Set to Push School Vouchers." *Philadelphia Inquirer*, January 20. www.inquirer.com/philly/news/homepage/20110120_Corbett_appears_set_to_push_school_vouchers.html.

Wuthnow, Robert. 2014. *Rough Country: How Texas Became America's Most Powerful Bible-Belt State*. Princeton, NJ: Princeton University Press.

Young, David. 1994. Letter to Catholic Conference of Ohio. "Young to Catholic Conference." March 17. Box, Needles Files, Misc. – Education, Box 1KK. Folder, Non-Public – Catholic Conference. Voinovich Archives.

Young, Richard P., and Jerome S. Burstein. 1995. "Federalism and the Demise of Prescriptive Racism in the United States." *Studies in American Political Development* 9 (1): 1–54. https://doi.org/10.1017/S0898588X00001164.

Zackin, Emily. 2013. *Looking for Rights in All the Wrong Places: Why State Constitutions Contain America's Positive Rights*. Princeton, NJ: Princeton University Press.

Zlaket, Thomas A. 1999. *Kotterman* v. *Killian*, 193 Ariz. 273, Supreme Court of Arizona.

Index

Note: Page numbers in bold refer to tables.

CPSIA information can be obtained
at www.ICGtesting.com
Printed in the USA
LVHW092003130122
708400LV00003BA/59